DRUMMING TO A DIFFERENT BEAT

Serving God for over 40 Years in Nigeria

Dennis Deane Shelly

Printed in the United States of America

The Christian Witness Team, Inc., in Nigeria has permitted us to use the adapted Romans Road pamphlet in this book.

ISBN (paperback): 979-8-218-97618-7
ISBN (hardback): 979-8-218-97619-4

Table of Contents

Foreword

Dennis Shelly has spent more than four decades serving the Lord in Nigeria, an oil-rich country whose social fabric is stretched thin by the sectarian violence of Muslims against Christians.

His childhood is a simple story, some might even say naïve due to his lack of "worldly wisdom" (James 3:13–18), but his faith is a simple trust in a God who leads and uses those willing to take up their cross and follow Him.

I did not get to know Dennis well until he began his studies at Capital Bible Seminary in 1974. Then, I spent two weeks in Ikwa, a Nigerian village in 1976. It was a blessed time, and we became lifelong friends of Joshua and Elizabeth Ekpikhe, the co-founders of the Christian Witness Team, Inc., in Nigeria.

I not only shared with Dennis in the classroom, but I participated in his ordination and was delighted to see God sending him to Nigeria. During our prayer times through their missionary updates, my wife and I have followed the life and ministry of Dennis and later of Coletta during their ministry at the Bible & Missionary Theological College in the South and in the North of Nigeria at the Evangelical Church Winning All Theological Seminary, Kagoro. The story of God's work in the life of Dennis is one of God's grace at work. I believe you will be encouraged and challenged as you read his story.

Homer Heater, Jr., Ph.D.
Professor Emeritus
Capital Bible Seminary
Minister at Large, BCM Int'l.

Preface

Drumming to a Different Beat is a fitting title for this book. At various times in my years of ministry in Nigeria, I'd hear the beating of drums in Ikwa or Kagoro. Sometimes during the night, villagers could be heard drumming as dancers happily celebrated in an open square or compound. At other times, they'd beat their drums to mourn the death of a loved one in their compound or to call on the spirits to help them.

The town crier could also be heard using his drum early in the morning or late at night. He'd inform various village compounds to alert everyone to meet the chief for special messages. Once a village crier, late at night, used his drum to inform the next village that we were soon to drive along their main road. When we arrived, they already knew about us.

Drums are also an essential part of African worship. We saw this in various church settings at Ikwa and at Kagoro in the Hausa women's fellowship choir and student worship teams.

Keith Green said, "If you don't have a definite call to stay here, you are called to go."[1] My mother, after she graduated from Moody Bible Institute in Chicago, Illinois, wanted to be a missionary to China. She had several medical issues that hindered her from going. One of her prayers was that at least one of her children would go overseas for missions. I see myself as an answer to her prayers.

This book reveals how God prepared me for and led me into missions from my youth and through Washington Bible College (WBC). In 1973 as a senior, President George Miles challenged me to go and teach for one summer in Nigeria at a tiny Bible college. I said, "No." However, he challenged me a second time, like a drummer pounding his drum to get the villagers' attention. After I prayed about this with my parents, I felt God was leading me to go, so I said, "Yes."

Not everyone follows God's call on their lives. Not everyone goes for a summer, short-term, or lifetime career of serving overseas. Jesus said, "Many are invited (called), but few are chosen" (Matthew 22:14). This book shows how God, by His grace, led me to serve Him for over 40 years in Nigeria.

As a result, I've seen hundreds of men and women—many from Nigeria and some from other African countries—be— better equipped and involved in Christian ministries. Many continue in faithful service for Christ in various types of ministries, often under challenging situations. Some are laymen who are active in their churches. Some have gone to be with the Lord. Others have retired but stay active in their local church. We're always happy to hear from alumni who share how God has been using them to bring children, youth, and adults to Christ. Others are just beginning their journey with the Lord in service for Him.

I have endeavored to honor as many of you as possible, but it was impossible to mention everyone, whether you were from the U.S., Nigeria, or other counties. Please forgive me if you aren't included in this book. I have appreciated your contribution to my life and trust that God will honor you for your service.

I continue to wholeheartedly share the vision of the mottos of the two Nigerian training institutions where I served. First, "Come—Learn! Go—Teach!" from II Timothy 2:2 is the Bible & Missionary Theological College (BMTC) motto. Secondly, "You are my witnesses," from Acts 1:8 is the motto of the ECWA (the Evangelical Church Winning All) Theological Seminary, Kagoro (ETSK). No matter what major our students chose in their studies, my prayer for each of them was that they would be missions-minded in all that they did.

May this book encourage you who've prayed for, supported financially, or had a part in our ministries over the years. Some of you and your local churches have partnered with me since my first summer of teaching at BMTC in 1973, and when I began full-time teaching at BMTC in August 1977. We couldn't have done this without you! May God also use this book to encourage you who've served with me at BMTC or ETSK or who graduated from there to "keep on keeping on" for the Lord, even when it would be easy to be discouraged or give up.

Finally, may He use this book to challenge many of you—whether you are a child, youth or adult, single or married, across cultures or oceans—to consider God's call on your lives. God wants each of us to be His active goers and senders (Matthew 28:19–20; Romans 10:14–15). He'll use you to "drum to a different beat" as you take a step of faith to become totally available and completely involved in ministry for His glory! He promises to guide you one step at a time in this process (Psalms 32:8). As you do this, the joys and rewards of seeing others come to Christ and go on to serve Him will be worth more than this world can ever offer!

Dennis D. Shelly, Ph.D.

Dedication

Although they are both now with the Lord in heaven, this book is dedicated to my parents, Heber Becker, and Ethel Mae Shelly. They were my most faithful supporters since my childhood.

It is also dedicated to my four sisters and their husbands: Teresa (Terry) and Francis Swann, Bonnie and Denny Sharp, DiAnna (Diane) and Bill Book, and Debbie and Dave Arndt. They've encouraged and supported me during my youth, my first summer trip to Nigeria in 1973, and right up to the present.

Finally, I dedicate this book to my wife, Coletta, who has been my close partner in ministry since our marriage in 1988. She's been the caring mother of our two children, Dwight and Stephanie. She continues to be my best advisor and prayer partner. You'll read her perspectives at the end of later chapters.

Acknowledgments

I thank God for each one who has prayed for and supported me for over 40 years as I, and later my wife and family, served Him in Nigeria. This especially includes my parents, along with my four sisters and their husbands.

Some of our supporting churches, which began supporting me when I first went to Nigeria full-time in 1977 (or in the late 1970s), have continued their faithful support until today. They are Word of Life Chapel, Bainbridge, Pennsylvania; Webster Bible Church, Webster, New York; Independent Bible Church, Martinsburg, West Virginia; and Mount Airy Bible Church (MABC), Mount Airy, Maryland.

Other churches have had a part with their prayers and financial support for many years, such as Lake View Bible Church (formerly Faith Independent Church), Manheim, Pennsylvania; Grace Brethren Church, Lanham, Maryland; and Warrenton Bible Church, Warrenton, Virginia.

Many individuals—extended family members, Christians from various churches who knew me from Washington Bible College (WBC), Child Evangelism Fellowship (CEF), Capital Bible Seminary (CBS), or Trinity International University also known as Trinity Evangelical Divinity School (TEDS), as well as the faculty and staff from these institutions—have also helped us with support, prayers, and advice. Some are now with the Lord.

After I married Coletta, her parents, Richard and Dorothy Shope, along with her twin sister and brother-in-law, Dee and Michael Lindsey, fully supported us and what we were doing. Her supporting churches partnered with us, including Calvary Church, Lancaster, Pennsylvania, which became our home church after I became a member in 1988. Since then, Berean Bible Fellowship, Fleming, Pennsylvania; New Life Center, Philipsburg, Pennsylvania; South Shore Baptist Church, Monarch Beach, California, and others have all faithfully supported us with their prayers and finances.

My wife, Coletta, has been my closest supporter since our marriage in 1988. She has assisted me by editing many chapters of this book and adding her perspectives in most chapters that took place after our marriage. She has kept our house going while I was researching and writing. Our children, Dwight and Stephanie, along with my Aunt Heidi Keller and Cousin Judy Roth, have read various chapters and given me suggestions. Linda Cribbs, from Rochester, New York, gave me many helpful suggestions to sharpen or clarify what I wrote. Jemi Rohrer has proofread the final copy of our book. Josh Pritchard has also guided me through this process. Other friends gave me ideas to include in the book.

Many of our Nigerian friends at the Bible & Missionary Theological College (BMTC), Ikwa, and ECWA Theological Seminary, Kagoro (ETSK), have been praying for us and encouraging us along this journey! Some have been mates as faculty, staff, students, and alumni. Others have been members of the Board of Governors, the Ikwa Christian Assembly (ICA), and ETSK's Seminary Church. All of you have played a part in encouraging us along this journey!

Many of you, as individuals and couples, have regularly prayed for and supported us over the years. Some have gone to be with the Lord, some of whom were in their 90s and 100s. Some, like Dr. Eric Crichton, who married us in 1988 and is now 102 years old, have prayed for us faithfully over the years.

Without each of you and your churches, many of whom I've not mentioned, I couldn't have ministered in Nigeria nor completed this book. May the Lord reward each of you who've been behind us (Colossians 3:23–24). Thank you!

List of Abbreviations

ABF	**Adult Bible Fellowship**
ALSCON	**The Aluminum Smelting Company of Nigeria**, based in Ikot Abasi, Akwa Ibom State, ten miles from Ikwa
BCMI	**Bible Centered Ministries International**
BMTC	**The Bible & Missionary Theological Centre**, later renamed the Bible & Missionary Theological College, the Bible-training arm of the Christian Witness Team, Inc.
BUTH	**Bingham University Teaching Hospital**, Jos, Nigeria
CBS	**Capital Bible Seminary**, the graduate school of Washington Bible College (WBC). In 2012 WBC and CBS merged with Lancaster Bible College and Capital Seminary.
CEF	**Child Evangelism Fellowship**
CWT	**The Christian Witness Team, Inc.**, founded by Dr. Joshua Ekpikhe, his wife Elizabeth, and Brother Mishael Nathan in 1961
CWST	**The Christian Witness Support Team**, represented the CWT in the U.S.
ECHO	**Educational Concerns for Hunger Organization**, based in north Fort Meade, Florida
ECWA	**The Evangelical Church Winning All**, formerly The Evangelical Church of West Africa and the national church of SIM in Nigeria, where Dennis and Coletta joined to minister in 2007.
EMS of ECWA	**The Evangelical Missionary Society of ECWA**
EMU	**Eastern Mennonite University**, Harrisonburg, Virginia
ETSK	**ECWA Theological Seminary, Kagoro**
FIM	**Fellowship Independent Mission**, later renamed Fellowship International Mission, the U.S. mission under which Dennis served since 1977 and Coletta since 1988 when she married him

FMC	**Fletcher Memorial Clinic** later became Fletcher Memorial Hospital
FMH	**Fletcher Memorial Hospital** named in memory of Orville and Virginia Fletcher, the parents of Ted and Harry Fletcher
HCJB	**Heralding Christ Jesus' Blessings**
ICA	**Ikwa Christian Assembly**, the church where Dennis was an elder. It worked closely with the CWT
JETS	**Jos ECWA Theological Seminary**, a sister seminary of ETSK
LBC	**Lancaster Bible College**, Lancaster, Pennsylvania
LCS	**Lancaster Christian School**
LMS	**Lancaster Mennonite School**
MABC	**Mount Airy Bible Church**, Mount Airy, Maryland
MK	**Missionary Kid**
MRH	**Miango Rest Home**
NEPA	**Nigerian Electric Power Authority**, later changed to the Power Holding Company of Nigeria
NYSC	**National Youth Service Corp** requires Nigerian graduates to serve the country for one year, like the U.S. Peace Corp
PACTeam	**Prayer and Care Team** of Calvary Church consists of about eight members who provide prayer and personal support for individual Global Partners sent out from the church
SAC	**Skill Acquisition Center** at ETSK
SIM	Formerly known as the **Sudan Interior Mission**, later known as **Serving in Mission**. Now it's known simply as SIM
SMF	**Student Missions Fellowship**
TCK	**Third Culture Kid**
TEDS	**Trinity Evangelical Divinity School**, Deerfield, Illinois
WBC	**Washington Bible College**, Lanham, Maryland
YFC	**Youth for Christ**

Chapter 1

Our Family Roots Are Important

"'Honor your father and mother'—which is the first commandment with a promise— 'so that it may go well with you and that you may enjoy long life on the earth'" (Ephesians 6:2–3).

I thank God for allowing me to grow up in a Christian family. A person's family roots are essential. God used my parents' backgrounds to lay a solid foundation for me and my four sisters. The following reveals some highlights from my parents' lives.

My Father, Heber Becker Shelly

My father, Heber Becker Shelly, was born on February 6, 1925, on the Amos Hershey farm one mile east of Manheim, Pennsylvania, where the Noah Kreider family now operates. After living there for six months, his parents, Ephraim and Daisy, bought the 77-acre Fahnestock farm north of Pleasant View Communities on Penryn Road outside of Manheim. On that farm, they raised their five children: Milford, Elwood, Heber, Harlan, and Heidi. Their family attended the White Oak Church of the Brethren in Manheim. He lived in Pennsylvania his entire life.

Heber Becker Shelly

Daddy attended the Pleasant View Elementary School with Mrs. Breitigan as his only teacher. Because World War II started in 1941, male teachers were drafted. The result was that no men were available to teach. He was the first in his family to graduate from high school in Manheim in 1942.

In 1943, Daddy was asked to teach the vocational agriculture course for one year at Manheim High School. Although he was never a certified teacher, he tried his best. He was awarded the Future Farmers of America Keystone Farmer's certificate based on his outstanding ability in farming practices. It was reported, "Heber is one of the class's most sincere, willing, studious, and prompt members."

Daddy also taught elementary education for half a year for grades one to eight at the one-room Union Square School in Rapho Township in Manheim. His sister, Heidi Keller, said, "He played the piano by ear and the students loved him." Later he was a Veteran's vocational agricultural instructor at East Donegal Township High School in Maytown.

While he was teaching, his joy for music led him to become actively involved in singing bass in the Gospel Four Quartet. His brother, Harlan, Bob Rohrer, and Ken Hershey were the other original members. They used a pitch pipe to sing acapella. They were very popular in Lancaster County, singing at weddings and church revivals. My mother's brother, Rev. Bill Longenecker, was often the preacher on such occasions.

Gospel Four Quartet

On one of his singing engagements, he met Ethel Mae Longenecker. Their first date was at the Florin Church of the Brethren in Mount Joy. They bought a plot of land on West High Street in Manheim, adjacent to Daddy's parents' home to build their dream home. They broke ground on his birthday, February 6, 1950. They were married on June 4, 1950.

During that same year, Daddy chose to change his career from being a teacher to working for the Lancaster County Farm Bureau in Manheim and Lancaster, which later became Agway. For 20 years, he worked in various aspects of the Farm Bureau, starting as a salesman and then becoming the manager in Manheim. Later he was transferred to their Lancaster branch where he became assistant general manager. Because of his keen ability to manage, he was soon appointed the Agway Supply Center manager in Lancaster.

God saw fit to change his career again. In 1972 he took on a job as the nursing home administrator at Pleasant View Rest Home in Manheim for five years. After that, he changed jobs to serve for 17 years as the nursing home administrator under Lutheran

Social Services at Luther Acres in Lititz and Spang Crest Nursing Home in Lebanon until he retired in 1994.

Over the years, Daddy was active in church ministries, serving on various committees and boards. While my sisters and I were in elementary school, our family attended the Florin Church of the Brethren. He served on their building committee and helped them with their new building project. For several years, he and Momma were Vacation Bible School directors. They also hosted a Scofield Bible Study Course in their home from Moody Bible Institute. Pastor Abram Gish, pastor of Word of Life Chapel in Bainbridge, Pennsylvania, was one of their first teachers.

Daddy and Momma later left Florin to help start the Faith Independent Church in Manheim, now known as Lake View Bible Church. For 11 years, they attended Calvary Bible Church in Mount Joy. He served on their pastoral search committee and building committee.

Heidi, Elwood, Heber, and Harlan

Retirement didn't slow him down. He actively served as the Calvary Bible Church Forever Young group's chairman. For several years, on Wednesdays, he and Momma drove to Exton to volunteer at the Swann Pantry, owned by my sister and brother-in-law, Terry and Francis Swann. He lovingly cared for his grandchildren who kept him going and gave him much joy. He enjoyed get-togethers with the Shelly clan and his siblings.

In April 2007, he had a blood clot in his lungs. Then, in late June 2008, he had a stroke. He was admitted to Pleasant View Communities in Manheim. From there, his health gradually declined. When he was 83 years old, he went to be with the Lord on August 7, 2008. He died at Pleasant View Communities within one mile of the two farms where he grew up as a child and youth.

My Mother, Ethel Mae Longenecker Shelly

My mother, Ethel Mae Longenecker Shelly, was born on the William Longenecker farm north of Mount Joy on June 23, 1922. She lived in Pennsylvania her entire life. Momma had four sisters and six brothers: Arthur, Earl, Ellen, Mildred, Lynn, Sam,

Dorothy, Bill, and Verdella. One brother, Chester, died when he was two months old. She attended Grand View Elementary School, as did her mother, grandfather, and great-grandfather.

Ethel Mae Shelly

She graduated from Mount Joy High School in 1940 and then went to Elizabethtown College for a one-year business course. That summer, she worked as a secretary at Benach's Furniture Store in Lancaster. Sometime later, her brother, Lynn, helped her get a job at the Union National Bank in Mount Joy. Then, in 1943 she felt the need to study the Bible and was accepted to attend the Moody Bible Institute evening school in Chicago. What a change for a country girl!

While going to Moody, God gave her a burden to serve the Lord as a missionary in China. However, after her graduation in April 1947, the political climate in China drastically deteriorated. Foreign missionaries were not allowed to enter the country. Another challenge was that when a medical doctor examined her, he found that she had a heart murmur. After taking an X-ray, they found a white spot on her lung. Because of these medical problems, she decided not to pursue being a foreign missionary.

That dramatically changed her direction. It was at that time she met Heber B. Shelly. During her dating years, 1947 to 1949, she taught 42 children in a one-room school at Milton Grove. Daddy taught her how to make a fire in a pot-bellied stove, keep attendance records, etc.

On June 4, 1950, Daddy and Momma were married at the Church of the Brethren in Hershey. Because of their love for music, they chose that church facility because it had an organ. The entire wedding program, clothing, and honeymoon cost about $550.00. On their honeymoon, they visited various western states. In Texas, they visited Momma's sister, Mildred, and her husband, Isaac Earhart. Uncle Ike took them to Mexico for a day. They also visited Momma's sister, Dorothy, and her husband, Lewis Minx, in Dallas. They spent 21 days traveling.

When they came home, their house was not yet finished. They rotated living with each set of parents for about two months. They finally moved to their 405 W. High Street home in Manheim on August 14, 1950.

Daddy's brother, Elwood, was a carpenter. He was the primary builder of their house. The cupboards were mounted and painted, floors were finished and polished, doors were stained and painted, pictures were hung, food necessities were bought, and the house became a home. They completed the work in time for Christmas. In their beautiful home, they raised five children.

Momma's knitted farm show items

Momma saw the importance of staying home with us children, especially while we were in elementary school. After that, she worked with Daddy as a bookkeeper and caretaker at the Agway Supply Center in Lancaster and as a bookkeeper at Pleasant View Communities. In 1976, Momma worked for Roman Mosaic and Tile Company as their secretary. Due to a ruptured disc in her back, she retired in 1985 when she was 63 years old.

Momma had a great heart for children's ministries. She taught Child Evangelism Fellowship (CEF) Good News Clubs from 1960 to 1994. She later volunteered with CEF in East Petersburg by helping with mailings and cutting materials for teaching.

Despite being retired, she found many hobbies to fill her days. She loved to keep her hands busy. Besides being an avid reader, she knitted, crocheted, cared for several neighborhood children during the day, kept a neat house, painted, cared for her flowers, worked in the garden, and fed the birds. In addition, she made baskets, afghans, latch hook rugs, baby outfits, blankets, and pinecone wreaths. These items were sold publicly and won many prizes over the years in the Manheim Farm Show. Besides this, she volunteered with Daddy for several years one day weekly at Swann's Pantry in Exton by restocking shelves.

Married 58 years

After Daddy passed away on August 8, 2008, Momma lived at her 405 W. High Street home until late that same year. Then, she sold it and moved to Pleasant View Communities in Manheim. She continued to pray for the family and others. She never liked to be idle, so she made afghans for many members of our extended family.

In 2019 she crocheted over 600 baby caps; in 2020 almost 700 baby caps; and in 2021 over 400 baby caps. All in all, she made over 2,000 baby caps for Chester County Women's Services and Operation Christmas

Child (a division of Samaritan's Purse) to include in their boxes to give to orphans and children. She continued this until the final week of her life. She went to be with the Lord on February 28, 2023, at 100 years old.

Chapter 2

God Cares for Us Every Day

"But as for you, continue in what you have learned and have become convinced of, because you know those from whom you learned it, and how from infancy you have known the Holy Scriptures, which are able to make you wise for salvation through faith in Christ Jesus"
(II Timothy 3:14–15).

My Early Childhood and Our Neighborhood

I was born in St. Joseph Hospital, Lancaster, Pennsylvania, on August 23, 1951, at 11:17 p.m., weighing almost nine pounds. I was delivered by Dr. William Hartman. Daddy and Momma took me to our home at 405 W. High Street in Manheim eight days after my birth—Momma said she needed to stay in the hospital because I needed to be circumcised first. This was my home base until I was married.

Happy at four months

While growing up, I was often prone to accidents that could have easily ended my life. God has kept me until today because He had and still has some jobs for me to do. He will keep us until our work on earth is done (1 Thessalonians 5:24).

Momma told me that one day at our house when I was little, I could have had my head smashed. Daddy and Momma had some cats that were allowed to enter the basement. The two outside basement doors over our steps were wooden and heavy. I must have been playing when the trap door somehow closed. I was right on the path where it came down. My parents kept a box at the top of the steps to let the cats come in and out.

When the door came down, the box blocked the door from closing fully. It protected my head from being crushed. I could have been hurt badly or killed if it had not been there.

I have many good memories of living at home that were enjoyable and fun filled. Momma recorded that our meal table prayer was, "Father, we thank you for this food. Help us to be kind and good." Daddy and Momma helped us while young to learn to get involved in praying at our meals, along with leading family devotions. We'd each be in charge for one week. Sometimes we'd get silly and begin laughing when it was prayer time. Momma would tell us, "Stop laughing." Then we'd ask her to pray, but she'd laugh too. However, we were able to be serious during most of those times.

Daddy and Momma were very active in serving in the Florin Church of the Brethren. Momma worked hard on Saturday nights to get all of us bathed and ready to go. She'd clip our fingernails while we'd watch the Lawrence Welk music hour on TV. When several of us needed to wear glasses, Daddy would line up our glasses in the kitchen and wash them one by one, so we'd be ready to go to Sunday school on time the next day.

In our house, Daddy enjoyed making real lemonade by cutting up oranges and lemons and squeezing the juice into a big kettle. He'd add some sugar and water, and we'd have a great time drinking a nice, cold glass of lemonade. We also made homemade ice cream with an ice cream maker which we'd turn by hand. We were always happy to taste and eat some of it at the end when we couldn't turn the handle anymore.

Once we kept the ice cream container outside with an old rug around it to keep it cold. Later when we brought it inside, a mouse was in the rug and jumped out into our kitchen. It resulted in some screams. Some of us stood on our breakfast nook table—and not on the floor—because we didn't want the mouse to crawl up our legs.

My Fulton Street neighbors

Momma was a great cook and baker. She'd often make cookies or a cherry or blueberry pie, along with delicious meals. We'd enjoy eating mashed potatoes, pork or Sunday pot pie, and a frozen vegetable from our garden, like green beans or cut corn. Daddy was also good at making Saturday morning breakfasts. They included hash-fried potatoes, bacon, and toast.

Our local neighbors were friendly. Some of my young playmates were from the row apartments on South Fulton Street just behind our backyard. We'd often play baseball or other games together. I wasn't too athletic, but I tried. Our neighbors, the Kings, had a vacant lot next to our garden, so we'd often play baseball there after school or during summer breaks.

One day I was stung by a bee. Unfortunately, I was allergic to bee stings. The result was that I had a very swollen face. I tried to eat a hot dog at lunch but couldn't because my face and throat were swollen. The next day I was back to normal.

Momma babysat two of our young Fulton Street neighbor children, Greg and Cindy Miller. One time we were all eating together at noon. We were seated around the wooden dinner table, eating homemade potato soup that was piping hot. I was sitting on a chair at the corner of the table. Somehow, I spilled the hot potato soup on my lap. I jumped up quickly and shouted. I could have turned over the entire table with everything on it. I didn't have bad burns on my skin and soon moved on to other daily items.

On a weekday, at the same table, I turned around quickly and caught my eye on the corner of the back counter behind where we sat. That caused me to have a black eye for several days.

Another day, while playing outside, one of my neighbors threw a stone over a row of tall hedges near the Yecker's apartment. It hit the back of my ear, which bled severely. I was quickly taken to a local doctor to get some stitches.

One winter, after a heavy snowstorm, our neighbors, Mike and Isaac Ruhl, helped me build a snow fort by piling the snow into a big pile in the middle of our backyard. Later we dug a tunnel inside and put down an old rug to sit on. We stayed inside for some time, as it was warmer and quieter inside than in the cold and wind outside.

Our family enjoyed playing hide-and-seek when we were young. Inside our house, we had many great places to hide. Some were risky, like our kitchen lazy Susan, which was built in a corner cabinet to store Momma's pots and pans. It swung in a circle, making it easy to get a kettle or pan from its shelves. When closed, no one would see the kettles inside.

In elementary school, while playing this game, I'd sit in the open space of the lazy Susan and wiggle my small body back inside so only the pots and pans could be seen. While my sisters were searching around in the kitchen, I'd be quiet. When they couldn't find me, I'd make noises. They'd eventually come to see where I was hiding. I don't know how I did that when I was young because I've become very claustrophobic in my later years.

I also crawled under the breakfast nook area where we ate our meals. Under the wooden seats was a small opening. I'd crawl inside one place where no one could see me. I also crawled inside a small kitchen door in that same breakfast nook or under the kitchen sink where there was room to hide. Another area was inside a clothing closet. I would climb up on the wooden shelves to the top, just below the ceiling. Unless someone looked up, no one could see me.

Since I was two and a half years older than any of my sisters, it was often easier for me to play rougher than they did at our house. More than once, I got in trouble when we wrestled or played together. My sisters would cry, and Daddy or Momma would quickly come to their rescue. Then I'd have to do two things I didn't like: say, "I'm sorry," and kiss them. Maybe that caused us not to want to give each other kisses often while we were young. As adults, we did better at hugging each other, especially when we'd go away to college, or later when I or my family traveled to Nigeria.

Daddy and Momma wanted us to watch our words when we became angry. They didn't want us to say words like gee, gosh, shut up, hell, or damn since they saw these words as taking the name of God or Jesus in vain. One time Momma wasn't happy with us and said, "Shut up." We responded, "Momma, you shouldn't have said that!" Members of our family continue to be cautious in what we say, although many people use these words in everyday conversations.

My Salvation: A Child Can Be Saved When Five

I decided to become a born-again Christian when I was five years old. It happened at a CEF summer 5-Day Club across the street from our house on West High Street. We sat on our neighbor's front porch and listened to a summer missionary share the gospel. I saw that I was a sinner and that the Lord Jesus Christ could save me from my sins, so I responded. She counseled me after one of those sessions.

Over the following years, I heard various gospel presentations and messages where, at the end, the teacher or speaker would say, "If you know that you're a sinner and want the Lord Jesus to save you from your sins, raise your hand." I would often respond. I wanted to live for the Lord Jesus, but I never had full assurance of my salvation during those years. I don't know how often I invited the Lord Jesus Christ into my heart in different Christian meetings. This problem haunted me until I went to Bible college.

School and Family Activities

Since my birthday was August 23, and I was the first child in our family, my parents admitted me into kindergarten probably one year earlier than they should have. However, I enjoyed my teacher, Mrs. Brenneman. We had great times together as a class. She did many special activities with us, such as drawing a silhouette of our heads and sending the big, cut picture back home to remember what we looked like at five years old. The outline showed me with a piece of hair sticking up in the air at the back of my head.

When I entered first grade, I liked my teacher, Miss Risser. Because of my birthdate and early admission, I initially had problems doing well in my studies, but as I continued elementary school, I began to pick up, improve, and enjoy them.

As first-grade students, one day we went to the school playground for our recess. A big German shepherd dog somehow entered the school playground and began to run after some of us pupils. It probably picked me out because it knew I didn't like big dogs. I ran inside the school and hid behind the entrance door. It came inside after me, sliding on the slippery, waxed floor. I was taken to my classroom for protection and to calm down. Because the dog was thought to be rabid, it was caught and put to sleep to avoid more problems.

Since both of my parents enjoyed music, they encouraged us to get involved in taking music lessons. Right from elementary school, I showed an interest in music. Daddy's singing bass in the Gospel Four Quartet was one area that caught my interest.

The men sang acapella at our house for weekday evening practices before singing at a wedding or church meeting on a Saturday or Sunday. These practices took many hours of work. Sometimes Daddy allowed me to go along to a church where they'd sing, and I'd sit on the front church pew and listen. Some of my interest in music over the years—and being persistent in it—probably came through such exposure.

Accordion practice

Daddy also sang bass when we'd sing at church. Our family would all sit together in one pew for worship services at the Florin Church of the Brethren. Momma sang alto well. We'd sing from the hymnbook and hear Daddy and Momma sing their parts for each verse. Over time, I learned how to read music and pick out the four parts to sing.

When I was in second grade, my parents faithfully took me weekly to Main Street in Manheim to begin taking accordion lessons from Mr. Streeshock. Daddy would drive me to my 30-minute class. The first little accordion I used was just my size. There were only 12 left-hand buttons, which had to be learned by heart, like learning the keys of a typewriter. On the right hand, there were two octaves of black and white notes. On the left hand, I couldn't look over the side and see what button I was to play. The C major bass note had a slight indent, so I'd use my left finger to feel and find it and then know where to start.

I'd practice various times during the week. Regular practice on my accordion (and later piano lessons) wasn't always easy. Sometimes, when it was practice time, I was tempted to stay outside and play baseball or other sports with my neighborhood friends, especially during the spring or summer. However, I usually came in for my practice without any struggle when Daddy or Momma called me. As time went on, with my parents' persistent guidance and encouragement, I began to enjoy playing songs easily from my accordion books.

After several months of lessons, my parents bought me a large gold and white accordion. It had 120 bass notes on the left with more octaves on the right and several right-hand switches to get higher or deeper tones when I'd play the notes. Being only in second grade, when I'd put its straps over my little shoulders, people could only see my head and my little arms and legs holding up this huge instrument. I continued accordion lessons for four years until sixth grade.

Accordions were a big fad while I was in elementary school. Mr. Streeshock had us learn various songs. On several occasions, we gave a special accordion concert at Franklin & Marshall College in Lancaster in one of their halls. About 50 students from Lancaster County would gather on a Sunday afternoon to play chosen songs together in front of a large audience of our parents and friends. Such experiences helped me learn to work together with others and play music better.

I realized that God gave me the ability to play music by ear, and that I had close to perfect pitch. I could usually tell whether a note was an A, B, or C (la, ti, or do) or if an instrument wasn't in tune. This ability helped me successfully play the introduction of a song for the family or a group gathering in a key that usually wasn't too low or too high. Likewise, if I heard someone playing or singing a song, I could play at least the main tune and often tell in what key they were playing without using a book to read the music.

Sometimes when I had free time on my hands, like after coming home from school late in the afternoon, I'd go up to my bedroom and play various Christian songs or hymns from memory on my accordion for half an hour or more without getting tired.

That expanded my ability to play music and chords. I experimented with various chords, major and minor, to help me begin or end a song a little fancier than usual with a new chord that I liked. Little did I know that all of this would be helpful to me later when I'd play my accordion at camps, churches, or various events in Pennsylvania, other states, and Nigeria.

Our family, which now included my four sisters, practiced singing different songs together at home. Occasionally, we'd be asked to sing several hymns or worship choruses at a Christian get-together or meeting. I'd play my accordion, while the family sang. We did it for the Lord and enjoyed it, even though we weren't professionals.

I wrote the hymn's title and the key that I should play it in on a small card taped to the top of my accordion. This helped me to give an introduction and accompany the family while they sang. Once I forgot the tune. I had to ask Daddy and Momma, "What's the tune for this song?" They quickly hummed it for me. That's all I needed to play the introduction. The family went on to sing the song well.

One year while Daddy and Momma were Vacation Bible School directors at Florin, I memorized about 150 Bible verses over the two-week program for a competition and won the first-place trophy. During those years, we'd drive the nine-mile trip from Manheim to Florin. We'd watch Daddy as he drove. Because he was very friendly, he'd often wave to people as he was driving. We'd ask him, "Daddy, do you know that person?" He'd say, "No," and we'd laugh. He loved people.

When I was nine years old, in 1960, I was baptized at the Florin Church of the Brethren. In 1962, our family left that church. Daddy and Momma became founding members of the Faith Independent Church in Manheim. It started with some Bible studies in our home and later met in the old Union Hall building at Grant and Ferdinand Streets.

Along with church activities, Daddy became a member of the Lancaster County Youth for Christ (YFC) Board. Over the next years, it was very easy for him and Momma to take my four sisters and me to various rallies and other Christian activities, often on Saturday nights.

Momma was active as a CEF Good News Club teacher for over 30 years. She regularly led one weekly Good News Club in our home and a second one several miles away in the country at the home of Bill and Janet Groff. She used these CEF materials to also teach in our children's church services.

Attending these clubs during my early years helped me to learn many CEF songs, hymns, and Bible verses. I'd go with Momma to some of the CEF Friday evening training sessions held in Mount Joy. Seasoned teachers, like Miss Katherine Hershey and Miss Edna Mae Glick, demonstrated the coming week's lesson. Then Momma and the other ladies attending would return home to teach the same lesson to their GNC children's clubs the following week.

Sledding was one activity that our family enjoyed doing together during wintertime. As children, we looked forward to having our sleds to use when it snowed. On one Christmas day, shiny, new sleds were waiting for us in our basement next to the fireplace. We had to go and try them out. Daddy and Momma took us to a big hill about one mile outside Manheim, next to Kreider's Church of the Brethren. We enjoyed these rides immensely. When it was my turn to go down, I laid on my sled and descended as fast as possible.

At the bottom of the hill, I tried to turn my sled into a farmer's lane. Unfortunately, one lonely mailbox was at the lane's entrance. I ran my sled right into it and was knocked out. Daddy and Momma saw what had happened from the top of the hill. Because I wasn't moving, they hurried down to rescue me. Only my lip was cut, but it could have been much worse.

During my school years, I often rode my bicycle to school using back alleys and streets because several times I was hit by cars on Manheim's main streets. Once, just a block away from home on busy West High Street, a car came out from Penn Street and didn't see me. The driver knocked me and my bicycle down in the middle of the street but drove away without stopping to see if I was hurt. I quickly got up and was all right, so I kept riding to school.

Once during junior high school, I wanted to find out exactly how far our house was from the school. I figured out that if I added up the number of revolutions on my bicycle tire that it took to get to school and then multiplied the total by the circumference (3.14), I'd easily discover the correct distance in feet. So that morning I began riding the back way from our house to school. After crossing High Street, I kept counting, "15, 16, 17," and then boom! I ran into something solid. It was our neighbor's parked tractor-trailer!

Because I was counting my tire's revolutions, I didn't see the trailer. I rammed into its greasy front, where the cab connected to the trailer. I didn't hurt my bicycle badly, but my white, fall jacket was all greasy. I had a small cut on my nose, and my glasses were bent out of shape. I quickly went home and told Momma what had happened. She cleaned me up. I thought that she'd allow me to stay home that morning, but instead, she told me to ride to school. I was late for classes and never was tempted to set out on such an antic again!

Another afternoon after school, I rode my bicycle as fast as possible from my house through the town square to see one of the high school track meets. As I was riding, I caught the fender of a car turning onto South Charlotte Street and was knocked down. The driver stopped to check if I was okay. I was shaken up over the incident, but I rode home safely. Unfortunately, I didn't get to watch the track meet that afternoon.

Often when parents buy children a new pair of pants or a shirt, and they wear it for the first time, that is the very day they fall and get a hole in that clothing at the knee or

Our home: 405 West High Street, Manheim

elbow. That happened to me more than once. Yet, Daddy and Momma were usually sympathetic and loving after hearing my stories in such situations.

I loved to watch junior varsity football games and track meets at Manheim Central High School, located about one mile from our house on the other side of town. Some of my schoolmates were on Manheim Central High School's football and wrestling teams. At least one in his senior year was a state champion and heavyweight wrestler. Because their athletic abilities appeared to be much better than mine, it was easy for me to believe that I wasn't very good at athletics in my gym classes when we all played together. Only after high school did I realize that I could play sports well, like volleyball.

God uses each experience in our lives to help us trust Him and be more ready to serve Him in the future. What I saw from Daddy's leadership roles in Christian ministries and at work, and from Momma as she worked with us and taught children over the years, positively impacted me later in my life to have a special love for music, children, and young people.

Chapter 3

Happy Family Bonds Through the Years

"A happy heart makes the face cheerful,
but heartache crushes the spirit"
(Proverbs 15:13).

Spending Extended Family Time Together

We did various activities with our nuclear and extended families during our childhood. Daddy and Momma's families were very close over the years. In various ways, this continues today, especially with the Shellys. The Longeneckers and Shellys would get together for a big meal, especially at Christmas. We'd dress up warmly, get into the car after church, and drive to the homes of our uncles and aunts. Bad weather, such as snowstorms, wouldn't usually stop us. If we gathered during the summer, we'd play outside.

Momma's parents

Momma's parents, William and Barbara Longenecker, and our family attended Florin Church of the Brethren. Her father was bald but had a hefty beard. He had big, strong hands. Their dress was very plain. Ephraim and Daisy Shelly, Daddy's parents, also dressed that way. Occasionally, our family would join Grandpa and Grandma Longenecker for a Sunday lunch after church. After the meal, he would often pull pink and white peppermints out of his pocket to give to us. We received them gladly.

Momma had nine living brothers and sisters. With some of her siblings also having large families, we could easily have fifty or more gathered for a Longenecker celebration. Only Aunt Verdella is still living.

Momma with her parents and siblings: Arthur, Earl, Ellen, Mildred, Lynn, Sam, Dorothy, Bill, and Verdella

During such events, we'd all enjoy a great variety of food and baked items, as many of my aunts were excellent cooks and bakers. No one ever went hungry. There was plenty of laughter, no matter which side of the family met. My Longenecker uncles Earl, Lynn, and Bill loved to tell funny jokes. We enjoyed hearing them, even if they were repeated year after year. We'd beg Uncle Isaac Earhart to pull out his false teeth and make a funny face with them sticking out of his mouth. These events kept our family in good spirits.

1958 - Shelly reunion at Uncle Harlan's

We also had great times with the Shelly family. After eating a delicious potluck meal, we'd open gifts from under the Christmas tree. Uncle Harlan was a good photographer and had a great sense of humor. During some of the Shelly holiday meals, he and his wife, Aunt Betty, liked to play tricks on unknowing family members.

For example, the Shellys would sit around their big dining table to eat. Uncle Harlan had a fork that would bend when being used to eat food. They'd put the fork at an innocent member's silverware setting. When the member would begin eating with the fork, their food would suddenly fall onto their plate or lap. The person would be embarrassed, but everyone would see it and laugh. They also had one cup that leaked when a relative drank from it, with the same results.

Uncle Harlan made a special animal cage with a long animal tail inside that looked like a mongoose. We'd all stand beside the pen and look in to see it. While doing this, Uncle Harlan would make the tail jump out. This surprised us and made us jump back or scream, with a good laugh at the end.

At most Shelly summer get-togethers at Uncle Harlan's, he would bring out his hand-cranked ice cream maker by mid-afternoon to produce a batch of delicious homemade ice cream. First, he'd have many of us take turns to briefly crank the handle. When it was thick enough, and we couldn't turn the handle easily, it was time to serve everyone a dish to eat.

My lamb chop face

Our families were also known for making crazy faces or unusual contortions. For example, Cousin Judy Shelly Roth made her big toe stand up straight while the other toes were in their normal position. Cousin LuAnn and others would add some funny faces when we'd take a group picture. I also joined in the activity by making my lamb chop face, where my lips would cross over to the opposite side of my face while crossing my eyes, or I'd make a face like a monkey.

I also enjoyed making farm-animal noises, like a cow, horse, pig (one of my favorites), chicken, donkey, goat, turkey, or duck. My sister, Debbie, was 12 years younger than I was. She took me to her kindergarten class one day to be her show-and-tell. I made these animal noises for her class. They enjoyed my visit that day very much!

When Momma was pregnant with several of my sisters, I stayed with my uncles and aunts. Uncle Bill and Aunt Peggy Longenecker lived on their sheep farm in Mount Joy. Uncle Isaac (we called him Uncle Ike) and Aunt Mildred Earhart resided on their dairy farm in Columbia, Pennsylvania. At Uncle Ike's, I'd get up early with him and his two teenage boys, Barry and Wayne, to milk their cows. One day we went out to check on a section of their pasture. One of the boys told me to touch their electric fence, which I innocently did. I didn't know that the power was on. The strong shock sat me right down on the ground when I grabbed it. For sure, I never touched it again.

Another day I asked Uncle Ike if I could drive his tractor. He asked if I knew how to drive it. I said, "Yes," so he allowed me to drive the tractor on my own. I was doing fine at the beginning. The tractor was easy to steer when going in a straight line. However, as the tractor moved in slow gear and got closer to the barn, I realized I didn't know how to put on the brakes. I managed to drive the tractor into one of the big barn doors, which made the engine stop running. I could have killed myself or had a bad accident if I had driven inside the barn and through the other side, where it dropped off one floor down to the ground level. Uncle Ike was very kind and didn't get too angry with me for the incident.

Riding in his truck in the afternoons was also fun. Once we went to buy an ice cream cone. As a dairy farmer, he said he liked chocolate ice cream because some dirt might be seen on it if he ordered a vanilla cone. Daddy also said that because he grew up on the farm and had to milk the cows, he didn't like to drink white milk. He remembered some cows putting their dirty feet in the milk bucket.

One of Uncle Ike's daughters, Barbara Ann, came to our house to babysit my sisters and me when Momma went to the hospital. We remembered good times with her, especially when she'd straddle her legs up on a door frame and climb as high as she could before coming down. We also had one of our neighbors, Blanche Mummau, come to babysit us several times.

Family Trips Locally and Outside of Pennsylvania

While we were young, Daddy and Momma took the whole family on many enjoyable trips. During the summers we'd drive to the Masonic Homes in Elizabethtown, Pennsylvania, to feed giant carp in a big pond. We'd take a bag containing pieces of bread and walk over a small bridge over part of the pond where we could see large carp swimming below in the water. They were of various colors—orange, black, and white—and some were over one foot long. When we threw bread to feed them, the fish would fight to get it. During such trips, we'd drive by some pigs—mothers with their piglets—on the Masonic Homes Farm. Daddy's particular interest in farm animals and agriculture helped us choose such visits.

We took day trips to local businesses or companies that allowed us to tour their facilities. We walked inside the Holsum Bakery, the Pensupreme Ice Cream facility, and the Hershey Chocolate Company. In today's world, we can't go inside them because of health standards and codes.

Our family didn't go out to local restaurants often, but our parents took us now and then to the Manheim Twin Kiss to buy a soft ice cream cone or a gallon of their homemade root beer. Occasionally, we stopped at an ice cream shop to buy ice cream sandwiches or delicious submarines at Chris' Sub Shop in Manheim after an evening church service. When we'd get home, we cut the subs into small pieces. Then, we'd all sit around the breakfast nook to eat them. Another treat was to go to Dunkin Donuts and buy a dozen of various kinds—filled, powdered, or with icing. We'd come home and cut them in quarters on Momma's cutting board with her favorite kitchen knife. That way, we'd taste various types until they were all eaten over the next day or two.

Our family visited Longwood Gardens to see flowers inside big greenhouses and many beautiful flower gardens growing throughout their many acres. Their orchid greenhouse was amazing to see.

A trip to Washington, D.C. to see the Capitol and the Lincoln Memorial was fun. When it was time for lunch, we entered one fancy restaurant where on the wall we saw pictures of presidents, senators, and members of Congress who had eaten there in the past.

When it was time for us to order from the waiter, we said, "We'll order hamburgers." He said in a disturbed voice, "We don't serve hamburgers here." That was below the restaurant's standards, so we proceeded to order several club sandwiches, divided them among us, ate, and left.

On the way home from one of these trips, we stopped at a restaurant. We all sat at one booth and waited for our food. Suddenly, one man at a nearby table said out loud, "Oih, oih, oih, oih, oih!" All it took was for our family to look at each other, and we almost died laughing. I had to crawl under the table. I nearly wet my pants from laughing so hard. We made it through the meal and arrived home safely.

Our family also traveled several times near Pittsburgh, Pennsylvania, to see Momma's brother, Uncle Sam Longenecker, and his family. The trip was more than five hours one way. We enjoyed going on the Pennsylvania Turnpike, which took us through several tunnels. It was fun to know that we were driving through mountains. Inside we saw all the lights that helped us know where we were going. We had Daddy beep his car horn while we drove through.

Along the turnpike, we needed to eat a meal at a Howard Johnson's restaurant. We enjoyed their ice cream cones with many flavor selections and giant lollipops, which took a long time to lick to the end. One time we ordered chili con carne. The pepper was so hot that we couldn't finish eating it.

In Chicago by Lake Michigan

In 1968 Daddy and Momma took us on a trip to Chicago, Illinois, by way of Detroit, Michigan. We saw where the U.S. car companies assembled their vehicles. We visited Battle Creek, Michigan, the home of Kellogg's cereals. Each of us walked out with a pack of six small cereal boxes.

One night Momma fell at the guest house where we were staying. She sprained her arm but recuperated quickly. When we arrived in Chicago, we saw Lake Michigan. Then, we briefly visited Moody Bible Institute on my sixteenth birthday. Momma wanted me to consider attending Moody since she was an alumnus. However, after that tour, I didn't feel like I wanted to study in that big city so far away from home.

Annual Sandy Cove Bible Conference and Camps

For over 40 years, our nuclear Shelly family went to Sandy Cove Bible Conference in North East, Maryland, near the Chesapeake Bay, for one week of vacation. On our first trip in 1960, we went with my parents, Terry and Bonnie, and Grandpa and Grandma Shelly. The facilities had no swimming pool then, so we swam along the Sandy Cove waterfront.

We walked down a long, wooden stairway to get to the swimming area along the bay. We waded in the water and tried to avoid hurting our feet on the rocky bottom. We enjoyed picking up smooth, flat stones and throwing them to see who could throw them the farthest and make them skip the most before they'd stop and sink to the bottom. We also loved petting or riding their horses at the barn.

At Sandy Cove, on our vacations early on, our family stayed in one half of a small duplex cabin that smelled very musty, like a pine tree, since pine trees were growing all around the buildings. Their property along Chesapeake Bay was many acres and nice and quiet, as cars weren't allowed to drive fast on the premises. Speed bumps on the road and driveways also slowed down drivers. In the cabin, we slept with the windows open and one or two little electric fans rotating at night to keep us cool. Some of us slept on the standard single beds provided in the room; others slept on a mattress on the floor.

Special invited Bible conference speakers preached daily in the morning and evening meetings. Examples were Dr. Theodore Epp of Back to the Bible Ministries and Dr. Clyde Narramore. Saturday night concerts in their big screened-in auditorium were packed with many outsiders driving in for the night. Their Choralaires choir, guest singers like Diane Susek, musicians like Greg Buchanan (who played his harp better than anyone else we ever heard), and the King's Brass were terrific! Their auditorium originally had several inches of sawdust under our feet instead of a concrete floor. When we as children became bored or tired of sitting during the service, we'd reach down and play in the sawdust.

Sandy Cove's family-style meals were delicious! We sat around round tables—seating up to eight people each—in their spacious dining hall. We had all we could eat, with waitresses and helpers always ready to bring us more food if needed. Many were college students who sang in the Choralaires, played in the band, or worked on the grounds. All guests would give a special offering at the end of each week to help toward their college tuition.

Over the following years, their founder, Pastor George Palmer, and his family and staff raised funds to expand the facilities. They built a new swimming pool and snack bar and renovated the Palmer Lodge and dining hall. My sisters' families gave money for one room in honor of Daddy and Momma.

Shellys swimming at Sandy Cove

One afternoon at the new pool, we dared Daddy to jump off the diving board. He reluctantly did with a big splash. With everyone watching, he didn't ascend to the top of the water as quickly as he should have. We became worried that he might drown. He later said he didn't know how to push off the bottom to lift his body.

Finally, he did come up. We were greatly relieved. He never jumped off the diving board after that. Instead, we enjoyed watching guests jump off the low and high diving boards. Some heavier swimmers made huge splashes doing a cannonball or other types of dives.

Going to the snack shop above the pool was a real treat. We loved eating their mint chocolate chip ice cream cones. That made our day!

As my sisters and I grew up, Daddy and Momma stayed at the main Sandy Cove campus for the week. On Sunday afternoon, they drove us to the Sandy Cove boys' and girls' camps for the week. I never enjoyed saying goodbye to my parents. However, once Daddy and Momma left and I settled in at camp in my cabin, I had a great time.

At the boys' camp, each cabin housed 10 or 12 boys and one counselor. During the week, all cabins were divided into teams for competitions. During those years of camping, I learned how to swim in their big swimming pool, make various crafts, and write home at least once during the week. I always enjoyed our times around the weekend campfires when campers gave testimonies of what God had done in their lives during the week.

1993 - The Shelly clan at Sandy Cove

Several of my sisters and I enjoyed attending Sandy Cove's Hilltop Ranch teenage camp, about 15 miles away from the Bible Conference. This was while Daddy and Momma spent the week at Sandy Cove.

These family activities and trips brought our nuclear and extended family members closer. After my sisters were married, their husbands and children joined Daddy and Momma for many years for part of or the whole week. These were great vacations. Daddy and Momma left a significant imprint on our lives through all of this. The Shellys especially continue to do our best to gather during yearly holidays or celebrations at their homes or in a mountain cabin for a weekend.

Chapter 4

Learning to Work Hard

"Whatever you do, work at it with all your heart, as working for the Lord, not for men, since you know that you will receive an inheritance from the Lord. It is the Lord Christ you are serving" (Colossians 3:23–24).

No family is perfect. Good and bad experiences during childhood and at home will be remembered for all of one's lifetime. We can all learn two things from each event we experience or from the people we meet and work with: what to imitate and what to avoid.

My parents were good examples of hard workers to my sisters and me. If you were a Shelly, you were expected to be a hard worker, so I always tried to do my best in whatever I did. We also learned that we should work to please the Lord. Over the years, I tended to be a perfectionist, as the first child in our family, whether working in the garden, mowing the lawn, etc.

When it snowed, I'd be happy. This was an opportunity to visit some of our neighbors who were elderly and couldn't shovel their walks and driveways to see if they needed any help. One winter, I became excited about buying a snowblower, hoping to make a lot of money. That year a small snowblower cost $189.00 plus tax. However, my father wisely advised me not to buy it. We hardly had any snow that winter, so I didn't make much money from shoveling. I was glad I hadn't bought it and learned to appreciate Daddy's wisdom.

When we were young, Daddy worked for many years with Lancaster Farm Bureau in Manheim. His job was to visit farmers in the county, take their feed orders, and help them diagnose poultry diseases when the flu or a virus would attack a flock. Occasionally, Daddy would allow me to ride with him for the day. We'd go together to a restaurant for lunch. He also took me various times to the Pennsylvania Farm Show in Harrisburg since he worked at the booth for his company. I learned to like animals through such trips, as he took me around to see workhorses, cows, pigs, goats, sheep, poultry, and other types of animals.

On a visit to a farm with Daddy, the family owned a big dog. Since I was afraid of dogs, Daddy let me stay in the car while he went into the farmer's house. The visit turned out to be longer than I expected, so I beeped the car's horn. The dog ran out to our car, barking loudly. I was safe inside but curled down in the passenger's feet area where the dog couldn't see me. Daddy soon returned to the car, and we drove away safely.

Later he was promoted to work at their Lancaster office. Agway, a larger agricultural company based in Syracuse, New York, bought out the business. For several more years, he served as manager of their Agway Supply Center on Dillerville Road in Lancaster.

Daddy's reputation as a very friendly and conscientious worker continued wherever he worked. However, as Agway was evaluating its presence in the area, one day he received a letter from them that the company was restructuring, and his position was eliminated. That forced him and Momma to trust the Lord for direction.

Several weeks afterward, God opened the door for him to become the administrator at Pleasant View Rest Home, several miles outside Manheim. While he worked there, he allowed me to work part-time. As a result, I sometimes rode the journey of two and a half miles on my bicycle. I shaved male residents and assisted the staff where needed, such as preparing vegetables for freezing.

Daddy served there for five years when he was informed that someone else would take over his job. Again, after prayer and searching for some weeks, he was hired to be the administrator at Spang Crest Nursing Home in Lebanon, where he served for 17 years until he retired at 69 years old in 1994.

Momma was always a very busy woman. She fit many of the qualities of a godly woman in Proverbs 31. She made it a priority to be a housewife while we were all in elementary school. That meant a lot to us, especially as we look back at this now as adults. She was there for us when we needed it the most. She saw us off when we went to school and welcomed us when we returned by late afternoon. When we came home and opened the kitchen door, we often saw her lying on her bed reading a book or her Bible.

As soon as I arrived home, I went and told her how my day went. Sometimes I'd be bullied by friends on the way home or have a rough day, but after talking to Momma, things were better. She and Daddy were there for us, even at night.

My fifth-grade teacher, Mr. Steinhower, was just out of university. His notes on the sciences were very demanding and hard for us at that level. Several times I couldn't sleep the night before he'd give our class a test. I'd go downstairs and peep in through their bedroom door, which was usually left slightly open, and tell them how I felt. They'd talk with me briefly and encourage me. That helped me feel better, so I could return to my bed and sleep better. Momma later began to work part-time outside of the house after my youngest sister, Debbie, went to elementary school.

Daddy and Momma loved to do outside work on the lawn and garden. We had a big garden about 30 feet wide and 150 feet long along the edge of the entire length of our home's property. In their garden, they grew sweet corn, white and sweet potatoes, green beans, tomatoes, sugar and garden peas, leaf lettuce, cucumbers, and squash. They constructed a small, wooden hothouse that was enclosed, in which they grew leaf lettuce and spring onions. It protected them from frosts and cold weather. This helped us to eat these fresh items before the normal vegetables were ready to be eaten.

Shelly flowerbed and garden

Momma loved her flower beds and kept the garden from getting overtaken by weeds. She planted beautiful flowers and meadow tea next to the garden or around the house during the spring and summer. She also grew rhubarb to use in making strawberry-rhubarb pies.

For the most part, I enjoyed helping them in the garden. I liked to push our little hand cultivator through the rows between the plants when I was old enough. It had a little plow and disc that could be easily exchanged with some wrenches if we were weeding or trying to pull up the soil toward the plants. This kept the weeds from growing.

When I went to college, Momma said she missed my gardening work. She thought I did a good job weeding between the rows. That desire to work in the garden and grow crops continued wherever I went.

Daddy and Momma learned much from their parents, all of whom were farmers their entire lives. They worked hard and did much canning for their large families. Sometimes Daddy and Momma would pick several half-bushel baskets of garden or sugar peas from their garden. Grandpa and Grandma Longenecker would come from Mount Joy and help us shell the peas or take off sugar pea strings. They did this sitting on our porch in the shade. Then Momma would blanch the items and bag them to go into the freezer to eat anytime during the year.

We picked strawberries from a local farm to eat fresh, freeze, or make jelly. We picked sour cherries from a friend's trees to freeze, so Momma could make tasty cherry pies. Our family would drive to buy baskets of peaches, pears, or apples from Stauffer's of Kissel Hill in Lititz. We cut the fruit in halves or made apple sauce and put the contents into a one or two-quart glass jar. We canned pickles, tomatoes, pickled cantaloupe pieces, or watermelon rinds and stored them in our basement's cold cellar. In addition, sweet corn, green beans, and peas were blanched and frozen. We could take them from our freezer or a jar from the cold cellar anytime during the year. They all tasted great!

Momma would make tasty drinks by adding ginger ale to canned grapes. We'd drink this while playing games like *Please and Thank You* to help us improve our manners or *Book* to help us spell our words correctly.

Momma's sand tarts

Momma was also an excellent cook and baker. The word entrepreneur would have suited her well, as she loved to find ways to raise money for the family or help someone. She made homemade doughnuts, sand tarts, sugar and molasses cookies, cakes, and pies. She made many batches of sand tarts close to the Christmas holidays. She packaged them in brown paper or clear plastic bags in sizes of one, two, or three dozen. Our dining room would often be full of these bagged items, ready to sell.

On Friday nights when the bank was extra busy, my sisters and I often went to the Manheim town square. Especially near the Christmas season, we'd stand outside the Manheim National Bank at their main entrance to sell Momma's baked goods. Since customers liked to buy these items, we'd stand out in the cold, dressed very warmly, to sell them from our full baskets. Momma also bought consignments of chocolate bars with almonds in them—five boxes of 20 bars each. My sisters and I sold them along with her baked goods. We often came home with none or very few of Momma's baked goods remaining. Momma paid us a nickel or dime for each bag of baked goods or chocolate bars that we sold to our neighbors and friends. From these ventures, she made money for the family.

In our house, we learned that not everything was a handout. We knew the importance of doing our daily chores, giving at least a tithe of what we earned to the Lord, and handling money wisely. I saved some of my earnings to buy my first red, 20-inch bicycle from one of my neighbors. It cost $11.00 when I was in elementary school. I later moved up a level and bought my own new, 26-inch, 3-speed bicycle from selling these items for Momma.

We also rode our bicycles or walked to our local grocery stores, such as Fink's or Albright's, to buy items needed for the family. Unfortunately, these stores were later forced out of business because larger stores like Weis and Walmart were built in Manheim and Lancaster.

As young, neighborhood boys, we bought packs of bubble gum with baseball player cards inside of them. We traded them with our buddies or put some of them on our bicycles with a clothespin because they were made of light cardboard. When we rode our bikes, and the wheels would go around, the cards would flap when the bicycle spokes went over them. The faster we rode, the louder the noises sounded, like a small engine. Everyone knew we were coming when we rode up and down our driveways or Fulton Street. That was one way we had fun! It's too bad that our parents didn't take many pictures of us during those years.

During high school and summer vacations, I earned money by selling beautiful flower bouquets for Mrs. Zug, an older lady living on Penn Street, one street away from our house. In addition, I mowed lawns for older people, picked cherries, bagged potatoes, picked baskets of tomatoes, and handed out paper advertisements for Longenecker's Hardware Store.

Such activities helped my sisters and me work hard and earn some money. Some days I'd pick up to 100 baskets of tomatoes when they were at their peak on the Jesse Dourte farm. With many of them being large, it wasn't hard to fill a basket from a row on my left and on my right without moving the basket forward. We'd come home at the end of the day tired and smelling like tomatoes, with our hands all black from handling the tomatoes all day. Our clothing would be filthy. We were all ready for a good shower! I also worked part-time at Sprecher's Shoe Store in Manheim Square, earning $1.65 per hour, which was big money for me as a teenager.

I used my bicycle to ride one mile to the other side of town to junior high and high school. I rode it whether it was rainy or snowy, cool, hot, or freezing. Sometimes I'd ride it after school to watch a football game or track meet. Riding my bicycle was good exercise and helped me get around more quickly than if I had walked.

I still used my bicycle for several years when attending Capital Bible Seminary (CBS) in Lanham, Maryland. I rode thousands of miles over the years. These activities helped me use what I had rather than go into debt to buy a car. I learned the dignity of hard work. Many thanks go to my parents for their example and encouragement to my sisters and me.

Chapter 5

Learning to Serve in High School

"For this reason, since the day we heard about you, we have not stopped praying for you. We continually ask God to fill you with the knowledge of his will through all the wisdom and understanding that the Spirit gives so that you may live a life worthy of the Lord and please him in every way: bearing fruit in every good work, growing in the knowledge of God"
(Colossians 1:9–10)

During junior high school, I didn't stop playing my accordion but shifted to taking weekly piano lessons for several years from Mrs. Marilyn Stoner. Knowing how to play the piano allowed me to be one of the pianists for our small church, Faith Independent. Sometimes I'd play for other occasions where needed. I was shy when in public, but through these events, I began to be more confident in front of people.

Our entire family attended the CEF summer camp in Quarryville for two years. Momma taught the Bible lessons while Daddy and Bonnie were camp counselors. Terry and I helped in the kitchen, washing dishes and pots. I had fun putting a mop on my head to be in a skit. Diane helped serve food in the dining hall, while Debbie enjoyed running around as a little girl.

Working in the CEF camp kitchen

In high school, I took my studies very seriously. I didn't get involved in sports or extra-curricular activities at school but was active in Manheim Central High School YFC events. I attended their regular meetings and special activities, like roller skating and rallies.

During these years, I enjoyed riding my bicycle to attend school and watching football or track and field events to see some of my YFC mates play in them. They were good Christian role models for me.

I also enjoyed singing in the high school choir. Mr. Dowhower was our director. I sang tenor, but later when my voice changed, I moved from tenor to bass. I passed tryouts and was qualified to represent Manheim Central in a Lancaster County choir concert. During one senior high choir concert, I was too hot in my gown and fainted while standing on the stage risers. I later found myself in the choir practice room, sitting in a chair, waiting to be taken home.

Manheim Central YFC quiz team

I became active on Manheim Central's YFC Bible quiz team for several years and attended weekly Bible quiz practices. Two young ladies, Linda Musser (now Ansel) and Naomi Groff (now Parke) were our Bible quiz coaches. My quiz teammates were Anita and Jim Metzler, Daryl Hollinger, Joyce Kilmer, Cindy Watts, and Marlin Haldeman. Our team participated in the Lancaster County YFC Bible quiz team competition during some of their monthly Saturday night rallies at McCaskey High School. I did well enough to be chosen as a member of the Lancaster County YFC Bible quiz team to represent them at their regional conference in Ocean City, New Jersey. We quizzed in front of hundreds of people.

Our team never won first place, but these interactions helped us learn more about teamwork, gave us a greater love to read and study the Bible, helped us become more confident in public, and laid a solid Biblical foundation for the future ministries God had for each of us.

One year I played my accordion in YFC's Lancaster County musical instrument competition. The winners would later represent them at Ocean City. I practiced "Wonderful Grace of Jesus" for weeks in our dining room. My family probably became weary of me practicing that hymn over and over. I tried my best but didn't get chosen. However, it was another good experience for me.

One other YFC activity that I immensely enjoyed was competing on the WDAC-FM radio station to personally plan a one-half-hour program as a disc jockey. We had to choose different recorded hymns to be played, with a theme and transitions. I did this several times. I never won first place, but I benefited from this exposure. One Lancaster County senior higher who competed against me was Nelson Groff. He had a pleasing radio voice. After he graduated from high school, WDAC hired him to serve as a radio announcer with them for many years. I greatly appreciated my parents' dedication to driving me many miles to these Christian activities. That took many, many hours.

Some of our YFC members at Manheim Central High School agreed to meet regularly before morning classes began for a few minutes of prayer. We enjoyed these times, encouraging each other to stand stronger for the Lord in our classes. These good friendships through high school helped us avoid being tempted by other high school class members who were involved in bad habits, like smoking cigarettes, drinking alcohol, having immoral relationships with girls, or taking drugs. I Corinthians 15:33b is true, "Bad company corrupts good morals."

I've never smoked a cigarette in my life. Once when I was mowing our front lawn, I saw an empty beer bottle lying along our High Street gutter. When I picked it up and smelled it, the strong, fermented odor turned me off. From that moment on, I have had no interest in drinking alcohol.

In my senior year, at least one of my high school classmates, whom I wasn't close to, was beginning to get involved in using drugs, like marijuana. We knew then that such activities could occur in the inner city, but we were more surprised to see them affect Manheim after graduating.

As a high school senior, I was asking the Lord where I should go to college. During the spring of 1969, Mary Ann Kilmer, one of our former Manheim Central YFC members, was already a student at Washington Bible College (WBC). She invited me to attend their spring banquet when their campus was still in Washington, D.C. It coincided with their week of evangelism. That Friday, I attended some of their classes and heard student testimonies on how God had used them to witness to people on the city streets.

Our family in 1969

The prospect of studying the Bible at WBC excited me. I thought, "Wow! I want to attend this college and get involved in Christian service activities, like passing out Gospel tracts to people on the streets of Washington, D.C." After that visit, I promptly applied to attend WBC and was accepted to begin classes for the August 1969 semester.

After my high school graduation, I volunteered to work during the summer at Hilltop Ranch in Rising Sun, Maryland, to wash pots and dishes for the campers and staff. Those weeks were another excellent step in becoming more independent from my family. We worked hard during the day in the kitchen. Then we had fun times in the evenings playing games and having competitions with the campers and their counselors.

I learned to work well under Bennie, the chief cook, and with others in the kitchen. I played my accordion several times during that summer at their Friday campfires. During those times, I enjoyed sitting on a log watching the fire embers burning or sparks flying into the sky. The weekly speaker would share a brief message. Campers testified how God had worked in their lives throughout the week's messages and activities. That made our work worth the effort!

I enjoyed getting to know some of the Hilltop Ranch staff, such as Director Bob Palmer and Stew Brady, one of their administrative staff. Stew later became a staff member at Lancaster Bible College (LBC) in public relations. As a fellow resident now at Calvary Homes, I still see Stew weekly at our Thursday morning Men's Fellowship meetings.

Some of the weekly Hilltop Ranch guest speakers had a very positive impact on me. For example, Butch Hardman was the pastor of Barcroft Bible Church in Virginia. Over the years, he had a thriving youth ministry at his church and in contexts like Hilltop Ranch. One day, after speaking, he came into the kitchen and asked the dishwashers our names.

I didn't think anything of it, but that next semester when I began my studies at WBC, Pastor Hardman came to speak at one of our chapel services. He saw me and said, "Hi, Dennis." I thought, "Wow! How did he remember my name?" From that challenge, I decided to try to learn the names of as many people as I could whenever I met them.

In high school, I took several years of French but still couldn't speak a complete sentence fluently. On one weekend occasion at Hilltop Ranch, when we were preparing for our Friday night banquet, a delivery truck brought various boxes of food items to store in the camp's freezer. On the outside of several boxes was written "hors d'oeuvres." I pronounced the words "horse douvers." I asked myself, "What are these?" I should have recognized those French words. Only later did I realize that those were appetizers for the banquet. I had a lot to learn!

After I went to college, my parents continued attending YFC activities with my four sisters. Several of my sisters met their husbands there. They all now have Christian husbands and families. I thank God for supportive families, Christian friends, and leaders who had an interest in seeing us grow up to love the Lord and serve Him. When I graduated from high school, I wasn't sure what God's plan was for my future. I did have an interest in becoming a missionary. However, there were two things I never thought I would want to be: a teacher or a preacher.

Little did I know that God's plans were different from mine, and that His plans were the best for me as I took one step at a time to follow Him. My favorite Bible verse became Colossians 1:10, "so that you may live a life worthy of the Lord and please him in every way: bearing fruit in every good work, growing in the knowledge of God."

Chapter 6

Going to Bible College

"Do your best to present yourself to God as one approved, a workman who does not need to be ashamed and who correctly handles the word of truth"
(II Timothy 2:15).

In 1969, WBC had just bought 69 acres of land and buildings from a Catholic seminary in Lanham, Maryland, 15 miles from the campus in metropolitan Washington, D.C. For that fall semester, WBC's administration decided to have all new students begin their studies at the new Lanham campus. At the same time, some upper-level students would continue living in the old city campus dorms and commute for classes. Thus, I never did get to live in the WBC dorm in Washington, D.C., or take any courses there. However, we did enjoy the new Lanham campus and its more spacious and modern facilities.

During my years at WBC, God continued to guide and provide for me. I never had my complete tuition fees in hand in time for each new semester's registration. Right from my first semester, I trusted the Lord to help me find a part-time job. Since I had learned from my youth not to be afraid of working to make some money for myself, I intentionally and willingly tried to find some part-time work to pay for my tuition.

WBC's Lanham campus

I took my studies and homework very seriously. For my first semester, I rewrote many of my class notes. That took time, but it helped me review what the faculty had taught me and do better on my quizzes and exams. I also didn't know how I might use those notes to help me teach others in the future. As the semester progressed, I became too busy to rewrite my notes. My handwriting also became harder for someone else to read!

WBC had various part-time work opportunities for students. That first semester I worked two or three nights weekly at Bob's Big Boy hamburger restaurant about ten miles from the campus. Since I didn't own a car, I had to travel with other WBC students working there who had room to take me in their vehicles. My shifts were from about 5 p.m. to midnight. I left the campus by about 4:30 p.m. and sometimes didn't return until about midnight or later. Working such hours forced me to plan well for my studies.

My two roommates, Dane Emerick and Wayne Seekell, and I lived in one of the dorm rooms on the first floor. We shared one three-level bunk bed in one corner of the room, with our three desks and dressers in other corners or rows. The quarters were tight. Because I was slim then, it wasn't a big problem. I slept on the top bunk, so I tried to be as quiet as possible when I returned from work late at night. When I climbed up the side of the bed, I'd make the bed shake and creak some until I settled in my bunk. Somehow, we made it. Dane and Wayne became good friends.

Dr. William Miller was WBC's Christian service director. He was a medical doctor from New Zealand, who later changed his vocation to come to teach at WBC. During my first year there, he counseled me on how to have full assurance of my salvation, which had been troubling me from my early school years. From April 14, 1970, I never had any doubts again. Now, when I counsel a child, teen, or adult after they pray to ask Christ to forgive their sins, I share a Bible verse to assure them of their salvation and have them put their name in parts of it to help this fact become more personal and practical.

One example would be John 3:16, "For God so loved Dennis, that he gave his one and only son, that if Dennis believes in him Dennis shall not perish but have eternal life." Another verse that helped me have assurance was Hebrews 13:5b, which says, "Because God has said, 'Never will I leave Dennis, neither will I forsake Dennis."

I ask them, "Can God lie?" When they say, "No," I remind them that God is the one giving this promise to us. As I say the five words, "Never will I leave you," I point at each finger—starting from my little finger to my thumb—as I say each word. When I come to my thumb, I point it back to my heart and substitute my name in place of "you." I help them do the same thing. When this is done, they often smile. The Bible gives us great assurance that once we believe in the Lord Jesus, we can know that we are saved from our sins and will go to heaven when we die (John 10:28; 1 John 5:12–13).

Life in the dorm was often noisy. The first-floor hallway next to our room had much traffic, as two other floors of men came by our room to go to classes, the dining room, and the chapel. The narrow hallway could quickly produce echoes because of not having any windows or curtains. We could hear noises whenever someone walked through. Various students would sing or whistle a song in the morning. Sometimes it had a good effect. If one of the fellows whistled a Christian tune, another student immediately picked up the same song and sang or whistled it.

One mystery stumped the dorm counselors and the leadership during one of my first semesters. We even thought that it was demonic. For several weeks, when we went to bed, we heard strange noises around midnight or later that were very spooky and scary. We made it a prayer point for God to help us solve it or for it to go away. Eventually, we discovered that several students were rolling some weight-lifting barbells up and down the dorm hallway on the third floor to make such scary noises. Later, when they were caught, the problem ended.

During my sophomore year, I was given a part-time job on the WBC campus in the kitchen. I washed dishes for several semesters. Later I was promoted to buying kitchen supplies with the kitchen manager, Mrs. Mary Ortendahl, or Mrs. O as she was called. She was retired but had much energy and tried hard to use her abilities to serve the Lord in the kitchen. She was very thrifty in her purchases. I often drove her in the afternoons to various places in the area to buy loaves of bread or other supplies that would be day-old or cheaper than retail prices.

At WBC, we became involved in a Christian service assignment. For my first semester, I joined other students on a Sunday morning team to go to a boys' home near the Washington, D.C., area. Orphans and boys who had rough family backgrounds lived there. We had the opportunity to befriend them and share the Gospel with them.

Since my mother had gone to Moody Bible Institute and had wanted to be a missionary to China but couldn't go because of health issues, she had prayed that at least one of her children would become involved in missions and go to a foreign mission field. Momma and Daddy were thrilled that I chose to go to Bible College. I was open to being a missionary but didn't know where God would lead me.

The Shelly family was always very close-knit. During my college and seminary days, I phoned my parents most weekends to tell them how my week had gone and to hear how the family was doing. My home in Manheim was two and a half hours away from WBC. My part-time work and Christian service assignments kept me busy, so I only went home during key holidays, breaks, or for special reasons, such as attending a family funeral.

In my sophomore year, other opportunities to get involved in WBC Christian service and missions opened to me. I became the North American Student Missions Fellowship (SMF) prayer band leader. That helped me learn more about missions, meet and chat with some of our WBC alumni who were missionaries, and get closer to some missionaries who came to speak at chapel. One missionary who had ministered with a cannibalistic tribe overseas told us some jokes about cannibals that made us laugh, but his love for those people to come to Christ also stuck with us. Would God lead some of us to such ministries after graduation?

My studies helped me gain a strong foundation theologically and practically. Mr. Paul Mangum taught Pneumatology-Soteriology. In that course, he shared three ways that anyone could discover their spiritual gift(s). First, the gift will give them joy as they serve. Second, there will be fruit in what they did. Third, mature Christians would confirm that they had that gift. My studies and being involved in various Christian service activities helped me explore different types of ministries.

1970 to 1971 WBC men's quartet

I enjoyed music very much and took piano lessons from Miss Nancy Schuppe, a WBC music department faculty member. As a sophomore, I applied to be the WBC men's quartet pianist and was accepted. I didn't major in music or know how to read by sight or play complex sheet music well. However, no other male student was interested in being the quartet pianist that year. I took this from the Lord to grow in Him and be a blessing to many. God gave me the ability to play music by ear and have close to perfect pitch. Any off-key music made me want to howl like a dog because I knew it wasn't correct.

Our first quartet had three seniors and two sophomores: Jerry Sprinkle, Gary Beard, Lee Button, Doug Cook, and me. During my second year as a pianist, I became the oldest member as a junior, while the other four members were sophomores: Dan Schwartz, Joe Stuckey, Paul Koelln, and Bob Brown.

The two years I spent in the men's quartet were invaluable to me. We traveled around Maryland, West Virginia, Virginia, Pennsylvania, New York, and Kentucky. We served for one week at the Scripture Memory Mountain Mission in Kentucky. Dennis Cline, a WBC graduate, was the director there. The camp was in the mountains or hollers as

1970 to 1971 WBC sophomore officers

the locals would say. Such outings made me bolder and more confident in front of people.

In that area of the coal country, we saw huge dump trucks that hauled heavy loads of coal. The camp was in Emmalena, Kentucky. That little town was named for twins Emma and Lena. It was also near another little town called Hell for Certain. Each little town and name had its own story.

Through such opportunities in camps, churches, and other Christian gatherings, we, as quartet members, gave testimonies, planned what songs we'd sing, interacted with each other, and had great times getting to know our hosts and church leaders. I was the member assigned to plan what we were to sing, testify, or preach. My general order in choosing songs that we knew and practiced and then sang publicly was the following: praise, salvation, the Christian life, and Christ's second coming.

During my quartet days, I wasn't free from accidents. We ministered for one week at a Christian camp in the Pocono Mountains in Pennsylvania. We were exploring the grounds and saw a high wooden ski slide where people could go down with their sleds in the winter. I tried to go down but slipped. While trying to stop my fall, I used my hands to catch myself on the wooden slide.

1971 to 1972 WBC men's quartet

It had many little pieces of wood sticking out its sides. My hands rubbed against the old wood when I tried to catch myself. Instantly, many little splinters entered my hands. They gave me much pain, so I was taken to the camp nurse. With a pair of tweezers, one by one, she pulled out a lot of little splinters. Thankfully, I was still able to play the piano for the quartet. I'm glad that none of my buddies had any mishaps like that.

My ability to play by ear and have close to perfect pitch wasn't always a blessing. Twice, when we went to Christian camps, their pianos were so out of tune that I couldn't play them. To my ears, a C was a C. I tried to play simple choruses, like "I Have Decided to Follow Jesus," in the key of C, which didn't have any sharps or flats. However, my mind knew that the actual notes being heard were not in that key—I had to stop playing. That made the quartet sing acapella without my accompaniment. They still did an excellent job without me.

One Sunday night, we sang and ministered in my small home church, Faith Independent Church, in Manheim. After the service, it was cool and foggy. It was my turn to drive over two hours in our black WBC station wagon back to campus.

About six miles after our departure, I drove over a small ridge near Mount Joy. Because of the fog, I tried to follow the painted line in the middle of the road. While I was driving, a small pickup came toward us, towing another car that didn't have its lights on. It was partly on my side of the road, so I sideswiped the towed vehicle.

We had to stop and get that driver's car's documents to report the incident to our WBC business manager the following day. Because I was upset, my legs shook when we talked with the other vehicle's owner, but we were all safe. Through those two years, God cared for us as we traveled back to the campus. Some Sunday nights after singing in a church, we wouldn't arrive back to campus until midnight or later. Thank God! We didn't have any other accidents on those trips.

In my second year with the quartet during our summer ministry, we ministered in the church of a WBC alumnus in New York. When we arrived on Saturday night, the pastor said, "I want one of you to preach in tomorrow morning's worship service." Every one of us looked at each other for a quick response.

Even though we were all in Bible College, none of us had ever preached a sermon. Since I was a junior, and my four quartet buddies were sophomores, they all looked at me to be the one to preach. I reluctantly said, "I'll do it."

That night, I worked hard and stayed up late to prepare. It was the first sermon I had ever preached. One of the church members afterward encouraged me by thanking me for the message. God was stretching me for bigger things ahead. I still have that 4x6 card with the outline of that first message. The idea of two things I never thought I would want to be—a teacher or a preacher—was beginning to change.

During those two years of quartet ministry, we learned much from our quartet advisors, Jim Schuppe and the College music director, James Bos. Mrs. Bos later taught me one year of organ lessons. In the 1972 Milestone yearbook, I stated, "Traveling with the quartet has shown me the importance of living a Christian life wherever I go as a representative of God first and WBC second." As a junior, I was appointed to be the student chaplain. I led various WBC chapels, gave announcements regularly at supper in the college dining hall, and asked different students to pray for the supper meal.

President Dr. George Miles, Dr. Miller, or another WBC or CBS faculty member would occasionally travel to preach and represent WBC on our quartet outings. Men like President Miles and Dr. Miller had real hearts for those who didn't know the Lord. When we'd stop to buy gas, President Miles gave out gospel tracts to people or tried to strike up a conversation to speak out for Christ. He gave us much practical advice for our ministries during such travels, like showing us how to tie a square knot for our neckties. Such memories challenged me to do the same over the years.

My involvement in part-time work and as a quartet pianist forced me to use my time very carefully while I was studying, working, or involved in other Christian service activities. Thus, I didn't have much time or interest in dating. I tried to invite one of the female students to the yearly WBC spring banquet or some student socials but never saw any deep relationships develop.

One challenging time for us WBC singles each year was the Sadie Hawkin's social, a campus event when the girls tried their hardest to tag a boy they liked or wanted to go with to the upcoming Friday night social. From Monday to Friday, if a girl tagged a boy, he was to go to the Friday night social with her. I did end up being nice and accepted invitations to go out with several of them.

One of those socials was a hayride. Somehow when I sat down in the wagon, a sharp object—like a knife or scissors—caught my leg between my ankle and knee. I began to bleed badly. I endured it throughout the social, but afterward, several buddies took me to a local hospital where a medical worker stitched my leg.

Dennis on the WBC Honor Society

When it came to dating during my time at WBC and later at Capital Bible Seminary (CBS), either I was interested in a girl, and she wasn't interested in me, or the opposite was true. So instead of dating much, as some others did, I chose to dig deeper into my studies and Christian service. I was praying that God would direct me to the young lady of His choice at the right time, which wasn't yet.

In addition, as a junior, I became a dorm counselor. The men under my care usually weren't hard to oversee. Some of them later became pastors, seminary professors, and cross-cultural missionaries.

In my senior year, my Christian service opportunity was to work with the children's church at the Grace Brethren Church across the road from WBC. It helped me learn to work more closely with children. The pastor and others at the church also got to know me better and were happy to see my interest in children. They became one of my supporting churches as I later went to Nigeria to teach full-time.

As a senior, I accepted the call to become the SMF president. This position helped me learn more about missions and missionaries and forced me to lead more in public and work with the other SMF student leaders to plan for WBC's annual missions conference.

That year we invited Brother Silas Fox to speak. He was a retired missionary who served as a church planter for many years in India. He and other missionary speakers shared from their experiences some heart-catching stories from India and their host countries. In addition, they shared how God used them cross-culturally and how people who came to Christ also became church leaders.

When I introduced Brother Silas during that missionary conference, I mistakenly said, "Brother Silas Fox is an independent missionary to India." Immediately from the audience, he boldly and loudly corrected me by saying, "I'm not an independent missionary. I'm dependent on the Holy Spirit," which was accurate for him and all of us. I was more careful in what I said after that.

Such interactions with visiting missionaries on campus planted seeds in some of our hearts to consider getting personally involved in cross-cultural missions after graduation. Some of our invited missionary speakers slept in our dorm rooms and ate with us in the dining room, leading to good discussions. As a result, some of our SMF leaders and other WBC students became cross-cultural missionaries to Europe, Africa, Canada, Papua New Guinea, and other countries.

During my senior year from 1972 to 1973, I had one other duty as the dorm counselor for the rooms in the basement under the dining hall. Because WBC was the home of a former Catholic seminary, these rooms were where the Catholic nuns had lived. The fellows in my dorm joked by calling me Mother Superior.

That year we had good times together in the dorm. One of my dorm buddies, Bob Ellis, had designed a homemade gun that he filled with shaving cream. He named it the Splatsomatic. Bob was one of our dorm pranksters. Once while I was in the shower, he quickly entered the bathroom, pulled back the curtain, and pulled the trigger. I was blessed with shaving cream all over me that day, but it was easy to rinse off.

I continued to work hard during my senior year and graduated as valedictorian of my class. I just beat the second-place student, Lois Carlson, by a narrow part of a percentage point. I also did well in New Testament Greek classes. I thank God for all that I learned at WBC. Little did I know that soon I'd be teaching some of the same courses that I had just taken.

1973 - My family at my WBC graduation

Chapter 7

Getting My Feet Wet in Nigeria for One Summer

"I will instruct you and teach you in the way you should go;
I will counsel you and watch over you"
(Psalm 32:8).

Over the years, I've always enjoyed using CEF choruses and hymns. Their lyrics are often simple but very biblical and educational. CEF produced the song, "One Step at a Time," with the following words:

One step at a time, only one step at a time.
That is the way the Lord will lead you,
One step at a time.
Take that one step carefully,
Walk that one step prayerfully,
That is the way to victory,
One step at a time.[2]

Since some Christian leaders remind us that life is a journey, it's exciting to see how God continues to lead us in our daily journey as we seek His will. We must stay close to Him in obedience to His word in the Bible.

Joshua, Elizabeth, and Mishael

In 1973, during my senior year, President Miles was approached by Brother Joshua Ekpikhe, the president of the Christian Witness Team, Inc. (CWT) in Nigeria. He wanted President Miles to help him find two teachers to minister at his Bible & Missionary Training Center (BMTC) that summer. The BMTC and the CWT headquarters were in the little village of Ikwa, in the country's Southeastern State.

The CWT began in 1961. Brother Joshua came to know Christ as his Savior after finding a gospel tract in a gutter.

It was written by Oswald J. Smith and entitled "Be Sure of Your Salvation."[3] In it he found four steps to take to become a Christian. Later God called Joshua and his wife, Elizabeth, along with Brother Mensah Nartey, who had a great gift of evangelism—later renamed Mishael Nathan—to return to Joshua's home village of Ikwa to start the ministry. BMTC was the Bible-teaching arm of the CWT, while Baraka Press and Publishers, Ltd., was in Kaduna. The CWT had several Christian bookshops also in Kaduna, Aba, and Ikwa.

Brother Joshua was looking for an older and younger graduate of CBS, the graduate school of WBC. Both men would help BMTC start up classes again, as it was closed for one year because of the lack of teachers.

With God's help, President Miles found Chester Boyd to be the older teacher. Chester had a Plymouth Brethren Assembly background, the same as Brother Joshua's. President Miles was having problems finding a younger teacher to join Chester. However, he was watching me while I was the men's quartet pianist for two years, the student chaplain my junior year, and the Student Missions Fellowship president my senior year.

He approached me one day, challenging me, "Dennis, I want you to pray about going to teach in a small Bible college in Nigeria this coming summer." My first response was to laugh at him and say, "No." Even though I was heavily involved in missions and Christian service activities at WBC, I had never thought about going to Africa. I surely didn't know much about that continent or Nigeria.

President Miles continued to pray for a young man to meet Joshua's request. Brother Joshua and the CWT were also earnestly praying for this need. President Miles didn't give up. He asked me a second time, "Dennis, I want you to pray much about going to teach at BMTC in Nigeria for one summer. No other name comes to my mind who could go."

During my weekly phone calls to my parents, I shared this opportunity with them. I had already planned to go to the CEF Leadership Training Institute in Muskegon, Michigan, for the summer. My mother had received some inheritance money from her parent's estate. She wanted me to attend CEF's three-month training program to help me minister better to children. I was willing to go.

However, when this new opportunity to teach in Nigeria was presented, my parents advised me, "Such a chance might never come to you again. We'd be happy to see you go to Nigeria. You can go to the CEF Institute later." I agreed and quickly told President Miles I'd be willing to go. He was thrilled and passed on the good news to Brother Joshua. God had answered their prayers!

During that spring, as a senior, I began preparing to go to Nigeria. After graduating in May, I returned home to Manheim. I prepared to teach Principles of Biblical Interpretation and The Christian Life at BMTC, over 6,000 miles from home.

June 1973 - Preparing for BMTC courses

I had never taught these courses before. I didn't have any course guidelines to build upon, so I used my WBC course notes and other sources to prepare a set of notes to use at BMTC. Taking detailed notes in my classes paid off in this new opportunity. I had to pass on many essential truths to the BMTC students.

With the help of President Miles and his secretary, Eleanor Bergsten, tickets were bought for Chester and me to fly to Nigeria. Finally, in early June, we were ready to leave. Still, our visas were delayed in being approved by the Nigerian Embassy. I later learned that this would not be the first time such a delay would happen. Visas to Nigeria weren't easy to obtain.

The date for our planned departure passed. I asked, "Will we travel or not this summer?" We couldn't do anything about the situation, except to keep praying. I kept reading and studying more for my summer duties. We kept waiting.

Two weeks after we were to travel, President Miles called to inform me that our visas had finally arrived. He wanted us to prepare quickly to leave within several days. I was able to do that since I didn't have much to take to Nigeria. Daddy and Momma drove me to Washington, D.C., to meet Chester and have President Miles pray for us and send us off to Nigeria from the National Airport. This was my first trip overseas; I didn't know what to expect.

We said our goodbyes to my parents and President Miles, knowing they would faithfully pray for us. Both Chester and I had prepared for our teaching the best we could. He was to teach Romans and Galatians, along with Homiletics. We took copies of several textbooks with us for each of our courses so our students could read for their daily assignments from reserve materials.

Communication to Nigeria during the 1970s was mainly by airmail. That took several weeks one way. Phone calls to Nigeria were almost impossible, except in key cities. Brother Joshua had already returned to Nigeria.

He and his staff had thought Chester and I were arriving on our original date in early June. For several days, they waited expectantly for our arrival at Port Harcourt Airport. Unfortunately, many roads to Port Harcourt, which was about four hours from Ikwa, were not in good condition. Being in the middle of the tropical rainy season also kept the roads from being repaired. Since we didn't arrive on time, the CWT staff and BMTC students were very disappointed—they had to return to Ikwa without any teachers for their summer school.

With this lack of communication and without our Nigerian friends' knowledge, Chester and I flew to Nigeria in mid-June on a Boeing 707 jet through Brussels, Belgium. We were advised to take a daily malaria pill to prevent us from getting a severe attack of malaria. The one I had to take was a huge tablet. I had never learned to swallow a big pill before this.

When we ate lunch during our layover in Brussels, I drank several glasses of water to try to swallow that monster pill. No matter what I did, it wouldn't go down. Finally, I had to chew that very bitter pill. Over time I did learn how to swallow capsules, one of the many lessons I had to learn as a new cross-cultural missionary.

One does not become a cross-cultural missionary one day and the next day hop on a jet to fly to the country of one's dreams. Instead, God works in the person's life right from birth. God uses each situation—one step at a time—to mold the person for present and future ministries.

Before traveling to Nigeria, I wasn't a Missions department major at WBC, so I never had any official cross-cultural orientation, training, or exposure. So much of my learning when I first went to Nigeria was learned on the job, rather than from textbooks, mentors, or other missions leaders. The Lord helped us!

We were relieved and happy to see Brother Peter Zawua meet us at the Kano airport, over 700 miles north of BMTC. Because he lived in Kaduna City, which had better communication than Ikwa, he knew when we were to arrive.

Peter had come to know the Lord through Brother Joshua personally sharing the gospel with him at the CWT's bookstore in Kaduna. Before he came to know Christ, Peter worked at a Nigerian brewery and drank much alcohol. His wife, Dorcas, became a Christian before he did. After his conversion, Peter worked at this same CWT bookstore and was a vibrant witness for Christ.

So many things were very strange to us as foreigners in Nigeria. While eating our first breakfast at Kano, we looked out the window and saw a giant lizard about a foot long. I quickly jumped out of my chair to grab my camera. I had to get a picture since the lizard looked like someone had taken a paintbrush and painted various strokes with orange, blue, and white colors all over its body. Peter thought we were crazy, but we had never seen such a pretty lizard.

The bus drive from Kano to Kaduna took about two and a half hours. Kano and Kaduna's weather was very dry during June. Many fields were cleared and dry, looking very bare without crops growing in them. On our way, the bus suddenly stopped. The men walked to one side of the road; the ladies went to the other side. I asked myself, "What is happening?" I realized they were going to the bathroom. As Nigerians would tell me, "We must ease ourselves." This was necessary since many areas of Nigeria, especially in rural settings, didn't have public toilets like in the U.S. or Europe. The men stood up, and the ladies squatted down to urinate. When they were done, they all quietly returned to sit on the bus. The driver continued to drive on.

When we arrived in Kaduna, some Christian brethren gladly welcomed us. I quickly learned that Nigerians are very hospitable. We came to the home of the Essien family. Brother Essien was Brother Joshua's brother-in-law. His wife, Sister Comfort, politely asked us, "Would you like some squash?" I didn't know what to say. Before I traveled to Nigeria, I was warned that I shouldn't eat anything that wasn't cooked unless I could peel it, like a banana. This led me to answer politely, "No, thank you."

Little did I know that "squash" in that context wasn't a tiny pumpkin or gourd to eat but was a concentrated orange or currant-flavored drink. The hostess would pour a capful of about two ounces into a glass and then add water to it. The result was that it tasted like Kool-Aid or an uncarbonated soft drink. I missed an opportunity to have a nice drink.

Since our final goal was to get to Ikwa, we flew from Kaduna to Lagos and then to Port Harcourt. Upon arrival, no one was waiting for us. We wondered, "Now what should we do?" Those from Ikwa had given up on our arrival. Also, on our part, it was impossible to call Ikwa by phone, because there was no phone service in that area. Since we arrived early in the afternoon, we hired a taxi driver to take us and our suitcases to Ikwa, even though we had no directions to get there. Also, we weren't used to Nigerian time or sunsets, which occurred at about 6:30 p.m. much of the year.

We did know that the CWT had a Christian bookstore in Aba, about 60 miles from Ikwa. The driver willingly took us there, where we met the bookstore manager, Godwin Oji. He gave the driver directions on how to get to Ikwa. God again guided us one step at a time to finally find Ikwa.

We were happy to arrive late that afternoon. The driver drove us along Ikwa village's dirt road and through water puddles to the village's far side, where the CWT compound was located. Ikwa is in the tropics. Late June is the middle of Ikwa's rainy season, compared to Kano's and Kaduna's much drier weather. Much of the CWT's ten-acre compound had weeds and grass growing on it several feet high. When the summer school students learned of our arrival, they came running and jumping for joy that we had finally arrived safely with our luggage.

The location of Ikwa in Nigeria[4]

The taxi driver unloaded our suitcases, happy that we had reached our destination safely. After he departed, Brother Joshua and the CWT staff sadly learned that we had paid the driver much more than they would have allowed or paid. We needed to learn to bargain for the price of items or charges before agreeing on the final price. After that, we let the nationals deal with their people whenever possible regarding money matters.

For Chester and me living in the U.S., we never had to worry about living at night without electricity or sleeping under a mosquito net. Kerosene lanterns or candles gave us light at night. We learned how coconuts and pineapples grew. Flushing our toilet with a bucket of water and getting a drink from a water filter—often drinking it without being cold—were all new to us. This made me always appreciate having electricity and clean water back in the U.S.

In the early mornings and late afternoons, little sandflies flew in the air, attracted to our skin. They looked like tiny pieces of dirt or sand. They'd come and bite us on our arms, legs, and faces. When they bit us, our skin looked like we had chickenpox. Our bodies eventually became more resistant to them, and the spots went away more quickly. We learned to wear long-sleeved shirts and long pants to protect ourselves. We also avoided being outside during early mornings or late afternoons before sundown.

By a coconut tree with Chester

BMTC's motto was "Come—Learn! Go—Teach!" The students had a great hunger to study our courses. The names of some of the students in our first classes were Mfon and Unwa Ubak, Nsese Umoh, and Isaac Okon. They were already staff members of the CWT. Others, like Stanley Okoro and Andrew Omede, came from Lagos and Benue State. We had good times in the classroom, at Monday mornings of prayer, in daily chapels, and in Sunday church services at the Ikwa Christian Assembly (ICA).

We began learning a great deal that summer on the job. I already knew that one of the most important things that matters to someone is their name. That simple principle helped me immensely over the years, whether in the U.S., as we ministered to our supporting churches and our friends, or in Nigeria. I tried to learn the names of as many of our students and staff as quickly as possible. Many of their names we had never heard before, or they were hard to pronounce. Initially, many of the nationals looked the same, but as time passed, we learned more about their features and differences. We soon became good friends.

To help me apply this principle, when I'd meet a student for the first time or call their name on the class attendance sheet on the first day of class, I'd ask which one of their names they wanted me to call them. Unlike in the U.S., in Nigeria one can call a person by their last name (surname), and they won't be offended. I told my students that in the U.S. if someone were to call me Shelly, I'd think that the caller was angry at me or was trying to insult me.

In Nigeria, people are very proud of their family's last name. I needed to remember what country I was living in. So, if an African called me by my last name, it might be more out of respect for me as a teacher or adult than an insult. In such cases, I tried not to be offended.

Ikwa village was Brother Joshua's birthplace. There in his parent's home right inside the village, in 1961 God gave him the vision to make Christ known through the CWT. It was made up of BMTC, Baraka Press, the CWT's Mission bookshops, and later other departments. His father died when he was a young child. His mother lived in Ikwa and supported Joshua's vision as much as she could.

Brother Joshua's home in Ikwa village

Chester and I ate our meals at Brother Joshua's house on the CWT compound.

Elizabeth was a good cook. She tried her best to provide good meals for us. They both had been to the U.S. in past years, so they knew what we were used to. However, because we were in a village, they couldn't provide a lot of variety for us. We often ate rice and items like Heinz baked beans from tin cans. Meat was also hard to find.

We did lose some weight during our stay because of the tropical heat and limited food items to eat. If we'd drink a cup of hot tea, we'd add some sugar and pour in some evaporated milk from a small can. One of the first times I was offered this, I thought that they were offering me some "pig" milk. I heard wrongly. They were offering me some "Peak" milk, which is the name of an evaporated milk company. I felt better after knowing that. It had a good taste.

Chester also brought some garlic pills with him. He said that they would help the mosquitoes to stay away from him. That might have helped him, but I could also smell garlic on him when we were close together. Most of the time, we were very sweaty and wet from the hot, tropical weather and high humidity.

During that first summer of 1973, we needed to take an umbrella with us wherever we went, since it was raining much of the time. Our classes were held in a small building, with a zinc (tin) roof, on the far edge of the compound and the main room of our house. When a heavy downpour came, which was often, we'd be forced to stop teaching and wait until the rain stopped before we could continue teaching. The sound on the roof was often so loud that no one could hear us, even if we yelled at the top of our voices.

The summer went fast and was a great experience with the BMTC students. Chester and I immensely enjoyed our teaching and studies together. We came to know the staff and students over those weeks. We had good opportunities to speak in church activities and chapels. Time spent with students and staff was rewarding. We played volleyball and soccer (football in Nigeria—from now on I'll put the words that Nigerians are more familiar with in parentheses throughout the book) with them several times weekly. Discussions in and out of the classroom were also enjoyable. The students were encouraged that they were able to attend these classes and learn more about how to study the Bible and live the Christian life more victoriously in their daily lives.

In 1972, Nigeria switched from the British or European style of driving to the American style, so how Nigerians drove wasn't a culture shock to me. However, the local roads had many holes (gallops) in them. Even good drivers couldn't avoid missing all of them. They learned to stay close to the middle of the road unless someone was driving toward them on the other side. Most roads weren't marked with paint like in the U.S. I vowed that first summer that if I ever returned to Nigeria, I would never drive.

Some weeks before Chester and I returned to the U.S., Brother Joshua asked me to prayerfully consider returning to Ikwa to teach for the next August to December semester. Unfortunately, he didn't have enough teachers to teach all their planned subjects, so they could start up BMTC fully.

His request was an enormous challenge since I was already accepted to attend CBS to start my seminary studies that August. I had already come to Ikwa for that summer and postponed attending the summer CEF Institute in Muskegon, Michigan. I initially responded, "Okay. I'll pray about it." How could I get counsel on what to do? I decided to trust God to show me what to do by reading through the Psalms in my devotions.

I started reading Psalm 1 and continued reading more of the Psalms daily. In Psalm 16:7, the psalmist wrote, "I will praise the Lord, who counsels me." Verse 11 added, "You make known to me the path of life; you will fill me with joy in your presence."

I kept reading until I came to Psalm 32:8, where God promised, "I will instruct you and teach you in the way you should go; I will counsel you with my loving eye on you." These verses gave me peace from the Lord to tell Brother Joshua that I was willing to return to Ikwa to teach for that next semester.

Despite the slow speed of Nigerian mail, I was able to write my parents and President Miles about this. President Miles, who had challenged me early in 1973 about going to teach at BMTC, surprisingly felt I shouldn't return to BMTC but should begin my CBS studies. In addition, he thought I needed more education to do a better job teaching. Finally, he agreed, "If God opens the way for you to get a visa, I'll take it as God's will for you to return to teach."

1973 - With Joshua & Elizabeth at Ikwa

Brother Joshua had to drive about 100 miles to Port Harcourt and then fly to Lagos, about 400 miles away from Ikwa, to apply to the Nigerian Embassy for a visa on my behalf. Every trip by road and especially by air involved money. Visas also cost money. CWT finances were often very tight and limited.

However, through all of this, God was working. Brother Joshua was a man of prayer, faith, and trust in God's promises to meet his needs. He told us that on more than one occasion, he was traveling, standing in the check-in line without his ticket money in his hand. He believed that God would supply his need for money. Before he got to the desk, someone would come and give him an envelope with enough money for the trip.

The CWT staff also trusted God about such matters as visas. He was able to get my visa approved in one day in Lagos. He came back praising God for answering their prayers for me to get that visa. This gave me more peace that God wanted me to continue teaching at BMTC.

The CWT and BMTC had a send-off service for Chester and me. It wasn't easy to say goodbye. They sang the song, "Blessed Be the Tie That Binds," which didn't help to leave them without some tears.

When Chester and I arrived at Kennedy Airport in New York City, I called my parents. I shared that my visa had been approved and that I could return to Nigeria to teach for the next semester. Daddy quickly replied on the phone, "Well, I guess that's the green light for you to return." God's supplying my visa met President Miles' condition for my return. He readily agreed that I could return to Ikwa and begin my CBS studies one year later, in 1974. That's how God led me, one step at a time.

In 1973, costs for airline tickets and missionary support were not as high as today. God continued to lead me and provide, stretching my faith and that of my parents and President Miles. For this second airline ticket, neither President Miles nor WBC committed to paying for the cost. This time I had to personally pay for it. I only had several weeks in the U.S. living with Daddy and Momma before I needed to return to teach in August. How would God work this out for me this time?

One night at home on my top bunk bed, I couldn't go to sleep. I asked the Lord, "How am I going to get enough money for my ticket and living expenses to return to Ikwa for two semesters?" My concern was natural since various friends had only given me about $75.00 of the hundreds of dollars needed.

1973 - With Joshua & Elizabeth at Ikwa

As I was lying there, God gave me peace in my heart, assuring me, "I'm going to supply your needs and get you back to Nigeria. Don't worry!" After that, I was able to sleep well. Soon some friends and donors gave me enough money to pay for my airfare with enough money to care for my needs. Thus began another step in my journey to teach at BMTC for the following two semesters.

Chapter 8

More Training Needed before Full-Time Ministry

"I press on toward the goal to win the prize for which God has called me heavenward in Christ Jesus" (Philippians 3:14).

In late August 1973, I returned to Nigeria to teach two more semesters at BMTC. I didn't join a mission board or need to raise much money for my monthly support or expenses. Those at WBC and CBS readily understood why I was postponing my seminary studies for one year and approved this step of faith. Those two semesters of teaching were not a mistake. I knew that my experiences teaching the Nigerian students at BMTC would stretch my faith and increase my motivation to go to seminary.

For this trip, I traveled by myself. Once I arrived in Ikwa, I settled in my allotted house. I shared my home with Brother Sunday Got, another single Nigerian Bible college graduate from northern Nigeria. He also wanted to serve the Lord as a Bible teacher at BMTC. Between our teaching and studies for the next day's classes, we enjoyed working outside in the garden, playing volleyball and soccer (football), and attending various chapels and church activities in the ICA.

Our BMTC students back in the 1970s learned how to study the Bible well and were taught the importance of not being ashamed to use their hands and work hard. They'd rise at about 5:00 a.m. for morning devotions. About ten hours of compound duties were built into their schedule each week.

1973 BMTC faculty & students

To survive, they had to spend time each day walking from the CWT compound to collect water from the village stream one mile away. At that time, the CWT compound didn't have a borehole or well. They'd fetch one bucket of water from the stream for the kitchen and then make a second trip for their baths.

They used machetes to cut several acres of grass on the Ikwa compound and harvest cassava tubers to process garri. To make this, they'd dig out the cassava tubers from the soft, brown soil on the CWT farm. Cassava was like big, long, sweet potatoes—some more than a foot long. They'd peel the tubers, then take them in a wheelbarrow or carry them in a basin on their heads to the village grinding machine. Then they'd put the contents in a cloth bag to squeeze out the juice.

Unfortunately, the liquid contained arsenic, which was poisonous, so they had to be careful. The ground-up mass that remained in the bag was fermented overnight, then fried and dried the next day over a smoky fire in a metal basin. The result was garri, which was often mixed with a bit of palm oil to make it yellow. Garri was one of the main staple foods of the Ibibio people, the tribe of Brother Joshua's family and the villagers of Ikwa. These chores helped the students learn the dignity of hard work and prepared them more for future Christian ministries.

BMTC students responded well to these disciplines. By putting them into practice, they could support themselves through farming or other skills, having a greater chance of success in their later Christian ministries. Moreover, they wouldn't have to depend mainly on their paper qualifications to see them through. This was one of Brother Joshua's goals for every BMTC student and graduate!

My oil lantern at my Ikwa house

My first year of teaching at BMTC forced me to study hard, even though they didn't have a large library of commentaries and Christian resources handy. One day that fall, I was teaching the course The Gospel of John. I had planned to cover John 3:1–36 for that day's class period. The students asked me questions from verses 4–5, such as, "What does being born of the Spirit and water mean?"

They kept asking tough questions I didn't know how to answer. I didn't get to the end of the chapter and was almost in tears before the class was over. I went home that day, continuing to dig deeper to answer such questions. Teaching also gave me a greater desire to go on to seminary to study and be ready to answer future questions that might come my way. My students helped me realize that I didn't know much and had much more to learn.

At Ikwa, as a teacher, I tried to practice how several of our WBC faculty members responded when students asked them questions in their classes. When unsure of an answer, Professor Willis Bishop would respond, "I'll write it down and come back with an answer next week." He did just that.

Mr. Jim Schuppe, who taught us Principles of Biblical Interpretation and New Testament Survey, gave a challenging answer to students after they asked him a question. He'd say, "That's a good question. Work on it!" In such situations, both teachers and students were challenged to continue studying as life-long learners.

We did a great deal of walking at Ikwa, especially in the 1970s. A major road was being constructed beside our CWT compound, but it wasn't ready for use for several years. We were forced to drive through Ikwa's main village dirt road to the CWT compound. At the front of the village, we had to go over a concrete culvert. That made us get out of our little cars, so the car could go over it first. Then we'd walk to the other side and climb back into the vehicle to proceed.

Driving on our Ikwa road

We enjoyed watching how God cared for nature. If we didn't have a watch, we could get some clues about the time from the local birds and insects. We could hear the African gray parrots talking as they would fly toward the ocean around 6:15 a.m. and return around 6:15 p.m. since the sun usually set before 7 p.m. any given night of the year. The flying ants would come out around 8:50 p.m. and return to their ant hill around 9:20 p.m. A wasp would come out and fly around 9:45 p.m. Most days were cloudy, while the night skies were often surprisingly clear, so we could see the stars easily.

During my first Christmas break in Nigeria in 1973, I traveled about four hours in several taxis to Umuahia to visit and stay with two veteran missionaries, Dad and Mom Piepgrass. One old Peugeot 504 station wagon taxi that I boarded was packed full of people. Even though the passengers were very worried because the taxi's horn didn't work, we went ahead and made the journey to Umuahia safely. Dad and Mom had

Christian literature and bookshop ministries and had many tracts printed for distribution.

While there, I had the first of many problems with an ingrown toenail on my right big toe. Dad Piepgrass saw it and said that he had solved similar problems for friends over the years. He said that he could take his pliers and pinch them on my toenail. He'd then twist the pliers and the toenail would come off. I agreed.

However, when he twisted it, the toenail only came off partially, with the other part still pushing into my toe. I was racked with pain. After his plan failed, he took me to one of his good Nigerian doctor friends in Umuahia, who looked at it and knew what to do. The doctor had me dress in a hospital gown and lie down on a metal table. He then called several assistants, all in white outfits and with masks. They took me to their operating room (theater), numbed my foot, and removed the remaining part of my toenail. I hobbled around for a few days, ended my visit with them, and returned to Ikwa to resume teaching for the January semester.

The toe slowly healed, but over later years, I had numerous ingrown toenail operations in Nigeria and the U.S., including one operation in Lancaster where two of my middle toes were broken so I could wear hard shoes, as I had worn sandals for many years. That was also unsuccessful. Although my toes don't look very nice today, Romans 10:15 encourages me, "How beautiful are the feet of those who bring good news."

During one local visit to some villagers, the host wanted me to be assured that the soft drink (mineral) that I was to drink wasn't poisoned and was safe to drink. He opened the bottle, poured some into a small glass, drank it, and then served the rest to me. I also had some culture shock when I saw several Nigerians use their teeth to remove a soft drink bottle cap. I was sure that their teeth would break, but their teeth were very strong because they didn't eat or drink many sweet things.

Several times during those two semesters, I traveled with Brother Joshua to Uyo or Aba to shop or make contacts for the ministries. During one trip to Aba, about 60 miles from Ikwa, I stayed in the car while Brother Joshua went to the market. One young man saw a sticker on our car bumper that showed we were Christians. He wanted to know about the Lord. I gave him a gospel tract, and he walked away.

However, right after that, he returned and wanted to talk more. I felt the Lord prompting me to share the gospel with him since he had a Catholic background. Finally, he decided to trust the Lord Jesus as his Savior from sin. We exchanged our names and addresses, and I invited him to come to visit us at Ikwa.

His name was Geoffrey Madubuike. Some weeks later, he traveled to Ikwa to see me, bringing me a live chicken and some food items as gifts. One step led to another. He enrolled to become a BMTC student. After three years, he graduated and returned to minister in his village in Imo State.

Ikwa village's monkey bridge

When the roads were too muddy for cars to drive into Ikwa, we'd leave our car in the nearby village of Ikot Akan, one and a half miles away. Our tropical location brought heavy rains much of the year. We'd walk down a big hill and carefully walk across a monkey bridge (made of some tree trunks with bamboo on the sides) that crossed over the village stream to Ikwa. We'd finally walk to our compound. Sometimes it was at night. If the moon was shining, we could see better where we were walking and wouldn't need to use our flashlights (torches) to avoid mud and puddles along the way. God gave us joy in doing this.

After teaching those two semesters at BMTC from late 1973 until April 1974, I returned home to the U.S. That summer, I attended CEF's three-month Leadership Training Institute in Muskegon, Michigan. My parents adjusted their schedules to drive me there. The class was comprised of 38 students from various countries, such as Jamaica, Rhodesia (now divided into Zambia and Zimbabwe), and Ireland. Most of us came from the U.S. We desired to learn how to work more effectively with children and youth and to see them come to Christ and grow in Him.

CEF Institute missionary students

Those three months helped us to bond together since we had similar goals to reach children for Christ. We had excellent trainers who were either CEF teacher training team members or CEF headquarters staff. CEF President Roland Gerdes taught us some of the doctrinal courses. The courses weren't heavy academically but kept us busy doing practical tasks, such as making a visualized song or Bible verse, teaching a missions story or a Bible lesson, or planning a Good News Club session.

This training helped me teach children better. It helped me blend various CEF principles into what I'd later teach in my Principles of Teaching or Homiletics courses at BMTC. For example, in each Bible lesson taught to children, CEF trained us to use a practical application for the saved and a practical application for the unsaved.

I was elected the president of the CEF Institute class, so our executive members met to plan various activities. The three months went by quickly. When it was time to depart, we said our goodbyes. Some of us kept in touch for many years afterward.

In August 1974, the Lord led me to CBS for my first year of seminary studies. My major at CBS was New Testament Greek. I lived about one mile off-campus in the home of a Christian family, the Skinners. I paid rent money to stay in one of their bedrooms and eat my meals with them. I rode my bicycle back and forth as much as the weather permitted.

My first day of CBS classes, a Monday, was a big shock to me. As a WBC senior, the most I was required to translate was three or four verses for a Greek class. However, the pace dramatically increased at CBS in my four new courses that met four times weekly. I was to translate about ten Greek verses, learn the Hebrew alphabet, and read about 30 pages—for the two other classes—by the next day. I asked, "How can I do all this in so short a time?" My abilities were stretched, but such assignments became my average load without too much stress because God helped me.

Since I had completed the 1974 CEF Leadership Training Institute, the CEF Director of Maryland, Miss May Hoover, approached me about working part-time in nearby Montgomery County. They wanted me to help make more contacts and encourage current Good News Club teachers and helpers to keep on reaching their local children for Christ. I consented.

Various Christians were praying that someone would fill this spot. One lady was Mrs. Roberta Bedi. She and her husband, Steve Sr., lived in Riverdale near the University of Maryland. They were committed to loaning their car to me to use so I could drive about 20 miles one way to Montgomery County. There I worked with their son, Steve Jr., and his wife, Phyllis, who were the CEF committee members in that county. Steve was their chairman.

On scheduled days for me to serve with CEF, Mrs. Bedi would drive about ten miles to pick me up at CBS. We'd return together to her house. I'd then drive their car to Damascus, Maryland, to Steve and Phyllis' house to make contacts for CEF by phone, which I did during the afternoon and evening. On my return trip, I'd drive back to Mrs. Bedi's house, and she'd take me back to CBS late that night.

Those trips to CEF gave me good experiences in public relations and working with people on behalf of the children. I also earned a little money for my CBS studies. After CBS and back in Nigeria, I assisted the CEF of Nigeria to establish it nationally. Later the ministry was led by nationals.

1975 - With Pres. Miles & Olah

During my CBS studies, I was asked to teach one WBC evening school course on Principles of Biblical Interpretation. That was already one of my favorite courses to teach when I was at BMTC. The class had about 40 men and women. Some were Sunday school teachers, workers from the suburbs around WBC and Washington, D.C., or had Afro-American backgrounds. I kept being involved in missions during my CBS years and was their student missions leader for one year.

During the summer of 1975, I returned to Nigeria and BMTC to teach with Olah Moore, an Afro-American CBS student from Norfolk, Virginia. Olah was a U.S. Army captain who served in Vietnam. It was great to return to Nigeria and connect with some of the Nigerian CWT staff, BMTC staff, and students with whom we had developed good friendships.

1975 - My family at Manheim

After returning from my 1975 summer teaching ministry at BMTC, I began my second year of CBS studies. However, a few weeks into my courses, I didn't have my usual strength. I saw that my urine was turning brown, and my eyes were yellowish. Daddy and Momma took me back to Manheim for some medical tests. My doctor discovered that I had hepatitis A, probably caused by poor hygiene from impure water or unsanitary conditions while at Ikwa.

The remedy for hepatitis A was to eat well and have plenty of rest. I gradually became stronger after more than a month and was approved to return to my CBS studies. If I had delayed a little longer in returning to classes, CBS wouldn't have allowed me to complete the semester. However, God continued to help me that semester to catch up without much difficulty.

I believed that God was leading me to complete CBS and return to teaching full-time at BMTC. Godly leaders, like President Miles and Dr. William Miller, from WBC advised me to apply to a small U.S. mission, Fellowship Independent Mission (FIM)—now Fellowship International Mission—as a missionary to Nigeria.

FIM was unique from many other missions. It was a solid, Bible-believing, evangelical ministry that allowed missionaries to apply who had already served the Lord overseas and felt called by God. FIM represented these missionaries, who otherwise didn't have an American mission, and passed on financial support to them with approved U.S. government regulations. This was my dilemma, and FIM met my needs just fine!

1977 - Shelly family at my CBS graduation

I graduated from CBS in May 1977 with my Master of Theology degree. I wasn't the valedictorian of my class, but I did my best. Although I was a Greek major, I never saw myself as a scholar. Two of my CBS mates, Todd Beall and Dennis Tinkler, did better than I did in most of my courses. We learned much together and saw God lead us all into full-time ministries. Todd and his wife, Sharon, have been faithful supporters of me, my family, and the Nigerian ministries from 1977 until today!

My ordination service at my home church, Faith Independent Church in Manheim, Pennsylvania, was held on June 10. I wanted to have it right after I graduated from CBS, so I wouldn't forget many vital truths and principles gained from my studies during the ordination interview.

I was honored to have key Christian leaders attend my ordination council to interview me. Pastor Lee Damon from my home church organized it. Others attending were

President George Miles, Dr. Homer Heater, Jr., our CBS academic dean, and several pastors from local Bible-believing churches. Our home elders, including Daddy, along with Momma, attended. Some godly leaders discussed with me that someone should be ordained not just to be ordained, but because they felt God's call on their life. The ordination would be one step that God would use to confirm that others felt God had called the person into ministry.

The ordination council took about three hours. Momma wrote down each question that the council members asked me. How many questions did they ask? The answer was 55. I passed successfully. The council recommended that I should be ordained that very evening in a church service. Dr. Homer Heater, Jr., gave me the challenge. All went well. Praise the Lord!

During that spring and summer, I shared my ministry with several churches and friends who had known me over the years at WBC and CBS or who I had served with in Christian ministry. As a result, FIM accepted me to go to Nigeria as one of their missionaries. President Miles and Dr. Miller also gave recommendations on my behalf. This again proved that, if I was involved in what God wanted me to do, He would supply my needs and lead me one step at a time to where He wanted me to serve Him (Psalm 32:8).

At least three churches became interested in supporting me to go to Nigeria in 1977. First was Webster Bible Church, Webster, New York, where I had done my ten-week CBS internship under Dr. Harry Fletcher. The pastoral staff gave me various opportunities to teach an adult Sunday school class on a book study of Colossians (my favorite book), lead in their children's church, visit youth, go to the county prison for the first time and share the gospel, preach in their Sunday evening service, and interact with many of the members. One phrase that Dr. Fletcher impressed upon me various times during my internship was, "Be flexible." If I hadn't kept that in mind later in ministries, I would have quit more than once! Several of the families who attended that 1976 Colossians Sunday school class at Webster Bible Church later attended other churches but still pray for and support our family financially.

Secondly, Independent Bible Church in Martinsburg, West Virginia, where our WBC men's quartet had sung, began supporting me. Their pastor, Charles Hanshew, was President Miles' son-in-law. Independent Bible Church had a great passion for world missions. He and Elder Elmer Fry visited us for our 1981 BMTC Christian Education Conference and graduation.

Thirdly, Pastor Abram Gish of Word of Life Chapel in Bainbridge, Pennsylvania, was a FIM Council member who recommended that their church support me monthly.

Other churches, like Lisbon Bible Church—now MABC, in Mount Airy, Maryland—began supporting me. These churches have continued supporting me and our family right up to the present.

My home church while I was at WBC and CBS, Faith Independent Church—now Lake View Bible Church—in Manheim, Pennsylvania, has also supported us over many of these years. Grace Brethren Church in Lanham, Maryland, where I did my Christian service ministry while at WBC, began supporting me. Several other churches played a part over the years in supporting me.

It was amazing to see how God began to raise Christian friends with whom I had ministered in the past to become blessings and partners with me. My team of senders who would support me with their prayers and financial support was beginning to increase.

By late August 1977, God helped me raise enough support to buy my airline ticket. In addition, I had several hundred dollars in monthly support to enable me to return for several years to teach full-time at BMTC. I said my goodbyes to my family and friends and returned by myself to Ikwa. This was another big step of faith to see how God would use me in a full-time teaching ministry in Nigeria!

Chapter 9

A Single Missionary Learning with His Mates

*"Preach the word; be prepared in season and out of season;
correct, rebuke, and encourage—with great
patience and careful instruction"
(II Timothy 4:2).*

I never had any official orientation training or exposure from WBC or FIM to prepare for my cross-cultural ministries. Much of what I learned as I first went to Nigeria was on-the-job training, and not so much from textbooks, mentors, or other missions leaders.

Many things in Nigeria and at Ikwa changed over the years that I lived and taught at BMTC as a single missionary. Some were good; others were not. When I first arrived at Ikwa, our school's name was The Bible & Missionary Training Centre, with the British/Nigerian spelling. Later, we changed it to The Bible & Missionary Theological College when we upgraded our curriculum and entry requirements.

1973 - BMTC's first signboard

During my first visits between 1973 and 1975, our state was called the Southeastern State. Later it became the Cross River State, with Calabar as its capital. Any trip to Calabar took three hours one way by Oron. We'd drive our car through Eket and Oron, then take a ferry.

Our former Local Government Area of Opobo was changed to Ikot Abasi, meaning "people of God." Years later, a major road and bridge were constructed through some swampy areas past Uyo and over a river near Itu, so we could drive the entire trip of 120 miles to Calabar. Over the years, we spent countless hours driving on primitive roads, many needing major repairs, especially during the rainy season.

Tree god in the middle of the road

On various trips to Abak and Uyo, we had to drive around one big tree that was standing right in the middle, with the road going around both sides of it. We asked about it. We were told that the village believed that the tree was a god, and that they couldn't cut it down when the road was being constructed. Several years later, we saw that the tree had died but was still left standing. Such beliefs showed how animism and the worship of ancestors controlled many of the local people.

The contrast between the Western and African worldviews was often seen in similar situations. If someone would die in the U.S., we'd try to find out the cause of the person's death. In Nigeria, if someone died, many of the people might ask, "Who killed them?"

I returned with Olah Moore to the U.S. at the end of the summer of 1975. We learned that the first BMTC graduation was held at Ikwa later that year. Stan Okoro and Andrew Omede received their BMTC Diplomas in Theology. Stan was the first BMTC graduate to go to WBC to do his B.A. in Bible, then on to do his Ed.D. in Adult Education. Andrew returned to minister to his people in Igalaland in Kogi State. Andrew is now with the Lord.

1975 - Andrew and Stan

During the summer of 1976, I was still in the U.S., working part-time with CEF in Montgomery County, Maryland. I was two-thirds through my CBS studies. A team from WBC visited Ikwa to build the foundation for the Fletcher Memorial Clinic (FMC) inside Ikwa village in memory of Ted and Harry Fletcher's parents. Overseeing that project was Leroy Blevins, WBC's maintenance supervisor.

The CWT had various Christian businessmen and laypeople represent them in the U.S. under the Christian Witness Support Team (CWST). Members who came to Ikwa for short visits and who supported the CWT through prayer and finances were Alvin Peters, Larry French, Ted Fletcher, Don and Phoebe Darling, Dr. Ron and Maryann Wall, along with others. Ted and Don coordinated the CWST in the U.S. for several years.

WBC visiting team at FMC foundation

When Ted Fletcher visited Ikwa in 1976, God gave him the vision of beginning the World Evangelical Outreach, later renamed Pioneers. According to their website at pioneers.org/core-values, "The mission of Pioneers is to mobilize teams to glorify God among unreached peoples by initiating church-planting movements in partnership with local churches."

Through the CWST's efforts, several WBC graduates joined us at Ikwa for ministries. Through first-hand exposure to cross-cultural missions at Ikwa, God led some of our U.S. missionaries who served at Ikwa to other ministries. Several examples will be seen below. Carol Baur came to teach for several semesters at BMTC. Ruth Wright, a registered nurse, served several years at the FMC, later renamed Fletcher Memorial Hospital (FMH). While at Ikwa, they made visits to local villages for ministry. Carol taught Bible stories. Ruth taught about basic health and looked after the sick.

Ruth returned to the U.S. in 1981 to serve with Pioneers. She was sent to Papua New Guinea for five years, then worked in the Pioneers' home office heading up their short-term missions outreaches. In 1992, she began working with internationals in Virginia and still faithfully continues reaching out to them. I was able to buy Ruth's VW Beetle when she left Ikwa. This was the first car I ever owned.

During the same summer of 1976, Ralph Sauers and Olah taught at BMTC. Olah later returned to teach at BMTC in 1978 and became our BMTC dean of students until 1985. He did a great job leading because of his military training as a captain. Ralph taught for several semesters from March to July 1976 and March 1977 to April 1979.

One life-changing event for Ralph happened during that summer. Ralph became very sick from malaria. Two young American ladies came to Ikwa with Dr. Andrew Foster. He directed the Christian School of the Deaf in Ibadan, near Lagos. They were coming to visit Brother Samuel Ijatuyi, the CWT's administrator, who was one of their ministry's board members.

One of the American ladies traveling with Dr. Foster was Pat Hiller from Maryland. When she met the team members from WBC, who were also from Maryland, she was so excited to meet friends from her home state. The other young lady was from California, Ralph's home state. Since Ralph had been in bed that entire week with malaria,

Leroy thought it would be a great idea if Ralph came out and said hi to this young lady. Weakly, Ralph turned to Leroy and responded, "I'd rather die in peace. Thank you!"

A few minutes later, Olah came into Ralph's room and said, "Ralph, you better get out of that bed and have a washdown (bucket bath) and come meet this young lady. If you don't, it'll be the worst mistake you've made in your life! It would mean a lot to her to meet someone from home." Ralph reluctantly got up, had a washdown, and joined the entire group for several hours before returning to bed.

That young lady was Miss Maridee Brandt. About nine months later, Ralph and Maridee began corresponding. The heart of their writing was sharing what God was teaching each of them in their lives and through His Word. Maridee encouraged Ralph to keep pressing on even though life could be hard at times. Four months later, Ralph did a very Nigerian thing and proposed to Maridee through a letter. Maridee's response was, "Let's wait until you return to the States next year and see if we like each other."

Ralph returned to California the following year. He and Maridee liked each other just fine and were married three months later in July 1979. After graduate training at CBS, being accepted by SIM in 1983, and learning French, Ralph and Maridee departed to Niger in 1984 to serve among the nomadic Muslim Tuareg people of Niger, West Africa. Ralph's zeal in the areas of teaching, evangelism, and church planting, along with Maridee's heart for serving and loving people, made them a great team.

Life wasn't easy for them to minister to the nomadic Tuaregs, who were constantly moving with their grazing herds of cattle and sheep. This caused them to be evacuated seven times for medical reasons during those years of ministry. In 2009, they returned to the U.S. to be close to Ralph's parents. Ralph and Maridee still serve with SIM in Charlotte, North Carolina, their international headquarters, in the areas of recruitment and member care. Ralph has since made several trips to Niger and Nigeria for ministry.

Ralph and Dennis at Ikwa

In early September 1977, I returned to Ikwa as a single missionary to join the BMTC faculty full-time. Soon after that, the CWT and BMTC Board of Governors appointed me as the director of studies to lead the college's various programs.

Ralph and I traveled during a semester break to Kaduna in the CWT's Landcruiser van. On our return, we stayed overnight in Enugu with Dr. Francis Ibiam, a well-known Christian medical doctor. Dr. Ibiam was the first governor of Nigeria's Eastern State after their independence from Great Britain in 1960.

On that trip, Ralph had a terrible stomach bug, so Dr. Ibiam gave him some tincture of opium to treat it. As we returned to Ikwa, the treatment caused Ralph to hallucinate. In the passenger seat, Ralph put up his hands, as he was sure I was going to run into the vehicle ahead of us, even though I was hundreds of yards behind it. We did make it home safely that day.

In my first years at Ikwa, if we'd accompany Brother Joshua to Kaduna, we could drive all day and night, arriving by 1:00 a.m. or later with no problems. However, in the 1980s and 1990s, robberies became more rampant, so we'd need to stop at a friend's home or hotel by sundown and then begin the journey again early the next morning. On one of our trips, we saw one of the highest ant hills that I had ever seen. It was twice my height.

Ant hill along the road

We saw God's protection over us on many occasions. On another trip, Ralph and I tried to return from Port Harcourt and Aba late one night. We drove through Ekparakwa (about ten miles from Ikwa in Annang land). We were able to drive through one village but were detained because there had been recent armed robberies in the area. On this trip, I was very sick. Ralph began to plead with the leaders to allow us to pass so we could return to Ikwa. Finally, they agreed. However, they said, "We'll let you pass, but the next village won't."

When we arrived at the next village's checkpoint, the town crier from the first village had used his talking drum to inform the second village leaders who we were, where we had come from, and where we were headed. At about 11 p.m., those second villagers blocked our car from passing. They forced us to sleep in our car until about 5 a.m. the next morning. We rested a little but had to stop and fight the mosquitoes since our windows were open because it was very hot and humid.

While at Ikwa, Ralph loved to play pranks on the staff and students. He brought a terrible-looking Halloween mask from the U.S. and named it Fred. Fred's head was bald, his face looked like he hadn't shaved for days, and he had a nasty cut on his forehead.

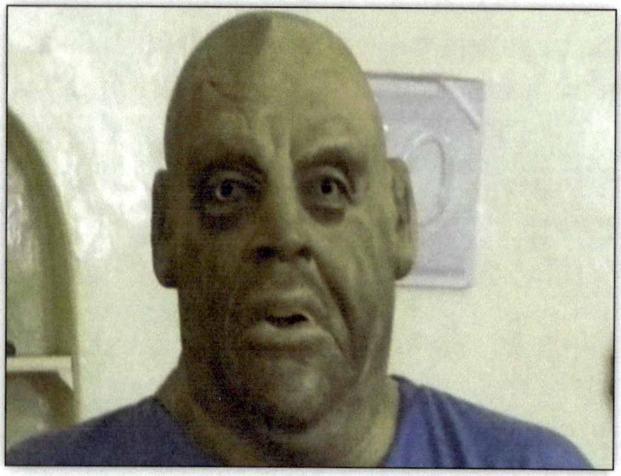

Saying hello to Fred

Over the years, we sometimes wore Fred to welcome a selected American visitor, new staff member, or student to our house. This caused some to scream or freeze, some to laugh or get annoyed, or some to run quickly out of our living room door. However, after a minute, everyone would be laughing over the incident.

However, working with the Ikwa villagers often brought a different response. The local people didn't like masked people. Their background for seeing people with masks was associated with masquerades (Ekpo), where masked people were the spirits of dead people.

Ralph told us some stories about living at Ikwa. One night, he noticed that the four CWT compound night guards were sleeping. He put on a long-sleeved shirt and borrowed some long welding gloves to cover any exposed skin. Wearing Fred, Ralph grabbed a machete and ran down the path toward the sleeping guards, screaming at the top of his lungs. The men woke up quickly and ran away towards the village, yelling and screaming all the way!

Ralph and the others with him thought that was hilarious. However, ten minutes later, the guards returned with about 20 village men, all armed with machetes and looking for this otherworldly creature. Ralph joined them in the search. When he went into the BMTC men's dorm, one of the students took him aside and said, "Brother Ralph, I know it was you wearing that mask. Don't EVER do that again because someone will kill you!"

On another occasion, Ralph returned from a long, three-hour trip to Calabar by motorcycle. As he pulled into the BMTC compound, he went into the village to see the progress of the medical clinic being built. At the hospital, he was immediately surrounded by six men with machetes. They were very belligerent. While they were verbally confronting him, Ralph heard the voice of a BMTC student pleading, "Brother Ralph, please help me! They're going to kill me!"

The student, who was from northern Nigeria, had gone out into Ikwa village to pray. The men accused him of lighting a candle and praying to evil spirits to cause havoc in the village. This wasn't true. The men then grabbed the student and forced Ralph to go with them to the house of the leading village chief.

They were led into the house. Before they knew it, the village crier used his talking drum.

Within minutes, there were about 100 people in front of the chief's house, demanding that both men should be turned over to them for calling on evil spirits. Brother Joshua and some of the CWT leaders heard the commotion and rushed to the house. After about an hour of negotiations, they were released, and all was calm again.

One aspect of this event that was so puzzling was that many of the villagers knew that Ralph and the student wouldn't call on evil spirits. There were various expressions of spirituality in Ikwa. Unfortunately, Ralph didn't realize that Ikwa village was the seat of witchcraft for about a 40-mile radius. People came from all over the area to receive special demonic powers.

The BMTC student who went to pray late at night used to venture out to pray in the bush in his part of the country. However, in Ikwa village, people who did that late at night were almost always intent on doing evil related to witchcraft. Ralph learned a very valuable lesson. Although people might verbally say they were following Christ, many had never truly found in Him the power to deal with their past lives that were centered around placating the spirit world.

Because of the lack of qualified teachers during various semesters over the years, I was forced to teach most of the courses offered in BMTC's three-year Diploma of Theology program. We as faculty members often taught 14 or more hours of classes weekly. We'd frequently be found after midnight seated next to our Aladdin kerosene lamps, studying or typing a duplicating stencil on our old, bulky Olympia typewriter for the next day's classes.

Because our house dining room wasn't screened in, we often chased away flying insects that were attracted to the lantern's light. The next morning we'd rush to the office before an early class to print out copies of an exam or class notes for the day on the duplicating machine. We were still young, with plenty of energy. With God's grace, we made it.

We as the faculty and missionaries were often asked to preach in the ICA on Sunday mornings or Wednesday evening prayer meetings or speak in a BMTC chapel. We'd also share a short meditation in the ICA Sunday communion (breaking of bread) services as we felt God leading us to speak. While Olah Moore and Ralph Sauers were at

1979 - Olah, Ralph and Dennis singing

Ikwa, we three had an opportunity to sing a special trio. It went well.

When we were all single men, we and three young boys, Daniel, Sunday, and Friday, lived together. The boys helped us to clean the house and its surroundings, worked in the kitchen, and washed our clothing. We believed that they all came to know the Lord and wanted to live for Him after they went back to their villages.

During my single years, we had many opportunities to speak at weekend or Christmas holiday conferences. During one weekend in Port Harcourt, I spoke at a youth conference. There were two interpreters to help the audience understand what I was teaching. After I spoke a sentence, the first interpreter spoke, and then the second interpreted in his dialect. However, the second one needed many extra words to convey what I taught. By the time he ended, I sometimes forgot what I had said originally.

Another weekend I spoke in Umuahia, Imo State, in a small church. It was near the livestock yards where Brahman cows were railed from the North to the East to be sold. While I was preaching, I looked out the back door and saw a cow with a long rope running down the street. It had gotten away from its owner. Right after that, I saw the owner running to try to catch it. During several Christmas breaks, I joined the Evangelical Church of West Africa (ECWA) for their youth conferences in Imo and Enugu States. Various Christian groups, such as the University of Calabar and Uyo, also invited us to speak in their Sunday morning Protestant services. One year the CWT was invited to have a one-and-a-half-hour TV program on NTV Calabar. Some of us preached, while in other sessions we used some of the Radio Bible Class TV recordings.

When we didn't travel to the U.S. for home assignments, we took opportunities to teach two-week BMTC summer courses. I taught one in Lagos, as well as several in Kaduna and Uyo. Other faculty taught them in Calabar and Uyo. Topics were on Personal Evangelism and Discipleship, How to Study the Bible, and Cults and Isms. All were taught in English.

I learned much personally from these studies and the opportunity to teach. While doing this, even though my CBS major was New Testament Greek, I became more interested in teaching missions courses. I saw the need for learning practical, hands-on activities alongside normal classroom studies. This coincided with the goal of our CWT president, who wanted all BMTC students to learn how to work hard with their hands and then continue with that same attitude in their future ministries wherever God led them.

The region around Ikwa didn't have many wild animals in the forests or water. Now and then, someone would come by on a motorcycle to sell us a small antelope they had killed or a large fish they had caught, hoping that we'd pay them good money for it. Occasionally, we went to Ibeno, about 25 miles from Ikwa and close to the Atlantic Ocean, to buy a freshly caught barracuda that was about three or four feet long.

Occasionally, we'd hear people shouting when a snake was seen. People would quickly run and grab a stick or a machete and try to kill it. Some were poisonous. No one would go back to their normal tasks until they knew that the snake was dead. Some of our Yoruba staff liked to eat snakes. Once when a python was killed, they cooked it. I ate part of it. It was tasty, like the white meat of a chicken or fish.

A snake killed at Ikwa

By our house, we saw some beautiful spiders that were about three inches big with black and yellow colors. They'd make their spider webs in bushes outside our house. We'd also have big crickets over two inches long make their noises right outside our office and bedroom at night. Little gecko lizards would often come out at night and crawl up our walls. They'd stay close to the top of the ceiling, close to the lantern or light bulb, hoping to eat some crawling or flying insects.

We also had soldier ants move around on our campus. When they came by the thousands to the back court of our house, we mixed kerosene with water and sprinkled it on them. They usually went away quickly. When we'd go to sleep, we'd either get under our mosquito net hanging over our bed or spray the room with a can of Raid and wait for about twenty minutes before entering.

One semester as the director of studies, I didn't have a faculty member to teach the course Daniel and Revelation. I didn't think that I knew enough about Bible prophecy, so I was afraid to teach it. However, since I had studied each of these Bible books before at WBC and CBS, I hesitantly agreed to be the teacher. To my amazement, I enjoyed teaching the course and learned many new things from my study. Usually, the teacher learns more than the student from diligent preparation. It was easier for me to agree to teach that course again for future semesters.

Some of our BMTC faculty were Nigerians, while some of us were Americans. Charles Cropper and his wife, Theo, came from Jamaica. After several years with BMTC and the CWT, the Croppers left the CWT in 1980 to minister in England as church planters. Several WBC and CBS faculty members came during different summers, such as Dr. Homer Heater, Jr., Mr. Jim Schuppe, and Wes Sweat.

In the late 1970s, Roy and Elvie Bridges joined the CWT for several years to use their years of experience to strengthen CWT departments and train the students. They came from Muskegon, Michigan. Elvie had many years of hospital experience as a nurse. Roy's background was in construction and maintenance work. As older, retired folks, it wasn't easy for them to adapt and understand the different worldviews of people in rural Ikwa.

However, they did well, with God's help. Elvie cared for many sick people. I turned my VW Beetle into an ambulance more than once to take her ten miles to the Ikot Abasi Hospital with a villager who was badly burnt by an explosion from contaminated kerosene or who had a medical crisis. Elvie, who had the heart to help the sick, would often go to the FMH late at night or at odd hours to help a sick person or accident victim. Roy was a very hard worker who upgraded the CWT's standards with better-constructed buildings, plumbing, and drainage systems. With his efforts, we had water piped into our home from the new, welded, water tank. These improvements saved everyone much time and effort.

Dennis, Olah, Roy & Elvie, Ralph, and Mutch & Barb Curtis

Over those years as a single man, I lived in my house with various other Americans, both singles and married couples, as well as several Nigerians. Each of the four bedrooms often had someone living in them. Because of our various backgrounds and worldviews, it was inevitable that we would have minor differences and opinions on issues like what types of food to eat, when to eat meals or go to bed, what types of music we listened to, and how loud to turn on the radio. By God's grace, we made it. When we'd offend a mate, we went and said, "I'm sorry. Please forgive me," and made it right.

While we were still single, other visitors from the U.S. came to teach and minister with us at Ikwa. One couple, Mutch and Barb Curtis, came for over one month. Barb was a registered nurse. Mutch had attended WBC. During their visit, they lived in one of the back bedrooms.

Since we missionaries didn't know the Ibibio dialect well, we depended much on CWT and BMTC staff to help us interpret to communicate with the villagers and local workers. Many of the workers didn't know English well either. They'd use pidgin English, which was used often in the markets for people of different tribes to communicate easily.

Once Ralph tried to ask a welding workshop helper where Silas Umoh, the CWT welder, had gone. The helper answered, "He don go." Ralph asked him again, "Where did he go?" The worker replied more emphatically, "He don go." Ralph asked the helper a third time louder. The helper replied louder too. Ralph had to walk away still wondering where Silas was. We later learned that the helper was answering Ralph correctly. "He don go," in pidgin English meant, "He has gone away."

Because the CWT had never published an official handbook for us as overseas missionaries to read before we came to Ikwa, we had to learn many things the hard way on the job. One example was that Elvie Bridges wasn't told before she arrived in Nigeria that women should wear a head covering when attending any church service or Bible study.

When I informed her of this after she had gone to church various times without a head covering, she asked me, "Why didn't you tell me this before?" Through such times over the years, the Lord helped us to show Christian grace and love to each other to keep making Christ known through the CWT ministries and wherever God has led us since then.

Andy Hunt came to Ikwa from Maryland in 1977 as a trained welder to work in the CWT's small welding shop. He helped the CWT construct a large, square, metal water tank mounted on high concrete pillars near the middle of the compound. A circular well about 30 feet deep next to the tower supplied the CWT and BMTC compound with water for many years.

One day a spitting cobra went down into the well. Andy brought the snake out of the well with a loop on the end of a stick. He took it to the courtyard at the back of our house and wore his welding gloves to remove it from the loop. That's when the snake spat into his eyes.

We immediately flushed out Andy's eyes. Ralph and I insisted that we should drive him to the Ikot Abasi Hospital to get his eyes checked by a doctor, and he agreed. The

Ralph returning from the stream

doctor said Andy would be okay. Ralph used a machete to kill the cobra, protecting his eyes by using his motorcycle helmet that had a clear plastic shield covering his face.

Ralph and Andy were very adventuresome. They loved to eat Nigerian foods, such as garri and vegetable soup. However, sometimes when they went to eat with various friends in Ikwa village, they'd return late in the evening with upset stomachs and loose stools. Probably the village water they drank wasn't boiled, or their bodies weren't used to eating the local foods.

We occasionally took evening walks for a break to visit Ghana, an Ikwa villager who owned a small supermarket. We'd buy a cold Coke from his kerosene refrigerator and have good talks with him while we enjoyed our drink.

Since we didn't have running water on the CWT compound for many years, we had to collect our water from the village stream for our home and cooking needs. Sometimes students brought buckets of water for us on their heads. We'd wash our clothes and sometimes take our baths in the stream. During the rainy season, we'd collect water that ran off our roof into an old bathtub or painted barrel. During a heavy downpour, the rain could fill the tub in several minutes.

Andy had problems renewing his visa, so he had to leave Ikwa. His training with the Navigators gave him a burden to see others discipled and growing in the Lord. In 1980 he married Patty Word in the U.S. In 1988 they returned to Nigeria with their four children, aged two to six, to serve with the Navigators for some years in Kaduna, Enugu, and Lagos. Their fifth child, Kent, was born in Enugu.

Andy Hunt's family

Later, when our children, Dwight and Stephanie, were in home school, our family stayed several times in the Hunts' home in Enugu when we traveled to the North. Andy spoke at one of our BMTC Pastors' Conferences on *Discipleship*. They still serve with the Navigators in Columbus, Ohio.

President George A. Miles of WBC and CBS came to visit Ikwa several times. He was a gifted Bible teacher and evangelist. Wherever he'd go, he'd be seen passing out a gospel tract or speaking to someone about the Lord. He had a great heart to see others come to know Christ.

1982 - Pres. Miles & CWT Leaders

In 1982 he came with Ed Hayward, a CBS student, and Ralph to lead a conference for evangelists. Several evangelists spoke: C.T. Taylor, from Jamaica; Brother Joshua, and CWT's co-founder, Brother Mishael Nathan.

In 1984, President Miles came to Nigeria to speak at several Prophetic Bible Conferences at Ikwa, Uyo, Calabar, Ayangba in Benue State, and Kaduna. Olah and I had the privilege of traveling with him. President Miles loved Bible prophecy, an important subject about which many Nigerian Christians had little Bible teaching. Those attending were eager to learn.

To strengthen the spiritual lives of the students, faculty, and staff at Ikwa, each semester BMTC had a one-day Spiritual Life Day. Before our May graduation, we'd have an annual Pastors' and Christian Education Conference. Various BMTC alumni, CWT leaders, and overseas friends of the CWT and BMTC were invited to come, such as a team from Bermuda and leaders from Olah Moore's church.

During the early 1980s, Olah and I had a part in writing various articles and editing the *Christian Witness Message* magazine. Brother Joshua usually wrote keynote articles. This was sent to various friends and supporters of the CWT for prayer and support.

As missionaries, we all joined the CWT members for various evangelistic crusades, held at least twice yearly. At one Calabar crusade, we did everything with the staff and students, eating their meals and sleeping with them on the floor of the home where we were staying. We were happy to see some children and adults come to Christ at those outings.

One night when we were with the CWT for an evangelistic crusade at Calabar, Ralph and I had to urinate badly. We weren't used to doing it in the open. Although it was dark, we went away from our accommodations down a dark path. We had to go so badly but couldn't because we were sure someone would see us. Finally, we were successful. Over time, we did better and weren't so bothered by what happened in public.

During my summer home assignment in 1984, I joined a group of Christians from WBC and CBS to visit the Holy Land in Israel and Egypt. The tour guides were Dr. Homer Heater, Jr., and Dr. Harry Fletcher. We visited Jerusalem, the Wailing Wall, Golgotha, Bethlehem, Nazareth, Megiddo, and Masada. Then, we flew to Cairo, Egypt, to see the pyramids and take an overnight train ride to Luxor before returning to the U.S.

Standing at the Wailing Wall

On our flight from New York to Tel Aviv, I saw some Orthodox Jews praying with their shawls and phylacteries (leather boxes with portions of the Hebrew Bible) tied on their foreheads. When we landed in Israel, we heard many heartfelt shouts and hands clapping for joy because they had arrived safely in their homeland. The trip helped me understand many Bible events and passages more clearly.

For Olah, God had also prepared a young lady for him to marry. While he was at CBS, he met Miss Debbie Carter, a registered nurse. His distant ancestry was probably from Nigeria or West Africa, as "Olah" is very similar to many of Nigeria's Yoruba tribal names that begin with "Ola" or "Olu."

After Olah taught at BMTC during the summers of 1975 and 1976, he returned to Ikwa to teach for the 1978 fall semester. He traveled to the U.S. to marry Debbie in August 1979. They returned to Ikwa for Debbie's first visit about three weeks after the wedding. That wasn't easy for them as newlyweds, and especially for Debbie, as that was her first cross-cultural experience over 6,000 miles away from her home. With a positive outlook and God's grace, they happily served at Ikwa.

Olah, Debbie, & Timothy Moore

Debbie used her nursing skills at FMH. While at Ikwa, she gave birth to Timothy in 1981 and David in 1984. Olah did well in teaching and administration. He also served as BMTC's dean of students and was an advisor to the BMTC Board of Governors.

In August 1985, Olah's family returned to Norfolk, Virginia, to become the pastor of his home church, Faith Community Church. He and some of his church elders came to Ikwa in 1991 to speak at the BMTC Pastors' Conference and graduation. He was a longtime member of the CWST in the U.S.

During my years at BMTC as a single man, I had various challenges with my health. I became sick with malaria several times a year for most years. Once I tried to attend an all-night prayer meeting. Since my body wasn't used to doing that in a hot, tropical context, I became very sick with malaria and couldn't go out with others to a crusade.

Later, when the CWT had all-night prayer meetings, I learned my lesson. I participated in part of the meetings but knew that getting my sleep as a foreigner was important too. I did the same when the CWT asked people to fast. Since my body would become very weak, I didn't do well during such times. I still tried to follow my normal meal schedule, so I could do my best and not get sick.

It was a blessing to have various trained nurses, like Ruth Wright, Debbie Moore, and Elvie Bridges, available to help us when we had minor health issues. Once I had boils develop under my arms. I had to go to a local hospital to have them opened. There a Nigerian nurse drained them before she put a bandage on them and sent me home. Elvie helped me with dressings before I returned to the hospital for more drainage. They finally healed. I also had issues with ringworm on my ankle. With some medicine, it slowly went away.

During one of my trips to the U.S. with Brother Joshua, I became sick on the 747 flight. We informed the stewardesses. They allowed all the other passengers to disembark. They called for an ambulance to take me to a hospital in Queens, New York. I was admitted into the men's ward, where various sicknesses were treated.

I told the hospital staff that I had malaria. They didn't believe me since they hadn't seen that before. They were sure that I was going to pass on what I had to others. Brother Joshua visited me every day, as he was staying nearby with Mr. and Mrs. Woods, who were faithful CWT supporters. Brother Joshua also informed my parents what was happening. Finally, after about three days, I was released and traveled home to Manheim for my short home assignment.

In August 1986, Vern Goertzen came to Ikwa with his wife, Kathy. He had many years of farming experience in California. Vern had a strong desire to find many acres of land in the areas around Ikwa to farm, so more food could be raise to help the lo-

The Goertzens with staff and students

cal people eat better and to help them find more means to support themselves financially.

However, many villagers didn't catch Vern's vision, since most of them had many traditionally owned small farm plots side-by-side all around the village. For them to give up their land for a foreigner to farm large-scale with his tractor and implements was risky and almost impossible. Their land was passed down to them from their families for many generations.

This was a big frustration to Vern and his assistant, Innocent. With his tractor and farming equipment, he succeeded in farming some acres of cassava in Edemaya. The Akwa Ibom State governor was greatly impressed when he came to visit the CWT compound and the Edemaya farm projects. Later Vern did some larger-scale farming in Imo State.

Vern helped the CWT grow many pineapples, orange trees, plantains, and bananas on the compound. He used drip irrigation hoses to help them grow better during the dry season. He also helped to set up a woodworking shop. The students and staff benefited from his efforts.

The Lord used each of our missionary visitors and staff through their years of training and practical experience. When they left Ikwa, God continued to use them back in their home countries in their churches and various mission agencies. Through easy and rough times, God used them to carry on the motto of the CWT, "To make Christ known."

Innocent and Vern in plantain plot

Chapter 10

A Single Missionary Learning with His Nigerian Mates and Students

"I thank my God every time I remember you. In all my prayers for all of you, I always pray with joy because of your partnership in the gospel from the first day until now, being confident of this, that he who began a good work in you will carry it on to completion until the day of Christ Jesus"
(Philippians 1:3–6).

Daily Routines

As a single missionary from 1977 to 1988, the Lord helped me to put my whole heart into teaching and ministering at BMTC. I tried as much as possible to be close to the national staff and students in their daily and weekend activities. Many of our expatriate missionaries did the same.

CWT Monday morning of prayer

We enjoyed the spiritual emphasis built into the daily routine of BMTC's programs. After the students had morning devotions, they'd do compound cleaning. Finally, they'd hurry to take their bath. Before the CWT had a borehole dug on the compound, the students had to walk one mile to the Ikwa stream to get their baths. They would often balance a bucket of water on their head to pour into a large drum for kitchen use before beginning their first class at 7:00. One student was assigned to ring a bell to tell the students when it was time for the next activity or class.

Later, they'd eat their breakfast and have another class before attending the morning chapel. On Monday mornings the CWT held its morning of prayer from 9:00 until noon. Helping the students learn the importance of prayer in one's ministry was a priority in the CWT's philosophy. As much as possible, we attended the ICA Sunday services, evening Bible studies, and prayer meetings. We also enjoyed attending their socials. Good bonding occurred. BMTC classes ended at 1:00 p.m. After lunch, the students did practical work on the compound, like cutting grass with their cutlasses, preparing garri outside the kitchen, gardening, or teaming up with a Nigerian or expatriate to learn basics in welding, printing, or other skills. After supper, they'd spend several hours studying before having evening devotions and sleeping.

At 4:00 p.m. on Tuesdays and Thursdays, the students and staff were required to participate in games like soccer (football) or volleyball. We enjoyed these times with the students and staff. My best game was volleyball because I was almost six feet tall. Most of the students were shorter. If they didn't like to play these outside games, they could play checkers (draft), ping pong (table tennis), or another table game.

We wanted the students to get a little physical break and have some fun with their mates besides doing their intensive studies and work. Because it was hot and humid much of the year, we'd get all sweaty from playing sports. These were good times to bond with staff, like CWT Vice-President Brother Mfon Ubak, and CWT Accountant Mac Ukpong, along with the BMTC students and staff.

Teaching

In my first years, as I taught full-time at BMTC, I was learning lessons on when and how to mark student papers and letters. I was noted for being tough on English writing, grammar, and speaking. When I was teaching as a single man, one BMTC alumnus wrote me a letter. It had some English mistakes in it, so I corrected the mistakes and mailed the letter back to him. I wondered why I didn't hear much from him again. My comments on the returned letter to him probably embarrassed or annoyed him, so he didn't write me another letter.

From then on, after a student graduated, I wouldn't comment on any mistakes unless they asked me for help. Now students can use helpful resources like grammarly.com or dictionary.com on the internet to check their mistakes and improve their writing and spelling. Even now, I use these websites regularly whenever I write letters, emails, and even this book!

Since I didn't have much specific training in cross-cultural missions before coming to Nigeria, I counted much on learning about life and culture from my Nigerian mates and students. Starting with the CWT President Dr. Joshua Ekpikhe and his wife, Elizabeth, I learned much. I did try to learn some Ibibio, the local dialect in the region around Ikwa, but I never learned enough to speak fluently in it.

However, from the first day that I began teaching at BMTC, I was to teach in English, so I never really learned Ibibio well. If I had been a church planter, I would have been forced to learn it well. The nationals were very kind when I had to use an interpreter to communicate with them, but most of the staff and students knew enough English to talk with me. All of our BMTC classes were taught in English.

I enjoyed serving alongside CWT President Dr. Joshua Ekpikhe, Vice-President Mfon Ubak, and CWT Administrator Brother Samuel Ijatuyi. They were men of prayer and commitment to the Word of God. Our faithful BMTC faculty and staff worked hard, even though life at Ikwa was difficult.

My faithful deputy for many years was Nsese Umoh, who was one of our early BMTC alumni. Other alumni, Akpan Umoetuk and Comfort Ekpikhe Davis, served on our faculty. Some of our students who showed leadership and teaching abilities helped us teach courses when we didn't have enough teachers, such as John Apeh, Olu Ijatuyi (Randee I-Morphe), and David Ekpikhe.

BMTC faculty with Nsese Umoh (arms folded)

Additional faculty joined us over the years, such as Pius Nnah, Christian Nwakunna, Emmanuel Inyangson, Moses Oluwole, and others. When I returned to the U.S. for home assignments, they carried on BMTC well. We kept in regular contact. Brother Nsese went to be with the Lord in early 2023.

Farming Crops

We worked together to grow various kinds of vegetables and crops on the CWT compound. We started a small poultry project to raise broilers and layers. We dug out a small pond behind our house to raise catfish and made a small, concrete-walled snailery with an overhead screen, so they wouldn't crawl away. Later we built a piggery, raising more than 100 pigs and piglets over several years. We raised rabbits, turkeys, ducks, and guinea fowl. We grew rice, corn, yams, sorghum, and other items to eat.

Later, Vern helped us develop several acres on the CWT compound to grow pumpkin leaves (like spinach), pineapples, plantains, and bananas. Some students learned basic welding and plumbing. Our willingly working alongside the students and staff, doing even the lowest of jobs and errands, helped them learn how to work humbly for God's glory. The spirit of hard work and integrity stayed with many of our BMTC alumni and helped them persevere in their ministries after graduation when things often became difficult.

Because our climate was very tropical, we sweated profusely whenever we worked out under the hot sun and in the humid air. Being under the sun in my early years and at Ikwa caused me to have some spots of skin cancer on my head and arms later in life. However, with visits to the dermatologist and treatments, including one small procedure to remove a lesion with melanoma from my face, I'm doing all right.

CEF

When I returned to teach full-time at BMTC in 1977, CEF asked me to voluntarily represent them in Nigeria since no one else held that position. I accepted. I began working with Brother Ayet Zemo in Kaduna State and Mr. Uwah in Uyo. I ordered boxes of various CEF flannelgraph stories and songs, like "Stop, and Let Me Tell You," "Good News," etc. They came through the Ikot Abasi Post Office. On free weekends, I traveled to cities like Enugu and Ibadan for weekend CEF training seminars.

Several key CEF leaders, such as Alan George and Tim Shorb, came for visits to Lagos and Kaduna to see how the work was progressing. I was invited by CEF of Ghana to go and teach for several weeks in their Leadership Training Institute in 1979. That never happened. Since I had never flown to another country outside of Nigeria, I had to go to Lagos several weeks before I traveled to apply for my visa. That first trip took me three days to get to Lagos from Port Harcourt because it was the rainy season, and

Nigerian Airways jets didn't have radar equipment to fly in foggy weather. Matthew and Victoria Ukpe allowed me to stay with them near the airport for those days.

Two weeks later, I flew to Lagos again to get my visa at the Ghanaian Embassy. Their workers told me that during those two weeks, there had been a coup in Accra. Only Accra could grant me a visa. That stopped my trip. I spent that weekend in Lagos at Peter Ekanem's home until I could go to the bank and get my traveler's checks refunded. Nothing was easy!

Between all my duties at BMTC, from July to August 1981, the Lord helped me to work with national brethren to plan for two two-week CEF training seminars at Kagoro Bible College in Kaduna State, and BMTC, Ikwa, with 41 students attending. Several CEF missionaries, Ira and Elsie Hovey and Janice Johnson, came from the U.S. to be the teachers. God kept us safe.

1982 - CEF's first Leadership Training Institute

On my bus trip back south from Kagoro to Uyo, sitting in the front passenger seat, I was sure that several times we were going to have an accident, and I was going to heaven. The driver drove excessively fast and narrowly missed several motorcycles and people. God kept us safe.

More interest in CEF training led to our having Nigeria's first three-month CEF Leadership Training Institute at Ikwa in 1982, with 22 students graduating. Several other CEF international trainers came to teach. Four students came from the Gambia, one from Burkina Faso, and the rest from Nigeria.

However, between my duties at BMTC and CEF, the work was becoming overbearing. Brother Joshua had to approach me and ask me to prayerfully decide between serving full-time at BMTC or with CEF. After that, I felt the best way to help CEF would be for me to serve full-time at BMTC. Through that means, I could encourage and train some of our BMTC students to get involved in CEF work in their home areas.

That's what happened. During those years, Daniel Sappor and his wife, Gifty, who were CEF workers in Ghana, came to study at BMTC and then returned to Ghana, where they later became the directors of Source of Life Mission in Ghana. Several of our BMTC alumni went on to attend the CEF Leadership Training Institute, such as Nuhu Shagaiya, who became a full-time CEF worker in northern Nigeria. They and other BMTC alumni helped to carry on the CEF work in Nigeria and their home villages and churches. I taught several courses for the CEF Leadership Training Institute in 1990 in Kaduna.

God was working. CEF arranged for Richard and Rebecca Acquaye and their two small children to come from Ghana to live at Ikwa and take over the work of CEF for Nigeria. Richard had a great love for children and was a gifted teacher and administrator. We traveled together during the summer of 1982 to challenge potential CEF Institute students to come for the training.

I officially turned over the duties of CEF to Richard on November 1, 1982. The Lord used Richard greatly to organize CEF in various states, later turning over the work to Nigerians who built their national headquarters in Kaduna, before returning to Ghana to become CEF's West African director.

Ministries at Ikwa

In 1981, I was asked to serve in the ICA as an elder. This opened the door for me to preach, teach, and work with the other elders to help lead the church while I lived at Ikwa. In the Assembly, we didn't have terms of three or four years before we'd end our service. Once we were elected as an elder, we were an elder for life, or until we couldn't continue to serve.

1982 - BMTC group with new bus

In 1982, God provided BMTC with a new Nissan van. It came just in time for us to take the students and some faculty on an extensive trip to visit several Nigerian seminaries, Yankari Game Reserve to see some wild animals, and Kaduna, where Baraka Press was located. The Lord gave us an enjoyable, safe trip. Many of the students had never been to other northern or western states. I drove my VW Beetle to carry several members.

During those years, several of our Nigerian BMTC faculty, staff, and alumni were married, including several who served their National Youth Service Corp (NYSC) year to teach with us. We traveled to Kaduna, Warri, Kwara State, Uyo, Calabar, and various locations in Akwa Ibom State to attend their weddings. Weddings and burials were big deals to attend in Nigerian culture. The couples felt very honored to have CWT and BMTC leaders and students grace the occasion. We often were invited to the high table for their wedding receptions.

Often the wedding invitations would say that the wedding would begin at 10:00 a.m. prompt. However, usually they'd begin late, because either the bride or groom or their family, or even the officiating pastor, was late. Once we drove more than three hours to the church. It began at about 2:30 p.m. instead of 10 a.m. Another time, the bride was late and was brought in an ambulance because she was a nurse, and they didn't have another car to chauffeur her and her bridesmaids.

Once we waited too long to attend a wedding in Uyo. We arrived when the recessional was in progress, so we missed the processional and the entire wedding but joined everyone for the reception. Another time we arrived at about 10:20 a.m., and the service was already in progress. Whatever happened, the wedding was a great time of celebration and joy. The event was the important thing, not the time it started.

Students, faculty, and staff went out regularly on the weekends for various types of Christian service assignments. Some witnessed to local villagers about the Lord. Others taught Sunday school or a local Bible study. Some went to the Ikot Abasi prison to preach. This was part of their practical training.

I was able to minister on several Sunday mornings with the students who preached in that prison. We'd get clearance from the wardens and then go into one of the buildings where prisoners were sitting on the floor on their mats. Some had shackles on their legs. It was very dark. At one end was their bathroom and toilet. The smells were not pleasant, but that's what they had to endure. Some were waiting for months for their trials to be called by the court. Through these ministries by BMTC and other local Christians, some of these men came to Christ and were doing Bible correspondence courses. They had a hunger to hear the Bible and read from it.

When I owned a motorcycle in 1978, I went with one of our BMTC students to Edemaya, about six miles from Ikwa, to teach a children's Bible club at the home of one of the village chiefs. A metal bridge crossing a big stream on the way to Edemaya wasn't fit for vehicles to cross because some of the wooden planks weren't in place. A vehicle's tires would easily go down through the open holes between the iron frames.

This didn't stop us from crossing. I'd ride to the edge of the stream. A boatman would lift my motorcycle into his boat. We'd then enter and sit down on a bench. Once on the other side, the boatman would remove my motorcycle onto the ground, and we'd drive several miles to the venue of the club. We'd conduct the children's meeting, with the student being my Ibibio interpreter. When we'd return after the club, the boatman would do everything in reverse to reach the other side. We'd pay him a little money for the ride. Sometimes I'd forget to wear a long-sleeved shirt on such trips, and the sand-flies would bite my arms and make me very itchy. This was part of life in the tropics. The privilege of reaching these village children for Christ was worth it.

During those years, the Lord opened doors for me to preach and teach boarding students in various local high (secondary) schools and teacher training colleges during their Sunday afternoon worship services. I often drove 20 miles to Eket to speak in the Scripture Union Bible study groups. These were excellent opportunities to challenge teens, youth, and adults to trust the Lord as their Savior and live for Him in their churches and communities.

Going for a crusade to Ikuru Town

BMTC's faculty, staff, and students were required to join CWT leaders and ICA members when they'd go out for crusades for up to a week to local villages, like Ete or Edemaya. We used all our vehicles to transport people and supplies several times for the Calabar crusades. Other outreaches were to Ikuru Town in Rivers State, where Michael Ikuru and Mine Acra, two BMTC students, lived. Because Ikuru Town was on an island, we rode for about 45 minutes from Ikot Abasi inside big, long motorboats. Over the years a church was planted in Ikuru Town. We traveled there various times for weekend follow-up trips.

Our Graduates

From 1977 until 1988, I continued as a teacher and director of studies at BMTC. Because of our affiliations with WBC, we were able to see 19 of our alumni have the opportunity to travel to the U.S. to become students at WBC for their B.A. programs.

Several of our BMTC faculty members, Okon Isaac and Nsese Umoh, were some of the first alumni to attend WBC.

Over the next years, after completing their first-degree studies at WBC, some of the men moved on to study at CBS or Dallas Theological Seminary. Other BMTC alumni, both men and women, have gone on from WBC to complete their M.A. or Ph.D. studies in the U.S. in missions, Christian education, education, business administration, and mass communication. Some have returned to Nigeria to serve in their local church denominations or to begin a ministry. A few have continued to live in the U.S. and have become educators in various professions. No matter where they live, we're always happy to see how God has been using many of our alumni for God's glory, as long as they live for Him.

Others in Nigeria went on to serve in crucial positions in ECWA and other denominations. A few have continued to live in the U.S. and have become educators to serve the Lord in various professions.

The majority of the BMTC alumni, who numbered over 300, never had the opportunity to travel overseas. They've served the Lord throughout Nigeria and Ghana as pastors, cross-cultural missionaries, church planters, school teachers and administrators, children's workers, and Christian laymen in their local churches. A few have moved into business ventures or have established nurseries and elementary (primary) and high (secondary) schools in their villages.

Brother Nsese later did his M.A. studies in the U.S. and returned to continue teaching at BMTC. He and other alumni returned to help BMTC have needed teachers. Since Nigerians who did their B.A. studies in Nigeria or overseas were required to do one year of NYSC service, the government usually assigned them to teach or use their area of discipline by going to another area of the country where they had never lived before. Southerners often served in the North or West, and Northerners served in the South or East.

Recruiting staff for the CWT and BMTC was always a challenge. We were able to request that several of our BMTC alumni do their one-year NYSC term with us at BMTC, such as Samuel Isaiah and Adejo Alao. Several who studied at BMTC, WBC, or CBS were willing to come to teach at Ikwa for a year or more, such as Mark Ogharaerumi, Enoch Apaibinyesim, and Emmanuel Inyangson.

We also used some of our upperclassmen to teach a course or two when we didn't have enough faculty during some semesters. Examples were John Apeh, Olu Ijatuyi (now renamed Randee I-Morphe), and David Ekpikhe. We successfully recruited several other Christian NYSC graduates who helped us for those months as secretaries and agricultural workers. David and Comfort Ekpikhe, along with other BMTC alumni, also taught at Ikwa over the years.

The Lord opened up a door to have a BMTC Extension School begin at Kaduna. We also began another extension school at Uyo where Moses and Kemi Oluwole resided in a home that we rented, so BMTC courses could be taught there. Several of us often traveled to Uyo on Saturdays to teach. We were happy to see God expanding BMTC, so that more men and women could be trained to study God's Word and become more effective in their local churches and ministries and beyond.

My Perspectives Broadened

During those years, God expanded and matured my perspectives in many ways. In my first years of ministry, I believed that all BMTC graduates should be pastors or become involved as full-time Christian workers. However, over the years I have seen that God can lead a student with a solid Bible college training into any kind of vocation to be a vibrant witness for Him, whether the person becomes a lawyer, businessperson, government worker, accountant, full-time wife, or lay person. It all depends on how God gifts and wires them. Everyone is different. God is ready to use anyone willing to serve Him.

Such Biblical foundations could greatly assist anyone to teach, preach, or serve in their local church in powerful ways. This is vital in contexts where the local people follow African traditional religions, are only nominal Christians, have Muslim backgrounds, or don't know the Lord at all. Many BMTC alumni took their motto, "Come—Learn! Go—Teach!" to heart, often sacrificing much and using these opportunities to be of great blessing in their home villages or cities.

I saw that wherever God leads someone to serve Him, He uses anything that the person has learned or experienced over the years to enhance that person's ministry for the Lord. Even if one doesn't know much about some skill or subject, like playing the piano or guitar, the person becomes an expert when others know nothing about the subject. The person can at least teach the little that they know and use it for God's glory.

For example, I always enjoyed working in my parent's garden when growing up. Later that experience helped me as I grew my garden at Ikwa and Kagoro and worked on farm projects with the students and staff. Right from second grade, I learned how to play the accordion and the piano. Over the years and right up until today, I've played these instruments hundreds of times throughout Nigeria and in the U.S. This has helped me to teach various students and staff basic staff notation, how to lead singing, and how to play the accordion. God gives us spiritual gifts and natural talents to be a blessing to others.

God can use His Word to have a positive effect on the lives of many men and women, whether they've graduated from Bible college, attended classes for only a few months or a semester, or caused troubles while in school. President Miles once told me, "God's word can work in anyone who comes to study the Bible." Isaiah 55:11 confirms this: "So is my word that goes out from my mouth: It will not return to me empty, but will accomplish what I desire and achieve the purpose for which I sent it."

Chief Ufot and his family

We saw this truth at BMTC. Seeing our students move on to various ministries and stand strong for the Lord through many difficult contexts, by God's grace, has been one of the biggest rewards that we've received over the years. Some have faithfully served the Lord with hardly any salary or financial benefits, yet they've been faithful. We've experienced firsthand what Paul said in Philippians 4:1, that the Christians he worked with, trained, and later saw moving on for the Lord were his "joy and crown." This was why we were happy to continue at BMTC.

I often went out with various CWT and BMTC staff for village visitations on Sunday afternoons to Ete and Ikot Akan, about one mile from Ikwa. At Ikot Akan, we visited Chief Ufot Ndah, one of the village chiefs. He was formerly a Jehovah's Witness. Eventually, he came to Christ, along with his wife and several of his children. He helped to begin and later lead the Ikot Akan Christian Assembly. One son, Peter, is now active in the Assemblies. Chief Ufot went to be with the Lord in 2022.

As we continued visiting homes in Ikot Akan, the Lord led us to Nsikan Uko's home. He was an agent for a pools betting company. Villagers would make bets on what European soccer teams would win. He came to know Christ. Through Bible studies and growth, he left that job and began a small drycleaning business in Ete. He continues to be active in the Assembly as an elder. These relationships at BMTC, in the CWT, and in the ICA were very rewarding as we served together for the Lord.

Chapter 11

It's a Wonder Why I'm Still Alive

"But he said to me, 'My grace is sufficient for you, for my power is made perfect in weakness.' Therefore I will boast all the more gladly about my weaknesses, so that Christ's power may rest on me. That is why, for Christ's sake, I delight in weaknesses, in insults, in hardships, in persecutions, in difficulties. For when I am weak, then I am strong" (II Corinthians 12:9–10).

Friday, May 13, 1983, was one day that caused me to wonder if I'd still be alive. What happened? One of our BMTC faculty, Emmanuel Inyangson, and I were returning in my VW Beetle car from a conference that never happened in Ibadan, Oyo State, about 300 miles from Ikwa. We had been invited several months before to attend an accreditation conference in May with other Bible colleges and seminaries across Nigeria.

Since we didn't have local phones to make calls within most areas of the country, and the Nigerian post office wasn't very reliable, we assumed that the conference was still scheduled and had reserved the date to attend. We drove all day on Thursday, May 12, arriving safely in Ibadan near sundown. When we met our contact person, we were happy to see him. However, he informed us that there was no conference. He asked us, "Didn't you receive our letter saying that the conference was canceled?" We surprisingly said, "No!" We never received that letter—then or today.

Emmanuel and I stayed overnight with Christian friends in Ibadan. We began our journey back home the next morning, Friday the thirteenth of May. By that afternoon we were getting close to Asaba and Onitsha when an oncoming car on the two-lane highway we were driving on speedily tried to pass the car in front of him. He couldn't return to his lane in time and hit my car on the side. The impact was so strong that Emmanuel said the car was in the air about four feet before it crashed into the bush on the left side of the road. The driver kept on going and never stopped to help us, so we never knew who hit us.

Back in 1983, we weren't as careful about wearing seat belts in vehicles as we are today, so we didn't have them on. From the car's impact, my chest went right into the steering wheel, and I was knocked unconscious. The car was demolished, as it landed in the bush and was not able to be driven again.

Asaba was near Onitsha, about five hours away from Ikwa. Some good Samaritans driving by our accident saw our license plate reading "CR," for Cross River State. Being from that state and recognizing our license, they kindly stopped to take us to the hospital. Emmanuel wasn't hurt as badly as I was.

I don't believe in superstition. Some people would have said that on Friday the 13th one could have some bad luck happen to them, like our accident. After we were admitted to the hospital, I woke up in a lot of pain. It was already dark, as the sun usually set by about 6:30 p.m.

Being a Friday evening, the X-ray staff at the hospital had already gone home for the weekend. There were no drugs to buy inside the hospital, and the electricity was off, which wasn't unusual for many places, even in Nigeria's big cities.

Ikwa didn't have phones for us to call and inform our people back at the CWT about the accident. We also didn't have access to call the U.S. to inform my family. I had no choice but to stay in the hospital. The next morning, Saturday, Emmanuel traveled to Ikwa by taxi to share the bad news, even though his neck and several ribs were stiff and swollen. He arrived in Ikwa late on Saturday. By about noon on Sunday, Emmanuel arrived at the hospital with several of our staff in Brother Ijatuyi's Peugeot station wagon to take me home.

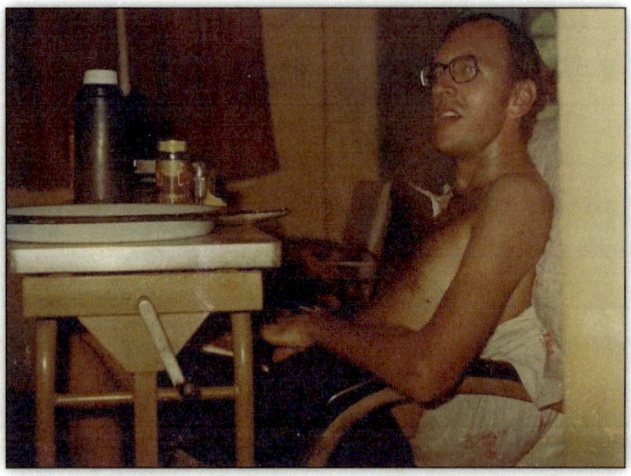

1983 - Trying to keep cool at Immanuel Hospital

The ride home in the car was especially difficult for me. I knew that I probably had some broken bones, so each time we went over a bump in the road, of which there were many deep ones (gallops) on the journey, they caused me pain in my ribs and chest. After the long drive all Sunday afternoon, they took me to be admitted at the Eket Immanuel Hospital early Sunday night, 20 miles from Ikwa. At the hospital, they put me on an old, metal, hospital cart and X-rayed me. They found that I had six broken ribs and a broken collar bone. They believed that I had some liquid in my right lung.

Over the next ten days, I stayed in that hospital, missing our BMTC graduation on May 21. I had to sleep at a 45-degree angle, as I couldn't lie down or turn on my side. To help me breathe better, they pushed a large needle through my right lung to withdraw liquid from it.

They did this two times before I was discharged. Externally, I only had a small cut on my elbow. One temple on the frame of my glasses was lost. Other than that, my injuries were all internal. There was no air conditioning in my room, so it was very hot and humid.

I had previously planned to fly to the U.S. in early June with Olah and Debbie Moore for our summer break. They were flying to their home in Norfolk, Virginia. I was able to return from Immanuel Hospital to Ikwa two days before we all flew to the U.S. I was still in much pain during the entire trip. Olah helped to bathe me at Lagos before our flight and helped me move slowly from the motels to the airports, through check-ins, and then on the flights.

Since we had no accessible phone service in our area of Nigeria, my family back in the U.S. still didn't know of my accident more than two weeks later. Once we arrived in Brussels, Belgium, Olah called Daddy and Momma from our hotel to slowly break the news to them. He asked them to come meet me at Kennedy Airport in New York City the next afternoon.

The Moores with me at Kennedy Airport

Inside the airports during our trip home, I had the privilege of being pushed by airport staff in a wheelchair through hallways and on elevators that other passengers weren't allowed to use. At Kennedy Airport, I was finally brought out in a wheelchair by an airport attendant to meet Daddy and Momma at the arrivals section. After we met, collected our suitcases, and said goodbye to Olah and Debbie, Daddy and Momma drove me home for our four-hour trip. We stopped at a restaurant for a meal. I wanted to eat a hamburger—like a McDonald's Big Mac—since I hadn't had one for almost three years.

At home that first night in Manheim, I couldn't lie on a normal bed because of my painful ribs, so I slept in Daddy's rocking chair in our living room. The next day they took me to St. Joseph's Hospital in Lancaster where I was admitted.

The hospital's X-rays showed that I didn't have just six broken ribs. Instead, I had nine of my 24 ribs broken. They used another big needle to draw out bloody liquid from my right lung. The first time, they brought out two ketchup-sized bottles of liquid. Later, another attempt was made, but the liquid was too thick to come out through the needle. The doctors had me use an accordion-shaped, plastic, breathing machine several times daily to try to expand my breathing capacity. It was only at about 40 percent then. I remained in St. Joseph's Hospital for almost one week before I was discharged.

1983 - My demolished VW at the Asaba police after my return to Nigeria

For the next five weeks, I had to sleep upright. I had no bandages or braces on my ribs throughout this period; they had to slowly heal on their own. Later that summer, one night while sleeping, I involuntarily rolled over on my side. That was the first time I began to move better and knew that I was slowly improving.

I appreciated visitors in the hospitals and later at our home during my recovery. One day my sisters visited me. When our family gets together, we usually laugh a lot. During that visit, I was laughing so much with them that I lost my breath and had difficulty getting it back. My sisters, three of them nurses, told me to relax and that I'd be able to get my breath back, although it was a little scary at the time. We all tried to not get too excited or laugh too much until I was better.

I continued to improve each day. By August I received approval from my doctors to return to Nigeria to continue teaching at BMTC. Because of the accident, the staff and students at Ikwa never expected me to want to return to Nigeria. However, I believed that God had some uncompleted jobs for me to do. He kept the doors open for me to return to continue serving at Ikwa. Everyone at Ikwa was overjoyed when I returned to resume ministering at BMTC.

It took two years before I received $2,000 from my car insurance company to replace my car. Even today, because of that accident and my broken ribs, I still do not sleep well on my sides.

From my accident and other physical challenges over the years, I'm learning that God not only answers our prayers in three normal ways—yes, no, and wait—but He often answers us by saying what He told the Apostle Paul, "'My grace is sufficient for you, for my power is made perfect in weakness.' Therefore I will boast all the more gladly about my weaknesses, so that Christ's power may rest on me. That is why, for Christ's sake, I delight in weaknesses, in insults, in hardships, in persecutions, in difficulties. For when I am weak, then I am strong" (II Corinthians 12:9–10).

Chapter 12

Two Special Visitors to Ikwa

"Have I not commanded you? Be strong and courageous. Do not be afraid; do not be discouraged, for the LORD your God will be with you wherever you go" (Joshua 1:9).

Daddy and Momma were my most faithful and long-standing supporters over the years. During my first ten years of serving in Nigeria, one step they never ventured to take was to visit me at Ikwa. However, in 1987, they felt that the time was right for the trip. They came for two weeks in May to attend our BMTC graduation. God supplied their visas. I met them in Lagos and brought them safely to Ikwa through Port Harcourt Airport.

The Ekpikhes, Daddy, and Momma at Ikwa

They stayed at my house. Momma helped me with some cooking and household duties. Their first night in their room was hot and sticky. Daddy especially felt hot and uncomfortable since we had no fans or electricity in their room to move the air. Although we had screens on the windows, the air at night was often still. The next day, I advised them to take a cool bath just before they went to bed. After that, they slept better.

I drove them to see various places in Ikot Abasi and Uyo. They visited Ikot Ekpene to buy some Nigerian souvenirs. We visited Chief Ekpe of Ikwa and Chief Ufot Ndah in the next village of Ikot Akan. Daddy and Momma attended our regular church activities at Ikwa.

They saw all the time it took for us to get through a day and prepare for the annual BMTC Pastors' Conference and graduation. The conference was in the CWT chapel, while the graduation was held in the Ikwa Methodist Church, the largest building in Ikwa village.

Many people were happy to have their picture taken with Daddy and Momma. They did well managing the daily challenges in Ikwa.

CWT and ICA leaders with the Shellys

After they returned home to the U.S., Daddy wrote me, "For all these years, I heard much about what life was like in Nigeria. Now I've personally experienced it and can pray better for everyone at Ikwa." Everyone else who visited Ikwa agreed.

In 1987, one important change was made in our state before Daddy and Momma's arrival. A state was created from the Cross River State and became the Akwa Ibom State. Akwa—also spelled Aqua, Kwa, or Qwa and meaning The Great One or The Essential One—is believed to be the ancestor of the people of Akwa Ibom State and Cross River State. It is currently the highest oil- and gas-producing state in the country. Ibom is an old word used by the Efik, Ibibio, Anang, Oron, and Eket people of Nigeria meaning the universe, the earth, or a community. The state's motto is "The Land of Promise."[5]

Chapter 13

Getting Married

"He who finds a wife finds what is good and receives favor from the Lord" (Proverbs 18:22).

Through the years, I continue to learn that God's timing is always best, even though we're often unaware of it. For example, in early 1987, the leaders of the CWT and BMTC at Ikwa challenged me to consider going to the U.S. for one semester to find a wife since I was 36 and still single.

In some ways, I was afraid to get married, as I wasn't sure if I would be a good husband or father. Whenever I'd return to the U.S. during the summer or holidays, I'd be busy visiting my family and supporters, making contacts for the ministry, or buying items to take back to Nigeria with me. Dating young ladies wasn't in my schedule.

After spending some time praying about this challenge, I finally said, "Yes, I'll go." Here's a prayer request that I included in my May newsletter:

> Please pray for planning and turnover as I prepare to go on furlough on June 13. We believe our faculty and graduates will do a good job for BMTC while I miss this semester. Pray for good health for me and a fruitful ministry with supporting churches and friends. Finally, I pray that God will use this time to help me find a wife. Let's see what happens.

That newsletter was printed and sent out to my friends and supporters in various places around the world. The couple who had been printing my newsletters from the time I began teaching full-time at BMTC in 1977 was Richard and Dorothy Shope. They lived in Bellefonte, Pennsylvania. In a letter from a year or two before, they had sent me pictures of their twin daughters, Dianne (nicknamed Dee) and Coletta, both single at the time. I wasn't yet interested in getting married, so I didn't write back to them.

However, as soon as they printed my May newsletter, they wrote to me saying, "You must meet our daughter when you come to Pennsylvania this summer." I had already wanted to meet the Shopes to see where they lived, and how they had been printing my newsletters for the past ten years.

I rounded up my duties at BMTC and had a safe trip back to the U.S. in mid-June. Anytime I returned to the U.S. for my furloughs, I lived with my parents in Manheim.

The Shope family

That summer Coletta had returned from serving in Quito, Ecuador, to take an Intensive Care course for one semester at St. Joseph's Hospital in Lancaster. In mid-July, her dad told her, "A nice, single missionary is coming to our house tomorrow." Coletta immediately knew that he was playing Cupid. She was very upset.

When I arrived at their house, neither Dee (who was home then) nor Coletta's parents were around to answer the door, so Coletta had to answer, and we said hello. The family was very nice to me. I saw their Missions, Inc. missionary newsletter printing ministry and chatted with the entire family. They asked me many questions, and I tried to answer them. Somehow, it felt like I was being interrogated, but that was okay. They were all trying to make me feel welcome, learn more about me, and make the best out of an awkward situation.

I returned to Manheim and was very excited about the visit. I also found out that Coletta's sister was already engaged and would be married that October. I didn't have any problems choosing whom I would date.

Coletta's parents were both committed Christians. Her mother led Coletta to Christ when she was six. As a child, her dad lost his job as a newspaper typesetter and began to print newsletters for overseas missionaries. Coletta and Dee were the only Shope children. At 12, she dedicated her life to the Lord. Then, at 16, she felt called into missions. As they were growing up, they had to proofread missionary newsletters. From this, she learned about various ministries around the world. Her favorite Bible verse was Micah 6:8, "He has showed you, O man, what is good. And what does the Lord require of you? To act justly and to love mercy and to walk humbly with your God."

Coletta attended nursing school and Lancaster Bible College's one-year concentrated Bible course. She was serving as a single missionary nurse with Reach Beyond ministries, formerly Heralding Christ Jesus' Blessings (HCJB) World Radio Ministries. During one home assignment in 1983, her cousin, Ron Shope, who served with SIM (formerly Sudan Interior Mission and later Serving in Mission) in Liberia, called her and said, "SIM is having a banquet in Lancaster. You should come to it."

Coletta agreed. This was a divine appointment. SIM gave away their most recent magazine with a centerfold showing people groups to be reached for Christ worldwide. Coletta removed the centerfold, placed it in her prayer notebook, and began to personally pray for them.

Lancaster was just ten miles from my home in Manheim. I had Coletta's phone number, so I called to see if I could take her on a date. She accepted, and we walked around the many stores at the Park City Mall in Lancaster. Afterward, we went to Wendy's to buy Frosty milkshakes. I later took her to Hershey Park one evening, and we enjoyed the time together. From there, we began dating and did more activities together. We went to Calvary Church in Lancaster for some services and Calvary Monument Church in Paradise, Pennsylvania, for a missions conference.

During that same summer while I was in the U.S., I also had friends help me meet some single ladies. My sister and brother-in-law invited one young lady and me for supper at their house. My parents were also invited. My other three sisters, all married, were also praying for me to find a wife. So that evening, they had me meet the young lady. We had a meal together, but Momma didn't get excited about my dating her, so nothing developed.

That September, I flew to California to be with some of our CWST board members. I stayed with Alvin Peters at his home in Dinuba. He and his wife, Annie, helped me have two dates in one night. We all met the first young lady by having pizza together for supper. Then he let me drive his Lincoln Continental car one hour away to meet a relative of another couple who were also good friends of the CWST.

While on the second date, I didn't know how to lock Alvin's car, so the car alarm went off. After trying several methods, I was finally able to turn it off. Alvin told me that if I had a good time with the young

1987 - Coletta

lady, I could extend my flight by a day and get to know her better. I stayed an extra day and spent the next day seeing some sights with her.

God opened and closed doors. After I returned to Lancaster, I had a few more dates with Coletta. Then, in October, I drove to Webster Bible Church in New York to attend their annual missions conference. The October leaves were gorgeous, and the missions conference was a good challenge for the members. I stayed with Mr. and Mrs. Giles Burtner, members of the church, who had a great heart for missions. While there, I received a nice note from Coletta, saying she missed me. I had never dated anyone before, so such words meant much to me.

When I returned to Manheim, Coletta and I met together more often. On one Wednesday night, I was to speak at one of my supporting churches, Grace Brethren Church, in Lanham, Maryland. Unfortunately, the weather was snowy and cold. My sister and her husband, Terry and Francis Swann, attended that church. They called me saying several inches of snow had fallen, and many people had problems driving on the roads and the beltway. They suggested I call their pastor and cancel the meeting, which I did.

Since I didn't mind driving in the snow at night, I quickly changed my plans and met Coletta at her apartment. She lived with three other young ladies in Lancaster. Coletta and I decided to play The Ungame, a game that asks players practical questions to get to know each other. On one of Coletta's turns, her card read, "What's one thing you'd like to see happen that hasn't happened yet?"

She answered, "If you're serious about our relationship and dating me, I'd like you to come to Quito in December and see the ministries I've been involved in for the past ten years." I didn't know how to answer her immediately. I'd have to first see how God would supply $1,000 to buy an airline ticket to escort her back to Quito when she'd return from her home assignment in early December.

In between all of this was the big weekend of October 24, when I joined Coletta to attend Dee's wedding to Michael Lindsey in Philadelphia. Coletta was the maid of honor. We also joined the Shelly clan for a weekend in the mountains with my parents, my four sisters, and their husbands. Such events gave us more time together to get to know more about Coletta's friends and my family members.

I didn't have much money saved up for the round-trip ticket from Philadelphia to Quito. I shared this as a prayer request with my supporting friends and churches, as I visited them during those next weeks. One couple said, "We'll give you $50.00 if you will truly go." Another friend gave me two $100 bills, while several others also donated. My FIM mission support funds for that month were several hundred dollars higher than usual, so I concluded, "Okay, Lord, I'm going to Quito!" I proceeded to buy my ticket!

Shelly & Shope Thanksgiving celebration

Our dating relationship continued to develop. Coletta joined me for several Shelly suppers and outings. My family members were happy with our relationship. Once, on her own initiative, Coletta was the first person at the Shelly family supper to get up from her seat after our meal to clean up the table and take the dishes to the kitchen. Momma noticed that and was impressed.

I gave Coletta my first kiss at Thanksgiving. Our home assignments in the U.S. were quickly coming to an end. We prepared to fly together to Quito from December 8–19. I also was preparing to return to Nigeria by the end of December, so that I could prepare for January's classes.

In my December newsletter, I wrote the following under my prayer items:

> For those of you who are interested members of the "Find a Wife for Dennis Club," be encouraged. December 8–19, I'll travel to Quito, Ecuador, with Coletta Shope to see her ministry in the HCJB Mission Hospital. She's worked there for ten years. She'll stay in Quito but plans to visit me in Nigeria in May 1988 for two weeks if funds are supplied. Pray for both of us.

December 1987 - At the Equator

The trip was delightful, informative, and of course, romantic. We stayed in separate bedrooms in the apartment of Coletta's roommate, Sara Risser. Coletta showed me various HCJB ministries, such as the Voz Andes Hospital where she worked. We saw their international radio ministries and tall radio towers at Pifo in the Andes Mountains, about 10,000 feet above sea level.

We ate a few suppers with some HCJB missionaries and staff. Next, we visited the tourist site at the equator, where the name Ecuador originates. Finally, we did some shopping to buy souvenirs, like carvings of a parrot and an equator stone paperweight.

The night before I returned to Philadelphia, Coletta took me to a fancy hotel with a restaurant on the top floor. During the meal, I started to cry. Coletta realized how much I dreaded leaving her, and that I was very serious about our relationship. It was hard leaving her at the airport the next morning.

When I returned to Philadelphia, Mike and Dee Lindsey met me at the airport. Mike asked me, "Did you give Coletta a kiss?" He knew that Dee was dying to know, but that she was too shy to ask. She told me later that if I had kissed her, she would know I was serious because I was a man of integrity. I answered, "Yes." They were very happy for us.

Between my travels, I visited Coletta's parents to report how our trip to Ecuador went. I took them some fruit and flowers. I also asked them for their permission to marry Coletta. They readily approved. In many ways, they had already indirectly agreed that I could marry Coletta. I was thrilled with their response. I was also happy that not one person disapproved of our relationship during our months of dating. God was confirming that we should be married!

My family also had the same response. Our Shelly clan Christmas supper with my parents and my four sisters and their families was at my parent's house. We enjoyed a great Christmas meal together. Since I was to return to Nigeria the next week, it was also hard for me to say my goodbyes to our family. Saying goodbye was always one of the hardest things for me to do as a missionary.

After that supper, while my four sisters were helping my mother wash the dishes, my mother gave them an update on how things were going with Coletta and me. They were very excited. They urged me that since our relationship was going so well, I should just go ahead and ask Coletta to marry me.

I responded that we had both wanted God's direction in all of this. Our agreed-upon plan was that I was first going to personally see Coletta's ministries, which I had just done. Then later, she would come to visit me at Ikwa. That would confirm if God wanted us to get married, and if Coletta could live in our tropical, buggy, humid climate. There she'd not have many conveniences that would make life easy for her. I remembered Dr. Harry Fletcher's statement in his Doctor of Ministry thesis on *The Pastor as Counselor*, that if God was leading a man and woman together, their ministries together as husband and wife should be stronger than if they were each single.[6] That's what we wanted!

Before the Shelly clan left our house that Saturday night, one of them secretly used a bar of soap to write on our upstairs bathroom mirror the words, "Don't forget to ask the question." I wasn't sure what to do when I saw it the next morning. I continued working hard to prepare to fly to Nigeria the following Tuesday.

That next night, Sunday, I called Coletta in Quito. This would be my last easy phone call before returning to Nigeria. It was great to talk to each other. We chatted about how we were doing and everything we needed to discuss. Then I recalled my family's challenge to ask Coletta to marry me. I took up the courage and went ahead and asked her the question, "Will you marry me?" I took her off guard. She paused and then said, "I guess so!" We rounded up the phone call with our hearts bursting, both happy and sad. Soon we'd be more than 6,000 miles from each other.

I was glad that when I became engaged to marry Coletta, I didn't have the burden of paying a large bride price to her family before I could marry her. Especially in southern Nigeria, there would be a traditional marriage, where the two families would officially meet. Her family would present a long list of items for my family to pay for or give before they finally approved my marrying her. This could involve buying a goat, yams, clothing, and sometimes even crates of soft or alcoholic drinks. Often this would take months to gather before the final presentation and approval.

Most young Nigerian men wouldn't have money saved aside to give to their fiancée's family, so each of the family members would need to contribute their share. Later they would have a formal church wedding. These challenges would often delay couples from marrying in a timely way. Sometimes they'd be tempted to have sexual relations before the wedding.

I had been working among the Ibibios in southeastern Nigeria during my entire time in Nigeria. The Ibibio tribe was one of the very people groups that Coletta had been praying for in the SIM magazine centerfold she had received in 1983. God was working things out for Coletta to join me to serve with these Ibibio people.

I returned to Nigeria that Tuesday in late December by myself. The trip went well. I slowly began to settle back into village life at Ikwa. It was always harder to leave the U.S. and try to adapt to Nigeria than to return to the U.S. from Nigeria. Once I stepped off the plane at Lagos airport, I'd face obstacles, like sweltering, sticky weather that would make me sweat immediately in the tropical climate. Other challenges would be irregular electric supply from the Nigerian Electric Power Authority (NEPA), more time needed to cook and buy food items, many knocks at my door, and much less leisure time. It was great, however, to see my Nigerian CWT and BMTC mates and friends again.

I made a habit of writing Coletta often. Once, I wrote her a 36-page letter over several days. I wrote several pages daily before combining it all into one letter to send her. After being at Ikwa for several weeks, I still hadn't received any letters from her. More than once, I volunteered to drive the ten-mile trip to the Ikot Abasi Post Office in my car to check the mail. When there was no mail from Coletta, I returned very sadly. This continued for about six weeks. I was asking myself, "When will I hear from her? Is she okay?"

My pace of life at Ikwa—teaching, studying, attending chapels and church services—often wore me out physically. I planned to go to a local hotel in Eket 20 miles away for a weekend to catch up on correcting my tests and homework. It was good to get some good meals at the hotel and more variety in eating than I had at Ikwa. As I was preparing to leave that Friday afternoon, a DHL (an express mail service) van drove into our compound and brought me a package from Coletta. Wow! Was I excited!

I took the package with me to Eket. Once I was settled into my room facing the Qua Iboe River, I opened it to find various letters and items from Coletta. She was receiving letters from me, but she knew I wasn't receiving any from her. The DHL package had cost her about $100.00 to send, but it worked and was definitely worth the cost. I read everything more than once during that weekend!

As I read Coletta's letters, she confirmed 100 percent that she was delighted to marry me. This began plans for a wedding in Lancaster, Pennsylvania, in September 1988. However, over the next few months, some of Coletta's HCJB mates—her roommate Sara Risser and other Ecuadorian Christian nurses—planned to attend a nursing conference in Philadelphia the last weekend of July. Coletta asked me if we could move our wedding date forward so these friends could attend. I agreed.

The semester went well. Coletta and I continued to correspond and always looked forward to hearing from each other. Knowing that it often took two or three weeks for our mail to get to each other, we wrote often and had much to read from each other when letters finally arrived. Even though we were already engaged, I still wanted Coletta to come and experience what life was like in Nigeria before we were married.

Once we agreed to marry and minister together, Coletta had the most challenging part of completing her eleven years of nursing ministries. She had to say goodbye to her missionary and national friends in Quito. Yet, God gave her the grace to do it well.

The CWT proceeded to officially invite Coletta as a visitor to Nigeria to attend our 1988 BMTC graduation in May. Her visa was successfully granted, and she came. I met her at Lagos airport, and we had a great reunion! We had a wonderful dinner together at the Sheraton Hotel and stayed overnight in separate rooms before we returned to Ikwa the next day.

Everyone at Ikwa was happy for us. Coletta attended our BMTC graduation and church services and saw many sights around Ikwa. Her two-week visit went by quickly. We both returned to the U.S. in June. There was much to do in preparing for the wedding. Dr. Eric Crichton, senior pastor of Coletta's home church (Calvary Church in Lancaster), and President George Miles from WBC were to officiate our wedding. The date was set for Saturday, July 30. Pastor Walt Jackson and our CWT president, Brother Joshua Ekpikhe, also had a part.

Friends pitched in to provide flowers, make a videotape of the wedding, and provide food for the reception. Sheila Druck sang "The Household of Faith" with Parke Duing playing the guitar. Ginny Spurrier and Heather Crichton welcomed guests at the church.

Coletta wore the same dress size as Dee. Since we wanted to have our wedding debt-free, there were various ways we decided to cut costs. Dee, who was to be the matron of honor, allowed Coletta to wear her wedding dress after a bridal shop told Coletta there was no time to fit a dress before the wedding date. Her only expense was to get it dry-cleaned. My four sisters were also willing to be bridesmaids. They had all been at other weddings over the years, and each wore one of those dresses.

My brother-in-law, Francis Swann, was the best man. My other four brothers-in-law and Daddy pitched in to rent tuxedos for the wedding. Because they all rented their outfits, I received mine for free. My brother-in-law, Denny Sharp, worked at Weaver Foods. He ordered many food items and salads at low prices for our reception. Momma baked several sheet cakes to use along with the official cake. God was putting it all together with minimum cost for us.

We had a smooth wedding rehearsal the night before the wedding. We ordered some Gino's fried chicken. Coletta and I arrived on time to pick it up, but the order was late. That made everyone wait to get started, but it all worked out. One of my young nephews somehow accidentally pulled a fire alarm in the church during the rehearsal, so the night was full of action.

July 30, 1988 - Our wedding

The wedding went well. The weather on that Saturday, July 30, was a scorcher. We were glad that it was inside Calvary Church's air-conditioned auditorium. It turned out to be very international. Coletta's roommate in Quito, Sara Risser; two Ecuadorian nursing friends, Cruz Quinonez and Nancy Mendosa; and Margaret Corin, director of nurses at Voz Andes, all came from their nursing conference in Philadelphia and were able to come. Diane Sheldon, a former roommate in Costa Rica and Quito, also joined the occasion.

Some of our CWT leaders, such as Dr. Joshua and Elizabeth Ekpikhe, Vern and Kathy Goertzen, Larry and Jenny Morrison, Rev. Sunday Umune, and some of our BMTC alumni attending WBC and CBS, were all able to join the celebration. They were Randee and Kasho I-Morphe, Emmanuel Inyangson, Udo Umoh, Samuel and Patience Ekwue and their children, and another Nigerian CBS graduate, Joseph Ezeigbo. In addition, we had Shope and Shelly relatives and friends from our home churches attend. It was a great day and a wonderful reunion of friends from all around the world.

After the wedding, Coletta and I planned to spend our honeymoon in Virginia. We wanted to start our journey by staying overnight at the Sheraton Inn in Harrisburg about 30 miles from Lancaster. We arrived just after 8 p.m. We had booked a room earlier and thought that all was well when we arrived. However, since we arrived after 8 p.m., the receptionist said we were too late, and someone had taken our room. Wow! Now, what would we do?

I told Coletta the news. We were both upset. However, the receptionist said, "Let me see what I can do for you." Soon he replied, "I think we can make another plan for you that you'll be happy about." He moved us up to stay in one of their junior suites, which was much nicer than the standard room we had originally booked. It all turned out to be for our good. We weren't disappointed.

Our honeymoon in Virginia was enjoyable. First, we visited Luray Caverns and Monticello, the home of Thomas Jefferson. Then, we spent several days in Williamsburg to see how life was in colonial times. One evening we enjoyed an organ concert played on an old organ. Finally, we drove to Busch Gardens, enjoyed some of their rides, and visited the famous Clydesdale horses that were driven in various parades around the U.S.

One night during our honeymoon, I played with my new wedding ring. I had never worn a ring, so it felt unusual to me. While we were at a restaurant waiting for our food, I pulled off my ring, and it fell. We couldn't find it. The restaurant staff had to help us by pulling out the booth. Finally, they found it for us, for which we were very grateful.

We rounded up our one-week honeymoon by joining our Shelly family members for the weekend at Sandy Cove Bible Conference. Our family loved to pull tricks on members. Some of my brothers-in-law called us late that night to see how we were doing as newlyweds.

The CWT and BMTC allowed us to remain in the U.S. for one semester after our marriage. We were advised to stay in the U.S. for this time—it would lay a good foundation for our marriage without too much cross-cultural shock. We rented a car from Jonestown Bible Church for five months and house-sat for a Christian couple from Calvary Church, Mr. and Mrs. Smiley, who were driving to Alaska in their camper for those months.

Their home was just what we needed. It was about two miles from our home church and was very close to many stores where we shopped for food and household items. That one semester in the U.S. helped Coletta and me immensely as 37-year-old newlyweds to get used to each other and be more ready to begin ministry together in Nigeria.

During that summer and fall, we visited many of our supporting churches for them to meet Coletta and wish us well. Some of these church members had faithfully supported Coletta and me since we both began our full-time ministries in Ecuador and Nigeria in 1977. They were praying that I'd find a committed Christian spouse, so everyone was thrilled to meet Coletta.

During those months, we both learned some of our strengths and weaknesses. My Aunt Elsie Earhart visited us once with Uncle Ike when we were at Daddy and Momma's house. She gave us some wise counsel to be sure to tell each other, "I love you," at least ten times a day. We weren't just to say, "I love you," ten times and stop. Instead, we were to find various ways to say, "I love you," by helping with housework, expressing our love with a hug or kiss, being kind to each other, etc. We've tried to do this since then. It works!

Arriving at Ikwa in November 1988

Somehow, one day at the Smiley's house, I lost my wedding ring again. Unfortunately, we couldn't find it this time, so I had to buy a replacement. While there, we purchased our first Toshiba laptop computer. It looked like a thin, little typewriter.

It used a small printer with a long ribbon, which we could reuse if we didn't have spare cartridges.

At the end of November 1988, we returned safely to Ikwa, ready to begin our new lives together. We were learning quickly that Coletta was an eternal realist, and I was an eternal optimist. Both perspectives were needed to keep us going at Ikwa.

The CWT, BMTC staff, and students were excited to see us again. They had been faithfully praying for us. Their prayers and support, along with our friends and supporters back home, would help us begin a new phase of our journey together in ministry in a new cross-cultural context. God's timing in all of this was indeed the best.

For each chapter from now on, watch for "Coletta's thoughts," as she shares some thoughts from her perspective on what I've written.

Coletta's thoughts:

No, it wasn't love at first sight, but Dennis was likable to me from the beginning. My Dad kept assuring me that Dennis was a man of integrity. The longer we dated, the more I recognized God's hand in our relationship. I was totally unprepared for his proposal over the phone that Sunday evening in late December 1987, but have no regrets.

The first year of marriage was hard for me—living on a new continent, in a village where there were few conveniences, a climate that was hot and buggy, with new foods, new diseases, and a difficult Ibibio language to learn. I was the only medical person in the ministry for my first years. I had a pact with Dennis that he would kill the creeping, crawling, flying critters. I eventually learned how to kill the cockroaches myself, but always left killing the rats and snakes to him or the villagers.

Chapter 14

One Startling Event at Ikwa

"As for God, his way is perfect; the word of the Lord is flawless. He is a shield for all who take refuge in him. For who is God besides the LORD? And who is the Rock except our God? It is God who arms me with strength and makes my way perfect" (II Samuel 22:31–33).

On November 8, 1989, one startling event happened. Larry Morrison was a BMTC faculty member who had returned that semester with his new bride, Jenny, to serve together at Ikwa. Dr. Ron Wall, an experienced, Christian dentist, and his wife, Mary Ann, a travel agent, visited us from California. They were active members of the CWST in the U.S. and were good friends of Vern and Kathy Goertzen. That morning Coletta, Jenny, Mary Ann, and Kathy drove 20 miles to Eket to have lunch with one of the Exx-on-Mobil staff wives.

Larry went to turn on the CWT compound generator, which produced 220-volt electric power (Britain's versus America's 110-volt power) to provide power for the CWT compound. When he returned to his house, he took off his shoes to keep dirt and mud outside. This was a custom in most Nigerian homes. He touched the kitchen stove while reaching to turn on one of the kitchen lights. Sadly, their house had just been wired, but some of the wires weren't properly grounded. He was severely shocked when he touched the stove and fell immediately.

Ron realized what had happened and began to use artificial respiration on Larry. He called us to come quickly. We ran to get the CWT van to rush him to a hospital in Ikot Abasi, ten miles away. David Ekpikhe, the president's oldest son and one of the BMTC faculty members, drove as fast as he could. At the same time, Ron continued with the CPR in the back of the van. I followed Ron's instructions to pump Larry's chest. I had never done that before.

We drove quickly to the Ikot Abasi Government Hospital and another private hospital there. Neither had any oxygen. We had no choice but to return, going past Ikwa on to

Eket. Ron continued trying to give Larry artificial respiration the whole way. We were all getting tired, but we were determined not to give up.

Larry preaching at ICA,
Pius Nnah interpreting

When we arrived at Immanuel Hospital in Eket, we discovered that their anesthesiologist was on lunch break at his home. Another staff called him to come quickly. Everything seemed to be against us. When we took Larry to the hospital, the team pronounced him dead.

Since the ladies didn't know anything that was happening, we had to go and tell Jenny the sad news. We met the ladies in their car as they were returning to Ikwa. When Coletta saw us, as a nurse, she knew that something terrible had happened. She saw that my face was as white as a sheet. We called her to our car and told her what had happened. She then went to tell Jenny. Larry and Jenny had been married for only four months.

Despite poor communication and the lack of facilities, like funeral homes, Larry and Jenny's families were promptly informed of his passing. We had Larry's burial at the Ikwa Methodist Church several days later. I presided over the service. It wasn't easy, but God gave me the grace to have good composure to lead the service. Immediately after I ended my part, my emotions hit me, and I cried. Larry's corpse was buried behind his house on the CWT compound. His parents and brother came from the U.S. several months later for Larry's more official memorial service, bringing a plaque to remember him.

Larry Morrison's plaque

Even though it was short-lived, the Lord used Larry's life and ministry at Ikwa to touch the lives of everyone in the CWT and BMTC. One of the BMTC faculty who was closest to Larry was Moses Oluwole. He later carried on Larry's burden for church planting by leading the CWT's church planting ministries while he served at BMTC. Moses' wife, Kemi, also led and strengthened the CWT's Life Foundation Nursery-Primary-Secondary School to where it is today. Moses continues his love for church planting and missions as he directs the Live School Missions Training ministry from Ibadan, Oyo State.

Chapter 15

Beginning a Family

"Be joyful always; pray continually;
give thanks in all circumstances,
for this is God's will for you in Christ Jesus"
(I Thessalonians 5:16–18).

As a single man, I did have the desire to get married, but I wasn't sure if I could be a good husband and father. In 1987, when Coletta and I became more serious in our relationship, she told me that she had a few medical issues that might keep her from having children. Many men might have stopped dating her after hearing that.

However, I quickly replied that if she couldn't have children, we'd instead pour our lives into the lives of our BMTC students. We'd do our best to disciple them and help prepare them for more effective Christian ministries wherever God would lead them. I also told Coletta that I had some physical challenges with my back and a large hiatal hernia, which made me use some pillows to prop up my head when I slept.

During my years as a full-time single missionary, I had various single and married couples living in my house at Ikwa. We shared cooking and household duties. Some were Americans; others were Nigerians. Everyone's varying ideas and standards were often challenging, sometimes even clashing, but God's grace saw us through. Now it was just Coletta and me in our house. It was great to have her by my side.

Coletta and I agreed that we'd try not to have children for one year to get a good start in our marriage. Happily, she was able to get pregnant with Dwight. He was to be born in November 1989.

40 weeks pregnant

We could have chosen to fly to the U.S. for Dwight's delivery. However, we decided to have him in Uyo, Akwa Ibom State's capital. It was 45 miles from Ikwa. Two experienced gynecologists at St. Luke's Hospital, Dr. Ward and Dr. Itina, were willing to help with the delivery. While Coletta was pregnant, I frequently drove her to see her doctors. Dwight was due to be born on November 16 but was born on the 25th. Coletta had her routine doctor's check-up on November 24 and was admitted for delivery on Friday, the 25th.

The tradition in Nigeria was for family members to provide all meals for their hospitalized family members. The families would often stay nearby to visit and care for the members as needed. I stayed at a hotel in Uyo for several nights to be close to Coletta. I was able to take her good meals from the hotel.

When Dwight was born, he wasn't breathing. Coletta, as a registered nurse who had worked for years in various hospitals in the children's unit, observed this and quickly called the doctors. They promptly used a machine to suck fluid out of Dwight's lungs. Right away, he was able to begin crying.

Coletta stayed in the hospital for three days. Then, we proudly took her and the baby home that following Monday. Unfortunately, the hospital's maternity unit didn't have screens on the windows, so mothers and babies were susceptible to mosquitoes. With all the ups and downs of feeding Dwight, Coletta came down with malaria that Wednesday. This forced us to take her and Dwight back to the hospital. After she was treated, I brought her and Dwight home.

At Ikwa, we had better control over what we ate and where we slept. Our house windows and doors had good screens that didn't have holes. We also had one house girl, Comfort, who worked for us. She was of great help to Coletta in caring for Dwight and cooking for us. In addition, she enjoyed watching Dwight when needed.

Since Nigerians are extra happy when a mother delivers a baby boy, we didn't have many who were disappointed when Dwight was born. Having a male child would help the family carry on their name to the next generation. If a husband and wife had four or five girls, their extended family and the local people would culturally believe that they didn't have a real family yet. Sometimes this would lead the husband to take another wife, hoping to have a male child.

However, medical authorities today have confirmed that the husband's chromosome determines if their child will be a boy or girl, not the wife's. We're happy that polygamy and this past type of thinking have now become much less in various parts of Nigeria than in previous generations.

Coletta and I started our family later in life. In 1989, we were both 38 years old. Our family and friends in the U.S. quickly received the news of Dwight's birth. We had reserved the name Dwight Deane for him because my parents wanted to have all boys. They would have named their next son Dwight. However, God gave them four girls after I was born. They never had the chance to name a second son Dwight. His middle name is Deane, after my middle name.

Keeping this in mind, Coletta and I felt that if God gave us a boy, we'd name him Dwight, as the next boy in the Shelly line. So that's what we did. We took many pictures during those first days and sent them to our parents and family. We included pictures in our monthly newsletter. Indeed, parents often take more pictures of their first child than of the children who come later.

Ikwa leaders celebrating Dwight's birth

The CWT had a special celebration service to dedicate Dwight to the Lord. Ikwa's village leaders also wanted to celebrate, so we prepared a big meal for them and took pictures. Dwight began to grow. He was highly active right from birth.

Various toys were bought or received for Dwight. One was a blow-up plastic toy that he could sit on. He was put in a wooden crib to help confine him. We enjoyed reading books to Dwight. I enjoyed reading the story "Bambi" to him. I could press the recorded animated noises of the various characters when reading about them. I believe that I wore out that book! Coletta thought that I enjoyed this book more than Dwight. I also enjoyed making various barnyard animal noises, so I had much fun making them for the children.

WBC Alumnus of the Year Award

In May 1990, Dr. Harry Fletcher came to speak for our annual BMTC Pastors' Conference and graduation. During the ceremonies, Dr. Fletcher gave an honorary doctorate from WBC to CWT President Brother Joshua Ekpikhe for his years of faithful

Christian service to the Lord. Dr. Fletcher also presented me with the WBC Alumnus of the Year award.

We returned to the U.S. in August 1990 for our home assignment. This was the first time the Shopes, Shellys, and our supporting churches saw Dwight. We arrived at Kennedy Airport in New York. Because of bad weather, we had to fly first to Pittsburgh airport, then take another flight back to Lancaster.

Dwight with Grandpa & Grandma Shope

The weather was unusually cool. When we arrived in Lancaster, I draped my summer suit coat over Coletta to keep her warm. During the coming months, we had good times with the Shellys and Shopes. As grandparents, they greatly appreciated our time spent with them.

Being missionaries with Calvary Church in Lancaster had advantages. One was that they had six different homes or apartments for missionaries to live in when they'd return to the U.S. for home assignments. We had to request one several months in advance.

For our 1990 home assignment, we lived in Calvary Church's split-level home on Princess Avenue in Lancaster. While we were living there, Dwight learned to walk. In addition, we bought a large video camcorder to record short clips of Dwight to share such family highlights with our families and friends.

One day while Dwight was starting to walk, he was backing down some of the carpeted steps near our main entrance. I tried to record his movements. While I began recording, Dwight tumbled down the steps right in front of me. The carpet helped him not get hurt. I was happy that he was unharmed. I recorded part of his fall.

During that same home assignment, Coletta became pregnant with Stephanie. Our Shelly family had some interesting customs. When we'd gather for a Christmas or holiday supper, Daddy would ask us, "Are there any special announcements to make?" This could include one of us getting engaged, married, or having a baby.

At that Shelly Christmas supper, just before we returned to Nigeria to prepare for the January semester, Coletta and I had arranged to give a paper puzzle to the family. As they put the pieces together on the dining room table, they saw the words, "Arriving at Ikwa in August." Finally, one of Dennis' sisters guessed that Coletta would have a baby.

Everyone was delighted, even though they couldn't be in Nigeria to be with us for the event. We also told the Shope side of the family the news. Another chapter of our lives was about to begin as we returned to Nigeria right after Christmas.

Coletta's thoughts:

We believe that children are a gift from the Lord and were so excited when I became pregnant. God saw us through some complications of pregnancy and living in less-than-ideal conditions. As a new mother, I so missed not having my mother present to help me. God sent me another helper in Comfort. What a blessing she would be to us for the next three years. Not only was she a good cook and baker, but she was excellent with the children. We enjoyed her presence even on holidays. We fondly called her Auntie Comfort.

Chapter 16

A Little Daughter Joins Our Family

"The righteous man leads a blameless life;
blessed are his children after him."
(Proverbs 20:7).

We returned to Ikwa in early January 1991, so I could join the BMTC faculty to teach for the January semester. Traveling with Dwight and pregnant Coletta was indeed more difficult than before. God helped us return without any problems.

During Coletta's pregnancy with Stephanie, Dwight kept growing and was always "Mr. Action," especially as he learned to walk and run. He loved to use his hands, so if a carpenter was working, he'd want to pick up a hammer or intently watch what the worker was doing and imitate him.

Coming home from the hospital

Coletta's pregnancy with Stephanie started roughly but then progressed without any incidents. When we brought Stephanie home from St. Luke's Hospital in late August, we showed her to Dwight. He had much to learn. He quickly discovered that a new family member was entering the house and his territory. His face immediately changed from a smile to a scowl. He promptly sensed competition.

The day after Stephanie's arrival, Coletta heard Stephanie's cry being muffled. Dwight had taken a pillow and covered her face. When we went to investigate, we hurried to take it from him. Fortunately, she was okay.

Almost three weeks after this, Coletta began having pain in her right hip and limped when she tried to walk. Late on a Saturday afternoon, after I had ended a long BMTC Board of Governors' meeting, she strongly felt she needed to go to Uyo to see Dr. Ward. Although I was tired from the day's events, I finally agreed to drive her and Stephanie to the hospital. She did see Dr. Ward, who scolded her for not coming sooner to report her hip problems. Coletta was admitted and received antibiotics for her inflamed hip.

Dr. Itina, a Christian gynecologist, lived on the St. Luke's Hospital compound. He learned of Coletta's situation and kindly allowed me to stay overnight at his house. I said good night to Coletta and then returned to his home. At about 10:00 p.m., I felt an intense pain in my right side and told Dr. Itina. He quickly took me over to the hospital to get it checked out. The staff immediately admitted me and rushed me to the operating room (theatre) to remove my appendix.

We saw God working in this whole situation for Coletta and me. Little did I know that God was using my escorting Coletta to the hospital to get me closer to getting medical help for myself rather than being 40 miles away at Ikwa. There, I wouldn't have been close to good medical attention. It also wasn't safe to drive at night. Dr. Itina's wife kindly sent Coletta a lovely breakfast that Sunday morning.

After my operation, the hospital staff allowed me to stay in one of their private rooms—with window screens—for the days I was under their care. Coletta was discharged several days before I was. One morning, she came to visit me from Ikwa with the children. Dwight was so happy to see me that he came over and jumped up on my lap, right where I had my incision. Ouch! That hurt, although I knew he didn't do it on purpose. Several days later, I was discharged, and we returned home. We were most grateful to the medical staff for their assistance and hospitality during those unexpected hospitalizations.

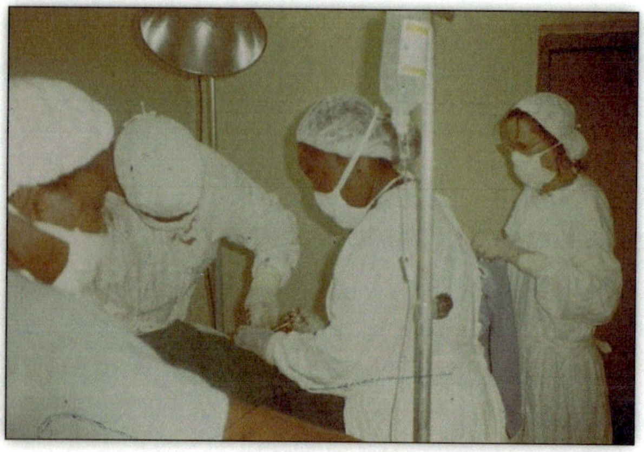
1992 - Coletta assisting the FMH doctors

Over the following months, Stephanie began to grow. She didn't have much hair when she was little. When seeing her, more than one Nigerian was sure she was a boy. Coletta asked a friend to pierce Stephanie's little ears, so she could wear earrings to help us convince at least some that she was a girl. When she did get more hair on her head, it was very blonde.

While Coletta was breastfeeding Stephanie, she also worked at the FMH. Two Nigerian doctors from Uyo helped the hospital do various operations, like hernias and appendix problems. Many had hernias because they had very physical jobs: farming, construction, and lifting heavy loads to and from markets. When a woman needed a hysterectomy, they arranged to have several surgeons from Uyo come to do the operation.

Dwight became Coletta's good little helper in watching out for Stephanie. Because he was usually very loud and vocal, we usually knew where he was and what he was doing.

Stephanie continued to grow and learned to crawl and walk. Dwight was also learning much and was becoming more independent. He learned early on how to kick a ball from his Nigerian friends and would visit various CWT children in their houses. The children were happy to play with him in and out of our house. Sometimes several boys would come to our house, sit on our dining room floor, and beat drums with Dwight. We thought Dwight would become a drummer; he loved beating things with sticks.

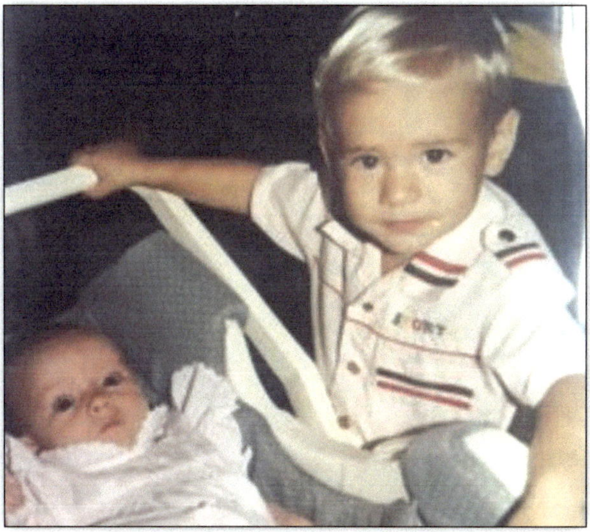

Dwight taking care of Stephanie

Dwight enjoyed eating various Nigerian meals, such as garri and soup. Later Stephanie also learned to eat them. These were very filling. After eating at a neighbor's house, he'd come home and wouldn't want to eat much. This lack of appetite concerned us until we figured out what was happening. The Nigerian families were very good at hospitality, happy to share their food with Dwight when he played with their children at their house. Often the children would eat alone, not with their parents, so they welcomed Dwight to join them. We served some of the Nigerian foods at our house, so the children enjoyed many of the local dishes.

We took many more pictures of Dwight compared to Stephanie. However, our new video camcorder helped us take many videos to send back to our families. This allowed them to see the children in action and what they were doing. For example, we recorded Stephanie as she ate, crawled, walked, and then played with Dwight and his friends. Our parents' and sisters' families were thrilled to see the children during regular days, holidays, and celebrations, like their birthdays.

In early 1992, we saw the need to buy a new car. Our old Peugeot was becoming less dependable on longer trips. A one-way trip to Kaduna from Ikwa was 600 miles.

Port Harcourt, where we occasionally traveled to buy food items or stay in a hotel for a weekend, was 60 miles away. Many Nigerian roads had deep potholes (gallops) in them, causing our shock absorbers and tires to wear out quickly.

We had asked the staff at Mandilas Motors in Port Harcourt to watch out for a newer Peugeot for us to buy. They advised us that we shouldn't rush in the process. If someone was trying to sell a used car, it was usually for a good reason—maybe the car was having a big problem with its engine, or it was in an accident and wasn't in proper condition, or the owner needed money.

One day we received word that Mandilas Motors had a brand-new VW Jetta Executive model car for sale. Someone had just won it in a national 7-Up contest but didn't want to keep it. He wanted to sell it within 24 hours. We quickly agreed to hurry and see it the very next day. The car's original color was bright green, just like a 7-Up soft drink bottle. It only had 230 miles on its odometer. We agreed to buy it and asked if Mandilas could paint it white. They agreed on a very reasonable price of about N4,000 (naira), or about $400.

Our new Jetta & Old Peugeot

The exchange rate in early 1992 was about N10 to $1.00. We took the money in cash to Port Harcourt the day we paid for the car. At that time, Nigeria's largest denomination in currency was only N20 ($0.20).

The Jetta cost N159,000, plus N4,000 to paint it white. The money we took filled my big briefcase and another bag. We were so glad when we finally turned this cash over to the company, not wanting thieves to steal it on the way.

It took several days to get the car painted. Afterward, we proudly drove it back to Ikwa. God helped us buy the car just before the exchange rate rose from N10 naira to N18 naira, equaling $1.00. That would have made us pay much more for the vehicle. We used the car for ministry trips, shopping, or taking the family for a weekend to a nice hotel.

At the hotel, we could eat meals that were more international or American. We'd enjoy air conditioning in buildings, swimming in their pool, and watching TV programs and news programs that we didn't often see. These were luxuries for us that weren't available in our rural area. Dwight and Stephanie especially enjoyed going swimming in the hotel's outside pool.

Getting dirty at our sandbox

On our first trip in the Jetta to Enugu (about 3 hours from Ikwa), while our car was parked at our hotel, someone slightly bumped its side and didn't tell us. We weren't pleased about this but couldn't do anything about it. Then, on our way home while driving through a village, a bicyclist rode in the middle of a newly paved road. He wasn't watching where he was riding. I almost hit him. I had to blow my horn loudly and suddenly swerve our car to avoid hitting him.

This is why during most of our trips, we'd begin our journey with prayer, trusting God to care for us. Many Nigerians did even better than we did. They'd start their trip with prayer and end it with prayer before disembarking from the vehicle. Day trips were also usually safer than at night.

Because Dwight was so active most of the time, whether day or night, this caused Stephanie to often be one or two steps behind him. After he learned to ride a tricycle, he escaped from our house one day without his clothes on. He pedaled his tricycle to the other side of the CWT compound to see Jenny Morrison's dog. We found him and brought him home.

1992 - Jenny Morrison with our family

The children weren't afraid to get dirty. We made a giant sandbox for them. Their friends loved to come and make castles or designs in the sand. One day they played with charcoal. Dwight led, with Stephanie following him. All of this was part of growing up at Ikwa!

In all our roles, our family members saw God teaching us much as we lived in the village setting of Ikwa. These experiences helped us learn how to work well with nationals and missionaries.

Even Dwight and Stephanie were beginning to learn how to live as third-culture kids (TCKs).

We're grateful for our prayer partners and financial supporters. If they had wavered in supporting us as our senders, we would have indeed failed as the goers. Instead, they were and continue to be a big part of our team!

Coletta's thoughts:

We *knew before Dwight was born that he was going to be a boy. The doctors who did an ultrasound didn't want to reveal the sex, but I overheard the conversation between the two doctors. With Stephanie, we had no such clue.*

We always named our babies long before they were born to help our families know what to call them. We did this because of poor communication. There were no cell phones or landlines where we lived. The nearest public pay phone at Uyo was open only during daylight hours, Monday through Saturday. A boy would be Stephen Andrew, and a girl Stephanie Dawn. I was secretly hoping for a girl this time.

Another fun thing we did was for our house helpers, Dennis, and me to guess a birth date. We all knew the expected date was August 23, Dennis' birthday. Whoever guessed the correct date would get a soft drink (mineral). Stephanie made her entrance on August 29, missing all our dates. We all had soft drinks to celebrate. We were all happy with one baby of each sex. Our lives were very busy with two little ones. We hired more house help to lighten our load.

One weekend I watched as the water tank emptied. We had two little ones in cloth diapers. I prayed for rain, and God sent a big storm. It filled our toddler swimming pool with water, which gave us water to wash our clothes! This is just one example of many answers to prayer. Wednesday nights were "uppers" for me, as I was confident many of our supporting U.S. churches were praying for us.

To keep tabs on Dwight while I was busy with a new baby, I put bells on his shoes. Our doors had hooks at the top, so he couldn't open them. As long as I could hear the bells, I knew where he was. If the bells stopped, I needed to find him. On several occasions, he managed to escape to the great world beyond our house. He loved visiting neighbors and eating whatever food they offered him.

Chapter 17

Going for Doctoral Studies

"And the things you have heard me say in the presence of many witnesses entrust to reliable men who will also be qualified to teach others" (II Timothy 2:2).

During my full-time teaching at BMTC from 1977 to 1993, I taught most of the courses from their three-year curriculum, including some introductory Greek and theology courses. I also enjoyed teaching various missions and evangelism courses. We thanked God for many of our graduates whom God led into full-time Christian ministries. They served as pastors, missionaries, teachers, children's ministry workers, and lay leaders in their churches. However, I needed to pursue more academic studies because of my increased interest in seeing our students receive more practical training.

The CWT knew that if I could get my Ph.D., it would help BMTC's status academically. So, they and FIM approved our family to go home to the U.S. for one year to begin these studies. However, my being away from BMTC would put an extra strain on the faculty. We lacked enough teachers to cover all courses in the curriculum. We needed to trust God to provide for them as we trusted Him to provide for our family. We didn't know what that would look like.

At the right time, in 1993, God opened the door for me to begin my Ph.D. studies. Rev. George Foxall, who oversaw the Accrediting Council for Theological Education in Africa in Nigeria, lived in Kaduna. He knew of my interests and encouraged me to consider doctoral studies at Trinity Evangelical Divinity School (TEDS) in Deerfield, Illinois. As an older SIM missionary from Canada who was close to retiring, he was doing his Doctor of Ministry studies at TEDS.

I followed his advice and investigated several U.S. seminaries with Intercultural Studies (Missions) programs. In early 1993, I applied to TEDS and was soon accepted. Some friends advised me to go for the Ph.D. in Intercultural Studies (Missions) program. This program would help me teach in a seminary or academic context more than a Doctor of Ministry program, which is more of a professional program for a missionary or pastor. Thus, I applied for the Ph.D. program.

Late that spring, our family returned to the U.S. to prepare to move to Illinois for my summer and fall semester studies. Dwight was four, and Stephanie was almost two. Calvary Church allowed us to live in one of their missionary homes until I traveled to TEDS.

I went ahead to TEDS in early August to prepare for my first summer course, while Coletta and the children stayed with Daddy and Momma for several weeks until I was settled in my studies. Friends warned me that I should be ready for Chicago's highways. Some were five and six lanes wide in each direction. This advice helped lessen the shock of driving there.

The week before my studies began, I drove over 700 miles to Deerfield, Illinois. I stayed with a Christian family for three weeks in Waukegan, about ten miles from Deerfield, until Coletta and the children joined me. I arrived on a Thursday evening.

On Friday morning, I went to the TEDS campus to find out where I would go for my first Monday course. I received my syllabus and learned from other Ph.D. students that I should have already begun my readings and known what topic I wanted to write on. Wow! I was about 300 pages behind before I started!

1993 - In the U.S. for doctoral studies

In late August, I was thrilled to have my parents bring my family to Illinois to live with me again. We celebrated Stephanie's second birthday on August 29 with Daddy and Momma by going to a Denny's Restaurant for a special meal before they returned to Pennsylvania.

My Ph.D. studies took two extra semesters to complete. My previous CBS Master of Theology major was in New Testament Greek, not in Missions. I had never studied missions courses at the M.A. level, so I was required to take 30 credit hours of M.A. missions courses before beginning the Ph.D. program. I enjoyed them immensely, such as Spiritual Warfare with Dr. Tim Warner, The History of Christian Missions with Dr. Ruth Tucker, and Folk Religions with Dr. Paul Hiebert.

One significant difference between my M.A. and Ph.D. courses was that the M.A. professors required me to write papers and take tests and exams during and at the end of each course. In contrast, my Ph.D. professors had me write various papers with much reading, but I didn't take exams. I preferred this second approach.

I never really completed any paper at the doctoral level since there was so much to read and learn from each course I took. Much of my reading was new and interesting to me and not too heavy, like some areas of theology or church history. The TEDS library usually had more resources than I could ever read. When a paper was due, I just stopped reading and writing on the specific topic. I handed in what I had read and studied in the time allotted. Then I'd move on to another course with the same format.

My doctoral courses were practical and interactive. Our professors were excellent facilitators during our weekly classes. We'd discuss assigned readings, and then share parts of the papers we were writing for each course. The discussions were lively since my mates were mostly cross-cultural missionaries from various mission boards. They had many years of experience and came from different countries where they lived or served. I was one of the younger doctoral students, beginning the program at 42. Others came from the U.S., Japan, Canada, Africa, and Europe and were in their 40s, 50s, and 60s.

That fall, we rented a small home at Gages Lake, about 15 miles from the TEDS campus. We lived right along a lovely waterfront and enjoyed watching different people boating. Pretty birds like lunes came to catch fish. They'd dive down at one spot and come up for air at another place many yards away.

That winter was the coldest we could remember, especially if we compared it with life at Ikwa in the tropics. One day it was so cold that I couldn't start my car. That year the lake froze deep enough that vehicles could drive on it for ice fishing. We had never seen that before.

At TEDS in the winter

We were happy when a two-bedroom apartment on the TEDS campus was available during my second year of studies. We lived there until I completed my studies. It saved me from driving many miles daily and gave me more weekly hours to devote to my studies and more time with my family.

After moving to the TEDS apartment, our family decided to take one summer Saturday to go to the Brookfield Zoo in

Chicago. This was the first big zoo that Dwight and Stephanie had ever seen. I took our camcorder with me. We enjoyed the day very much, seeing many wild animals in their pens or areas where they roamed.

We watched an exciting water show with dolphins as well as black and white whales jumping up into the air in a large pool. We saw elephants, lions, tigers, polar bears, snakes, monkeys, apes, and birds. We asked Stephanie what other animals she wanted to see. Her reply was, "I want to see the chickens." Dwight wasn't pleased with her answer.

We enjoyed that day and took various pictures and videos of the animals. Because we spent all Saturday at the zoo and I had a paper to turn in on Monday, I stayed up extra late on Sunday night. I wrote what I could with the time remaining before my class. I was tired, but it worked out okay.

Coletta did well in holding the family together during my TEDS studies. I spent most of my time in the TEDS library or our bedroom studying or writing, including Saturdays and Sundays, from morning until night. However, I did take some breaks to play with the children. We had good times wrestling in the living room or taking some walks to see the Canadian geese living on campus. This made us watch where we were walking, as their droppings were everywhere.

Once while we were playing in our living room, Dwight punched me hard in my chest. I almost lost my breath for a moment but was okay. We built a big playhouse in one corner of our living room out of refrigerator cardboard boxes. The children had fun with it. I also took a few breaks from my studies to watch some of Trinity College's football games on Saturday afternoons. After Sunday church services, I'd be back at it on Sunday afternoons and evenings, preparing for Monday.

My sister and her husband, Bonnie and Denny Sharp, with their two boys, Mike and Darren, visited us for several days in 1994. We wanted to show them Lake Michigan. After parking our cars, we walked down a large, steep stairway to get close to the lake. On the way down, Stephanie, smaller than Dwight and his cousins, tried to keep up with the other children. Unfortunately, she fell and hurt her forehead badly.

Coletta and I debated about taking her to a hospital. Finally, we decided not to take her and tried to care for her at our apartment. Stephanie's black and blue bruised face looked like a raccoon's. Over the next few days, she improved. The effects slowly went away.

On the TEDS campus, other families from around the world lived in our apartment building. Sometimes we had to learn new habits or put up with some that we didn't like. For example, we had a Korean family who lived right above us. Sometimes when they made kimchi with cabbage, many seasonings, and much garlic, we would quickly smell it through our apartment vents. Those smells stayed for a long time.

Our children enjoyed playing with the TEDS apartment children. Dwight had much to learn about following some of the boys. He did get into trouble when he and another boy broke one of the stairway railings. Both of our families shared in the repairs. We all were learning on different levels.

Our original plan to study for one year and then return to Nigeria was challenged during one weekly TEDS group meeting with my missions department mates and our advisors. Dr. Ted Ward warned us, "If you return to the mission field after only one year of studies completed here, you most likely will not return to complete them later."

With that wise warning, Coletta and I prayed for God to direct us. We were asking, "What will be the next step in our journey? Should we return to Nigeria or stay in the U.S. to complete my Ph.D. studies? What would our CWT and FIM leaders think?" Our staff back at BMTC would continue to be overstretched. As we continued to pray about this and receive counsel from others, we both had peace about staying on to complete my Ph.D. studies before returning to Ikwa. Others agreed with us. "For lack of guidance a nation falls, but many advisers make victory sure" (Proverbs 11:14).

That's precisely what we did. Our CWT and FIM leaders supported our decision. The Lord continued to care for our monthly needs. Housing and living expenses in Illinois were much higher than those in Pennsylvania. At TEDS in 1994, we paid over $600 monthly just for rent. Our supporting churches and individuals continued to support us during my four years of studies at TEDS. MABC in Maryland, along with supporting us monthly, once sent us a special gift of $3,000 toward my course tuition, being about $300 per credit hour then. Praise the Lord!

One ministry opportunity arose during our years in Deerfield. Harvest Bible Chapel in Rolling Meadows, Illinois, was looking for a part-time missions coordinator. Coletta and I were selected to assist them in this capacity since we already had some years of missions experience in Ecuador and Nigeria.

Serving in this part-time capacity for several years helped us encourage some of their church members to go on short missions trips or consider more profound involvement in missions. In addition, I taught a series of lessons using Paul Borthwick's book, *How to Be a World-Class Christian*. Their church paid us for this part-time position, which helped us pay for some of our TEDS tuition fees.

One Sunday afternoon after we returned from church, I decided to help Dwight find a short branch from the nearby woods for him to nail a small bird feeder on. Then, we could stick it in the ground and watch the birds come to get feed from our living room window. There was snow on the ground, and it was cold.

I found a nice branch about my height, but its roots were fast in the ground. I pulled and bent it, but it didn't want to come out. It sprung back and hit me right in my face. It scratched my face, causing me to bleed. I did finally loosen the branch but was embarrassed by the story when I came home. Coletta had to wash off some blood from my white winter coat.

During those years at TEDS, we drove back to Lancaster, mainly during the holidays, to see our parents and families. A one-way trip was over 700 miles, taking about 12 hours. On several trips, we stayed overnight at a motel with a swimming pool. The children loved that extra feature. Several trips were taken with much snow on the ground in freezing conditions. At home, our families were always happy to see us. The children grew more each time we went back.

When Dwight was five, we enrolled him in the Bannockburn Kindergarten just a few miles from the TEDS campus. His teacher, Mrs. Hampton, was a skilled, veteran teacher who encouraged Coletta and helped Dwight get a good start in school. He learned to ride a bus to school and began to interact with boys and girls his age. Stephanie did the same when she went to the TEDS preschool classes.

During my studies, I wanted to do my dissertation on some aspects of the family. I saw the need for many Nigerian Christian families to become stronger in their relationships between husbands, wives, children, and extended family members. This could happen if they followed biblical principles.

My professors allowed me to study and write my major course papers on topics that I was interested in as long as they fit into the perimeters of the course. That helped me read and write about various aspects of the family. For example, in my Introduction to Islam course, I wrote about "The Role of Women in Islam." These studies were enjoyable and educational.

My dissertation was a big challenge. I didn't get credit for writing it, but without writing it, I couldn't graduate! I learned much through the process, maybe even more about what not to do versus what to do. My chosen dissertation topic was "The Response of Evangelical Churches to Changing Family Roles among the Ibibio in Nigeria." The Ibibio were the local people group, and the Efiks lived around Ikwa and our state capital, Uyo, in Akwa Ibom State. Since this was a primary research paper, I needed to personally go to Nigeria and interview people instead of mainly reading books from the library or downloading them from the internet.

My research plan was to travel to Nigeria to compare two Christian ministries, the Qua Iboe Church and the Christian Fellowship (Evangelical) Nigeria, Inc., with both of their ministry headquarters in Uyo. I had to ask the same questions to the same groups of people in each ministry to compare and contrast their responses. I didn't know how much time this would take until I began these interviews.

Since our family lived in Illinois for all my Ph.D. studies, I returned to Nigeria alone to do this research for seven weeks, from late October to early December 1995. The duration wasn't easy for our entire family. Coletta had the most demanding job of caring for the children and keeping the apartment in very cold Deerfield.

When I settled in Nigeria, I was initially going to ask specific questions concerning only the father. I made one mistake that I only realized later after it was too late. I enjoyed the interviews so much that after asking my planned questions about the father in my first interview with one of our BMTC alumni, Rev. O.J. Essien, I continued by asking and recording answers on the mother, the children, and the extended family members. I should have limited my questions to only the father.

I later learned that these questions about each group could have been one selected dissertation topic by itself. Then, comparing and contrasting the two denominations involved at least two more dissertations. I asked myself, "What should I do?" If I had only asked questions following my original plan about the father, I could have completed my research much more quickly.

Those seven weeks of research in Nigeria kept me extra busy. I often drove the forty miles back and forth from Ikwa to interview various Qua Iboe Church and Christian Fellowship members. Some lived in urban and rural settings. In addition, multiple families graciously provided meals and sometimes overnight accommodations for me during my visits.

I learned much from these interviews. Some respondents wanted to give me the ideal and not the real answers to my questions. For example, they'd say, "Husbands should love their wives," but it was harder for them to admit that sometimes even Christian husbands would beat their wives or mistreat their spouses, children, or in-laws.

One family that I interviewed shared that their first four children were all daughters. They continued to pray and trust God for a son. God answered later with two sons. Another family had four daughters but no sons. They thanked God for their daughters, accepting this as from the Lord. They didn't allow their culture to overshadow the Bible. This became an excellent example to their extended family, church, friends, and community. Psalm 127:3 says, "Sons are a heritage from the Lord, children a reward from him." This includes both sons and daughters.

One man I interviewed admitted that his father told him and his brothers when they were young to never go into the kitchen. That was the job of his mother and sisters. He also shared that everyone perked up and wanted to be on their best behavior whenever his father came home. His father was stern and wasn't afraid to discipline the children if they were doing wrong. He said, "I never heard my father say, 'I'm sorry. Please forgive me.'" He now wanted to do better than that with his young children.

Communication was still a big challenge for Akwa Ibom State in 1995. Airmail letters took several weeks to travel to or from the U.S. Our plan was for me to go to the Nigerian Telephone Company in Uyo and make a weekly call to Coletta at an agreed-upon time. Sometimes Nigeria's being five hours ahead of U.S. time and the children's schedules made it hard to know when to call.

Those seven weeks in Nigeria, in some ways, went quickly. My biggest challenge was that I missed my family. I made a daily chart showing how many days it would be until I returned to see them. Each day was ticked off with a big *X*. Finally, the day to fly back to the U.S. came.

The night before I returned to Deerfield in early December, Coletta took the children to Dwight's Christmas program at his school. The weather was frigid, snowy, and icy. Sadly, she slipped and fell while holding Stephanie's hand because of the slippery conditions. Both fell but weren't hurt. The temperature was about -50 degrees Fahrenheit (-45 degrees Celsius). Thankfully, the weather had warmed up when I arrived the next day. I was sorry that I had missed the concert, but I was extra glad to be home.

Dec. 1995 - Dwight's kindergarten concert

The Nigerian weather in the Ikwa area from October to December was the end of the rainy season. The temperatures were in the 80s to 90s F, or 26 to 32 C, with very high humidity. Just the opposite met me when I arrived at O'Hare airport that December, with the temperature below freezing. Our family was extra excited to see each other again. I vowed that I'd never intentionally be away from my family for that long again. I've since kept it!

After returning to the U.S., I bought a transcriber and spent many hours daily typing what was recorded from the interviews for children, youth, young and older adults, both males and females. This process took much more time and effort than I had initially bargained for. I never had time to listen to and transcribe every interview I conducted. However, I learned much about the Ibibio people, which I should have known when I began working with them in the late 1970s. The time was not wasted!

From December 1995 until July 1996, I worked almost daily to transcribe interviews and organize the results. Coletta helped me to edit some sections. In addition, I often met with my supervisors, Dr. Paul Hiebert and Dr. John Nyquist.

That same spring, our family moved back to Lancaster to live at the Wycliffe apartments on Willow Street. Coletta began to homeschool Dwight and Stephanie in our home. The children did well.

About June, my advisors said, "Dennis, you've done enough work. Now go ahead and stop." My family was thrilled with their advice, as they were getting tired of my daily and nightly routines, seeing no end to them. This closure was also greatly welcomed toward the end of my writing. While talking to people, I'd also often be thinking about one more book or source to read, one more idea to write down, or one more improvement in another section of my dissertation.

Finally, in July 1996, I submitted the best copy of my dissertation. I successfully defended it and returned to Lancaster, relieved that I had finally completed this work. I graduated absentia from TEDS with my Ph.D. in Intercultural Studies in December. The Lord helped me to successfully achieve my goal of completing my doctoral studies!

My Ph.D. dissertation defense with Dr. Hiebert & Dr. Nyquist

Those years at TEDS helped me learn much from my professors and my studies. Although I was able to attend one of Dr. Ted Ward's courses on Non-Formal Education, one of his statements stuck with me. "We shouldn't say, 'I've learned,' but instead say, 'I am learning,' since we never will learn all that is to be learned in any particular situation." I appreciated the idea of being a life-long learner, having a desire to continue to learn new things until God calls me home to heaven.

With all my Ph.D. requirements completed, we were ready to return to teach at BMTC. Sometimes God opens doors and sometimes He allows delays to come into our lives. He might want us to slow down, teach us new lessons in trusting Him, or want us to wait to know why things happen until we get to heaven (if we need to know). For example, when we tried to apply for visas from the Nigerian Embassy, we worked hard to send them many copies of our credentials. Unfortunately, no reply came for about six months.

We researched and bought a Planet 1 satellite phone during that home assignment. Over the next few years, it helped us immensely to make calls and send emails easily to the U.S. from our rural context of Ikwa. The charges were high at $3.00 per minute. Some months we paid over $300 for this privilege, but it helped us connect immediately with our family, friends, and supporters. They were also grateful!

After much waiting and prayer, in July 1997, we were granted our resident permits from the Nigerian Embassy in the U.S. We returned to Nigeria that August. Another chapter in our family's journey was completed. We believed that God would use my doctoral studies and all that God had taught our family from 1993 to 1997 to be better servants for the Lord at Ikwa and BMTC.

Coletta's thoughts:

I was excited for Dennis when he was accepted into the Ph.D. program at TEDS. From the time of our marriage, we had discussed it as a step he would eventually need to take. I was happy to be closer to family again and join them at Christmas and for a month in the summer. Little did I know that those would be treasured memories with my parents.

For those four years, it was pretty much me hanging out with the children while Dennis was hunkered down in classes, in the library, or our bedroom reading and writing. When his dissertation was finally accepted, we celebrated by ordering pizza. Our budget was tight, so Dennis didn't return to Chicago for his graduation in December 1996. We lived for the next eight months with our suitcases half-packed on the floor in our apartment, waiting for our visas to be approved.

Meanwhile, my mother was diagnosed with terminal non-Hodgkin's lymphoma. This was one time in our marriage when Dennis and I were on separate pages. He was praying for the granting of our visas. I was praying for more time with my mom. As it turned out, God called her home in early March 1997. Our visas were granted in July.

That was one of the hardest returns to Nigeria for me. My Dad, who also was terminally ill with prostate cancer, had just given up his treatments. I knew he wouldn't have much time left and promised we would return when he needed me.

After our return to Nigeria, we made travel plans and canceled them each month for the next ten months until my sister informed us it was time to come home. I asked the Lord for a month with my dad, and He generously gave me five weeks. He went to be with the Lord on June 30, 1998.

Chapter 18

Training Our Children before and during Homeschool

"Children, obey your parents in everything,
for this pleases the Lord"
(Colossians 3:20).

Homeschooling Dwight and Stephanie while in ministry wasn't easy. However, God used our extended family and friends in the U.S. and Nigeria, along with our supporting churches and individuals, to empower us on this long and challenging journey. They also prayed for and supported us and various ministry projects financially. They encouraged us, primarily through letters and phone calls. Our families back in the U.S. were our biggest cheerleaders.

Coletta must get the most credit. Right from Dwight and Stephanie's births, she spent the most time with them. I was heavily involved in teaching and leading BMTC. I was also an elder at ICA. I helped her as much as I could in our village setting. We were usually in survival mode since daily routines took up much of our time. Murphy's law also worked well in Nigeria: If something can go wrong, it will, and usually at the worst possible time.

Coletta and I, as parents, had to depend daily on the Lord. We wonder how we raised Dwight and Stephanie effectively through our journeys between being in the U.S. and Nigeria. Yet, with God's grace and direction, we made it.

We often complimented our parents on how they supported us as we raised our children in Nigeria. They didn't make us feel guilty that we couldn't be close to them, so they could see Dwight and Stephanie in person. Some parents do this and become an obstacle to those called by God to serve cross-culturally. We don't remember our parents ever doing that! Instead, they encouraged us in every way. When we were in the U.S., we lived with them, especially my parents in Manheim.

Our dining room at Ikwa was large enough that it contained our dining room table and chairs with one highchair for the children, and it had a big red carpet on the floor. Before Dwight could crawl, we kept a playpen there that was made for him. When he learned to walk, we'd play games or wrestle together on that carpet. Dwight later learned to jump off the arm of one of our cane chairs onto the chair cushions laid out on the rug.

He loved riding his little tricycle around the compound and was usually very vocal in talking or shouting. No one had to guess where he was or what he was doing. As soon as Dwight began to walk and run, his Nigerian friends started to kick a ball with him. This helped him to enjoy playing soccer (football) on the CWT compound. Many of these boys learned to play soccer without their shoes on. Dwight usually wore a pair of soccer shoes when he was outside. Little did he know it, but as he sharpened his skills in soccer, this would help him play better as he grew up.

As the first born, there was no doubt that Dwight was the leader, while Stephanie was the follower. While learning to walk, she often got in the way of Dwight's tricycle and was knocked down, but soon she'd get up.

Right from Dwight's birth, Coletta did most of the children's diaper changing, bathing, and cleaning up. We did have Nigerian helpers, and that was a big help during daytime hours. Sometimes I'd give Dwight a bottle of milk. When he'd be close to sleeping, he'd grab one of my ears and hold on to it while sucking his thumb. I'd also have him sit on my lap while I read a short story to him on our living room sofa.

Life was usually non-stop at our house from morning to night. People would often come knock on our door to see the children, ask me a question about BMTC or the CWT, or sometimes ask Coletta to help them with a health issue. The best way to get a short, much-needed break was to travel away from Ikwa for the weekend or a holiday.

One of our favorite places to go was the Airport Hotel outside of Port Harcourt. The 60-mile drive took us about two hours, usually because of delays from bad roads or police checks. We'd leave Ikwa on Friday morning or afternoon, stay at the hotel for the weekend, and return on Sunday afternoon in time for me to prepare for the Monday morning of prayer and classes.

Staying at a hotel usually gave us the luxury of enjoying close to 24 hours of continuous electricity, some cool air conditioning, and quiet from the busyness of village life. We ate tasty meals at their restaurant and swam in their large pool with the children. In addition, the hotel's satellite dish provided a variety of different TV programs to watch, including world news. Sunday afternoons came too quickly, but even such short breaks helped us be more refreshed to face village life again.

1992 - Dwight's first day of nursery school

Kemi Oluwole was a teacher and the wife of Moses, one of our BMTC graduates who later became a faithful BMTC faculty member and leader in the CWT missions programs. In 1992, Dwight was Kemi's first white nursery school pupil to meet in her home. All these experiences helped lay a good foundation for him. The nursery school later developed into the CWT's Life Foundation Nursery-Primary-Secondary School at Ikwa.

Coletta and I were praying for Dwight and Stephanie to become born-again Christians. We wanted to see them have a heart for the Lord and serve Him with the talents and spiritual gifts that He had given them. We believed they could come to Christ while young—like I did when I was five, and Coletta did when she was six. While attending the 1974 CEF Leadership Training Institute, our teacher shared Charles Spurgeon's memorable quote: "A child of five, if properly instructed, can, as truly believe and be regenerated, as an adult."[7]

Dwight made this decision when he was four years old in March 1994 at Harvest Bible Chapel. A CEF worker who led the service invited the children to become Christians. Dwight prayed to receive the Lord into his heart then.

At six, Stephanie decided to trust in Christ in our homeschool. While Coletta was doing a Bible study with them, Dwight asked Stephanie in front of Coletta if she'd like to become a Christian. Stephanie said, "Yes," so Coletta led her to the Lord.

Dwight and Stephanie learned to make friends easily with the local Nigerian children. We invited them to special events, like birthday or holiday parties. These young Nigerian friends felt like they were big shots at these events, as they could drink part of or all a soft drink (mineral) or get a whole plate of food to eat all by themselves. Normally, they'd not have such privileges. They'd often be required to share a plate of food or a soft drink with their siblings.

During Dwight and Stephanie's years growing up at Ikwa, they not only played with their friends but learned to have a love for animals. The CWT president's wife, Elizabeth Ekpikhe, was a hard-working farmer. She and her family and house helpers often went to their small farm plots near the CWT compound early in the morning, only to return near sundown. Elizabeth also raised chickens, sheep, and goats. In addition, they'd

Dwight with Brownie and her twins

often have a cat around to keep away mice or rats.

Once Elizabeth gave Dwight an offer that he accepted. She had one ewe that she wanted Dwight to raise for her. He later called her Brownie. Whenever Brownie would give birth to lambs, the first set would be given to Elizabeth. The next set would be Dwight's to do with as he pleased. Over several years Brownie gave birth to twins several times. This was good training for Dwight.

Dwight and Stephanie raised some broiler chickens. In addition, Stephanie cared for several local cats named Mickey and Jerry. Jerry's nickname was Three-Legger because he once had an accident and lost one leg. They also raised rabbits, so we occasionally ate rabbit meat. At first, they gave their rabbits names, like Princess. However, we later discovered it was harder to kill a rabbit we treated as a pet, so we didn't give them names after that. Coletta often went along the main road with the children to collect green vines and leaves to feed the rabbits. Coletta wrote home about what happened once with the rabbits:

One of Dwight's rabbits had six babies last week, but we had a sad day on Thursday. We had a mason repairing some concrete work in our back court. We put one rabbit pen with three cages out in the hot sun. It was extremely hot that day. We only realized this after it was too late, as Dwight's best mother rabbit, Snowflake—who was to have babies the coming week—reacted badly to the heat and died in Dwight's arms. He buried it in our garden and put a cross over the grave. The next day his attitude was much better, and he still wanted to raise rabbits.

Another interesting pet they had was a turtle named Oscar. He had a fascinating personality. He would knock at our back courtyard door with his legs for us to let him in. If we didn't, he'd cry with real tears. Then one day, someone left the back door open. He walked out, and we never saw him again. We also had a pair of caged love birds and fish in our house at various times.

BMTC had a piggery building behind our outer wall. Depending on how the wind blew, we'd get some nasty smells from the pig manure. Several times a sow gave birth and couldn't provide enough milk for her piglets. As a good-hearted little farmer, Dwight would bring in any of the piglets that needed milk and feed them in a box in his bedroom to try to raise them. However, after a few days, each of the piglets died. He still learned much through this.

Our classroom for seven years

Coletta and I agreed that it would be best for us to homeschool our children. There were no homeschool co-ops in Nigeria. As a registered nurse and not a trained teacher, Coletta eagerly read from *The Teaching Home*, a Christian homeschooling magazine. This helped her know where to buy many of her teaching resources. She did a great job! Homeschooling demanded much work, discipline, and perseverance. She enjoyed the process of preparing lessons and then teaching the children through sixth grade. God helped her, and they all learned together.

Dwight was two years ahead of Stephanie in homeschooling. He had some auditory and visual sequencing problems as a youngster. To help him learn and read better, Coletta contacted Mrs. Becky Stonecypher, one of the American Hillcrest School's missionary teachers in Jos, Plateau State. Becky had special training in working with children who had learning disabilities. She was willing to test Dwight on one of our trips to Jos between his first and second grades. Becky gave Coletta some training and materials to help Dwight overcome these issues.

Homeschool reading class

Reading was challenging for Dwight as a youngster. We tried to help him read books he was interested in, such as those about horses. With much patience over time, he began to love to read.

Coletta used the Blue Book method to teach both Dwight and Stephanie how to read. Stephanie loved the *Little House on the Prairie* books. There were many similarities between people who settled in the western U.S. and those who lived in villages like Ikwa in Nigeria.

Dwight and Stephanie loved to climb some of the trees on the CWT

Climbing a tree at Ikwa

compound, which was about ten acres in size. This made Coletta work hard to clean their clothes that had stains on them from the cashew trees. They enjoyed visiting the compound children at their homes and playing games and soccer with them. Sometimes they'd eat a meal together.

As Dwight and Stephanie grew, we taught them how to do chores. We kept a wall chart containing a list of what they were to do each day, such as make their bed, take the garbage outside to the pit, wash the dishes, and brush their teeth. For each duty completed, they could put a star on their chart. To reward their efforts, we gave them a little money to begin to teach them how to manage it. They learned to give to the Lord at least ten percent of anything they earned or received. This has helped them learn to be faithful givers until now.

Stephanie learned to have a generous and tender heart for people. She started a small store selling small packs of cookies and candy to her compound friends and pupils at the CWT's Life Foundation Nursery-Primary-Secondary School that opened in 1992.

Coletta wrote in an email:

> Stephanie loves to climb the cashew trees and continues to tend her store. Life Foundation Nursery-Primary-Secondary School pupils on our compound (over 370 strong) are her chief customers, as many come to buy a pack of biscuits for a morning snack for about five cents each.

Stephanie's store at our house

Stephanie knew the times when the pupils took their breaks. Her store's downfall was that she was too kindhearted and often gave some of her items away to her friends. This dipped into her overall profits, but from this, she learned to manage money better and work well with people.

Stephanie wanted to help her friends whenever they were sick. Sometimes she'd bring a sick child to our house, so Coletta could see what was wrong. Coletta would clean cuts and scrapes and put a Band-Aid on when needed. She'd visit a child's parents if the child had malaria to encourage them to take the child to the CWT clinic.

Nigerian church services were often two or three hours long. Coletta volunteered to lead the children's church activities, so our children wouldn't have bad attitudes toward attending church. She began this in 1991 when Dwight was two years old. She continued this until 2006 when we left Ikwa. With several CWT staff assisting her, these services were taught in English in separate buildings from the adult church services.

During the Christmas holidays (during the years when Dwight and Stephanie were in homeschool and at Ikwa), we'd go Christmas caroling one night around the CWT compound and into Ikwa village. I'd play my accordion. Usually, we'd sing a verse of four or five favorite carols and end with "We Wish You a Merry Christmas (And a Happy New Year)." Often the members at the house where we sang would join us. The group would keep growing until we had 15 or 20 people singing. We'd return to the CWT chapel and serve a soft drink (mineral) and some cookies or biscuits. Everyone enjoyed those times together.

In January 1999, our family, BMTC's Assistant Director of Studies Nsese Umoh, and our house helper Ekaete, all packed into our VW Jetta for a trip to Kaduna. I taught Spiritual Warfare to 12 students in the BMTC Kaduna Extension School. While there, I preached in three churches and led a Saturday seminar on "Developing Christian values among our youth" to over 140 people.

This seminar was based on Josh McDowell's book, *Right from Wrong: What You Need to Know to Help Youth Make Right Choices*. He emphasized the importance of three Ps for youth to learn: (1) Precepts from God's Word; (2) Principles in how to apply God's Word; and (3) Remember the Person of God and how He wants us to respond when we're tempted to do wrong.[8] We conducted similar seminars at ICA for Ikwa and other assemblies at Ete and Ikot Akan. Uyo Christian Fellowship also asked us to conduct a seminar for their youth.

Included in the trip was a visit to Yankari Game Reserve, several hours from Jos. We stayed in one of their cottages for the night. The workers warned us that baboons could cause trouble for us, and that we shouldn't get too close to them.

As we unpacked, several baboons ran quickly to our open car door and took away our medicine box full of vitamins and health items. One took it about 30 feet from us, sat

Elephants at Yankari Game Reserve

Baboons at our car at Yankari

down, and took a quick look at the box's contents. Soon it left the box and ran away, so we could retrieve it. After that, we were more careful not to leave our doors open.

While at Yankari, we went on a short safari. We were fortunate enough to see a herd of elephants moving and eating. Yankari also had some enjoyable warm springs, so we swam there. Our eyes were alert to watch for the baboons, as they weren't afraid to come and try to steal food items where we kept our towels and handbags.

On one of our family trips to Kaduna, we drove past Zuma Rock, one of Nigeria's tourist sites. It's a natural monolith about 980 feet (300 meters) tall, near Suleja, Niger State. We also stopped one afternoon on our return to watch a total solar eclipse.

When we'd travel to Kaduna or Jos, we'd usually pass through Lafia, Niger State. That area of the country was known for its good yams. On our return to Ikwa, we'd often stop and bargain with the traders to buy some. Their yams were dried well and usually didn't spoil. We'd enjoy eating fried yam chips, boiled yam, or pounded yam for some weeks after our trip.

Zuma Rock near Abuja

In the late 1990s, the Reynolds Aluminum Company—an American-based company—partnered with the Nigerian government to build an aluminum-smelting plant ten miles from us near Ikot Abasi town. It was known as the Aluminum-Smelting Company of Nigeria (ALSCON).

We became friends with some of the American ALSCON workers and doctors. Some of these Americans and their wives, along with some of their Nigerian workers, were Christians. I preached several times in their Christian gatherings. We met with them during some holidays. They also occasionally allowed us to stay in one of their vacant workers' homes to give us a nice weekend break with air conditioning and cable TV.

1999 - Dwight's baptism

In February 1999, we had a baptismal for ICA in the Ikwa stream. I baptized six people, including Dwight. Several of the ALSCON workers, Gary and Mary Jane Smith, joined us for the occasion.

Once during this time, our Planet 1 satellite phone stopped working. We planned to take it to one of the ALSCON workers to take to the U.S. for repairs. Our family drove in our VW Jetta just after dark around 7:15. I drove with my dimmed headlights on, as I wanted to be courteous to drivers coming toward us in the opposite lane. About three miles from Ikwa, we suddenly saw a motorcyclist carrying a passenger right in front of us. The motorcycle had no lights on nor had any reflectors on it. They also wore dark clothes. I immediately put on my brakes and turned to the right to avoid hitting them.

The red soil on the side of the road was wet from the heavy rains. Our Jetta slipped in it and turned over on its side. It stopped after turning completely around on the other side of the road. Coletta and I wore our seatbelts, but the children didn't. Coletta told me to turn off the engine. Some villagers came running and quickly helped us climb out of the windows. None of us had injuries other than a few scrapes. We were taken back home to safety. The car was later repaired but never drove the same afterward. Later we did get the Planet 1 phone to the ALSCON worker, who took it to the U.S. and returned it working well again.

In the fall of 1999, Coletta had health problems with her thyroid gland. For this issue, the ALSCON doctors suggested that our family should return to the U.S. for her testing, which we did. We stayed with Daddy and Momma for two months in Manheim. After various exams, the U.S. doctors saw no need for further treatment for her thyroid. On Halloween, Dwight and Stephanie enjoyed dressing up to go trick-or-treating around the neighborhood.

Going trick-or-treating

We enjoyed our time with Daddy and Momma. They took good care of us with food and met our daily needs. Momma was a great cook and baker. Daddy also had the habit of cooking great Saturday morning breakfasts with scrambled eggs, bacon, fried potatoes, and toast. We enjoyed his snacks while watching a Sunday afternoon Philadelphia Eagles football game. He'd serve us ice cream, soft drinks, chips, pretzels, and cookies. We never went hungry!

All too soon we returned to our life in Ikwa. Everyone in our family had accidents that called for quick action. Once we cut down the beautiful bougainvillea bushes growing along our home's back walls. They had large thorns on their branches. Our house helpers dragged them out back behind the walls for them to dry and then be burned. Dwight came back to watch me bend some of the long branches to be placed on a pile. One of the branches whipped right into Dwight's face and he began to bleed badly.

All I could say to Dwight was "Sorry! Sorry, Dwight, sorry!" Coletta heard me and came running to see us. She took Dwight into our house and cleaned him up. We took him to the ALSCON doctor. He saw that the bleeding had stopped, and that he didn't need any stitches. Dwight soon was back to normal.

Another time Dwight had some rust get into his eye. We knew that it was annoying him, so we took him about one hour away to the Abak Eye Hospital. We had to wait for a while, but finally, a Nigerian doctor treated him. He and his staff tried to remove the rusty piece of metal from Dwight's eye. Dwight screamed as if they were killing him. Coletta was with Dwight, and I sat out on a bench nearby. I felt so bad for Dwight. However, the doctor did get the rust out of Dwight's eye, and the pain and annoyance soon left him.

We didn't have a good well (borehole) on the CWT campus for several years. This forced us to drive our car one mile to the village stream every few days and fill several five-gallon (20 liters) plastic containers (jerry cans) for our household needs. Dwight and Stephanie would often help me fill the containers in the stream. I'd lift them into our car's trunk (boot), take them back to our house, and carry them inside. We were later thrilled when the CWT had a large rig come to drill a water borehole at the center of our campus, next to the CWT's big water tank. We could then use a generator to pump water from the well into the overhead tank. From there, because of the efforts of Andy Hunt and Roy Bridges, the water then ran into our homes.

Another challenge was that we needed to regularly buy gasoline (petrol) for our car and fill plastic containers (jerry cans) with gas to run our small generator to provide electricity for our house. We'd go to a local gas station, haul the jerry cans back home, take them to our generator house, and fill the generator with gas when needed.

Dwight & Stephanie at Ikwa stream

These chores took much time over those years. Lifting them was probably another part of why I had ongoing back problems. Similarly, several times I could hardly stand up straight from carrying my heavy accordion back and forth from our house to the CWT chapel, even though the distance was only several hundred feet. Packing and carrying 70-pound suitcases over many trips to and from Nigeria also took a toll on my back.

Sometimes buying gas became a challenge. If there was a fuel shortage or crisis and our two local gas stations about one mile from our campus didn't have gas, we'd be forced to drive ten, twenty, or more miles one way to buy it. More than once I had to drive those distances, then wait in a long line (queue) of vehicles to fill our car and jerry cans. Sometimes gas station owners hoarded the gas, so prices would increase, and they could make more money. Other times people wanted to butt in line or get into a fight with words, pushing, or punching. Such situations made gas prices much higher than normal.

During the summer of 2000, we went to the U.S. for a home assignment. Coletta enrolled in an intensive two-week course with the National Institute for Learning Disabilities in Philadelphia. Two years later, she took part two of this course in Maryland. With this training, she taught Dwight with much better results.

Living at Ikwa wasn't easy for our family. We often had health and schooling challenges. We had many big decisions to make as a family and in the ministries. In an email from April 2001, Coletta wrote:

Our health has seen some general improvement. Because it's been extra hot lately, in our already tropical climate, Dennis had a very bad rash for several weeks. With some dermatitis cream, much of it has gone away. I still have some tendonitis, especially when it's about to rain. Dwight and Stephanie also have had some rashes from the heat, with Dwight having some skin infections.

In an email of May 5, 2001, Coletta wrote to her sister:

Dwight is making good progress [in homeschooling], but he'll need to stick with the [special needs] program for several more years. Dwight had his heart set on being "average" and being able to fit into a regular classroom, so he was disappointed.

We did a lot of talking between the two of us about his special learning needs. I told Dwight that he learned a different way than many other children. We checked on options for enrolling in Hillcrest School. We never knew it was so difficult to get in. We thought that we'd automatically qualify because we were missionaries, but that isn't so. Our mission [FIM] isn't one of the qualifying missions, so unless we find another group that has room to include our two, we're on the waiting list for at least two years.

Steph is open to going [to Hillcrest] in the future, but not now. She wants to live at home, so I am near if she gets sick. She also wants to celebrate her birthday at home. The cost is great. It would cost us over $12,000 a year to have them in school there. We came away feeling that homeschooling has been the right choice for us in the past and that it will be so for at least the next year or two.

Stephanie in homeschooling

To show some of the tensions we as parents had in trying to balance our ministries between working at BMTC and the CWT with caring for the needs of our family while they were being homeschooled at Ikwa, we wrote in our August 2001 newsletter:

> This past week Dwight and Stephanie were talking to Coletta while Dennis traveled to Uyo for BMTC contacts and purchases. They both said to her, "All Daddy does is work. We don't talk to him because he is always busy." This is a real challenge for me. This must change!

In that same newsletter, we shared that at BMTC's 27th graduation on May 26, "the BMTC Board of Governors officially announced that Dennis' new title will be provost, while Mr. Nsese Umoh's new title will be deputy provost, in line with our higher status at the university level."

To try to give a higher priority to supporting the children while at home, I wrote:

> I've already been trying to give the children more time. We've played several games of *Monopoly* and have gone out to eat at a nice fast-food shop in Eket that served fried chicken and soft ice cream. I've helped Dwight collect grass for the rabbits several times. Considering my new BMTC duties, the workload will get heavier, not lighter.

This was why our newsletter's title was *REINFORCEMENTS NEEDED ON ALL FRONTS*. We needed more workers, more prayer, and more financial support.

In our email update of October 28, 2001, I wrote:

> Coletta is going strong teaching Dwight and Stephanie in homeschool and leading the children's church for ICA. The children continue to care for their animals: nine rabbits, one new kitten named Jerry (Stephanie's former cat, Mickey Mouse, never came home last month), two turtles, three sheep, 14 chickens, and some snails. Since the CWT Life Foundation Nursery-Primary-Secondary School classes are in session, Stephanie's store is busy again.

Stephanie also did well in gardening. She grew some banana suckers that produced large bunches that tasted like strawberries.

In 2002, during our regular home assignment from July to December, the Lord helped us enroll the children into Lancaster Christian School (LCS). Coletta held

Stephanie's 3rd grade banana project

Dwight back from entering seventh grade. She felt being in sixth grade could help him adjust to the U.S. learning system and allow him to be on the LCS soccer team.

That suited Dwight just fine, as he loved soccer. We often drove the four-mile trip to the school after his soccer practice and enjoyed watching his team play some of their home games. He received some learning therapy that year from LCS staff member Myrna Adkins, who helped him improve his study skills. Stephanie entered fifth grade at LCS and did well in her studies.

This time we enjoyed living at Calvary Church's old farmhouse near their ponds and baseball diamond. The children enjoyed riding their bicycles, exploring the spacious grounds around the house, watching the Canadian geese raise their babies at the nearby ponds, and seeing various wildlife. There were no other houses near us, so the busy Route 222 traffic going by the church property caused us the most disturbance.

Air balloon landing in our yard

Once we saw a giant hot-air balloon land on our farmhouse front lawn. Somehow the pilot didn't navigate it properly. Thankfully, no one was hurt.

During those months, I wrote in our November newsletter, "Since July we've safely driven or flown over 10,000 miles, visited 14 churches, and shared pictures of the CWT and BMTC ministries 44 times." During that home assignment, our Calvary Church pastors allowed me to baptize Stephanie in the church baptistry on December l. We don't have a picture of that event, but we do have a certificate.

Every weekday morning that semester, Coletta would make lunches for the children and drive them up to the main road by the church for the school bus to take them to LCS at 7:10. After school, the bus would return and drop them off at the main road. Then they'd walk about half a mile down the hill to our house.

These experiences helped our family learn how to better serve the Lord, trust Him to lead us, and prepare for ministries together. We wanted God to use our family to be a blessing to others. After we returned to Nigeria, Coletta continued to homeschool the children.

Coletta's thoughts:

I look back on those homeschool years as some of the best years of family life. December was also Christmas school with Christmas carols as music class and homemade Christmas decorations as art class. We did weather experiments to compare and contrast the rainy season and the dry season.

Painting in home school

When we studied the stars, we sat out under the night sky and named the constellations. There is nothing like watching the stars when there are no lights to obstruct the view! We even saw satellites as they flew by. Each year we kept scrapbooks with pictures and examples of each area studied.

Chapter 19

The Children's Training during High School

"Train a child in the way he should go,
and when he is old, he will not turn from it"
(Proverbs 22:6).

Homeschooling Dwight and Stephanie until sixth grade helped us spend quality time together at Ikwa, which made our family very close. In sixth grade, Dwight had shown interest in attending a boarding school for seventh grade. That April, God opened the door for him to enter Hillcrest School in Jos, Plateau State.

It was (and still is) a Christian boarding school noted for its high academic standards. It has met the needs of many missionary children from Nigeria and other African countries over the past decades. Hillcrest's educational standards were higher than what could be obtained in many other Nigerian public high schools. Moreover, it was approved by several U.S. accrediting councils. This was a significant advantage for Dwight and Stephanie, as they both aimed to continue their college studies in the U.S. after high school. The Hillcrest instructors made them work hard academically, so they would be well-prepared to enter college.

Jos was 550 miles from Ikwa. Our family qualified to receive some tuition assistance to come under the Church of Christ in Nigeria's missionary quota for missionary children. (This church is not affiliated with the Church of Christ in the U.S.) They had several vacancies and allowed us to fill two of them. Unfortunately, our CWT ministry didn't have any direct connections with Hillcrest. The Church of Christ in Nigeria's kindness helped us immensely in paying lower school fees for the children. Their education at Hillcrest was another great tool God used to mold and sharpen them for their futures.

In March 2003, Coletta became very sick with malaria. She was admitted to the ALSCON hospital in Ikot Abasi for several days. The doctor allowed her to return home so she could attend the wedding of Bernhard Farnbauer, one of the German contractors from Ikot Abasi. He helped us with some of our CWT compound generator problems.

April 2003 - Calvary Church team

Bernhard wanted us to marry him and his Nigerian fiancée, Funmi. We had over 200 people from the company and area join us for the wedding. It was a great opportunity to share Christ with many.

However, after the wedding, Coletta still wasn't well and needed to return to the hospital until she felt better. One ALSCON couple, Sid and Gayle Steib, helped us greatly for about one week by taking Dwight and Stephanie in the morning and bringing them back home in the late afternoon. Dwight and Stephanie remember Gayle taking them to a supermarket near ALSCON and buying them a whole candy bar each instead of having them share one.

In April, Calvary Church (our home church) had a team of four visit us. It included, George and Mary Duff, Don Kitchen, and our missions pastor Dave Hall. Their visit encouraged us. They returned to the U.S. knowing how to better pray for us.

Then in May, we had our annual BMTC Pastors, Leaders, and Christian Workers' Conference. We invited Dr. Mark Ogharaerunmi and Rev. O.J. Essien to be our guest speakers. The conference theme was *Transforming leadership in the Church today: Impacting present and future generations*. We saw 37 students graduate that day!

Brother O.J. was a BMTC and WBC alumnus. He returned to Nigeria to become the president of the Uyo Christian Fellowship. He served with us for many years as a member of BMTC's Board of Governors. He's with the Lord now.

Brother Mark attended a year of studies at BMTC and then went to WBC to complete his B.A. degree. From there, he worked with Wycliffe Bible Translators and completed his Ph.D. in Linguistics at Aberdeen University in Ireland. God used him for many years in Nigerian Bible translation and consulting work from his home in Warri, Delta State. He's also now with the Lord.

In August 2003, Dwight began seventh grade at Hillcrest School and lived in Pine View, a boarding dorm on the school campus. He had a great time living in the dorm and learning to live with his mates from Nigeria, Korea, and Australia. Other students in the school were from Denmark, Yugoslavia, Senegal, and China. He loved soccer, so he played soccer and other games on the school's athletic field as often as he could.

In Coletta's email to her sister and brother-in-law on August 11, 2003, she wrote:

> It wasn't too hard to leave Dwight [at Pine View] because I felt that the timing was right, and we had been preparing for this for some years. I know he has many more opportunities in Jos than we could ever provide for him here in the village setting, where it is hard to get beyond survival. He phoned us yesterday, and we were able to let him know that we had arrived home safely and that all his animals were okay.

During that year, we learned how to break up our long road trips—one and a half days one way to Jos—into three sections of about four hours each. Because of armed robbers, it wasn't safe to drive after sunset. Horrific accidents also happened, often at night. There was no police protection or 911 if we had an emergency. Gas stations were often closed after sunset.

We'd typically try to drive two sections in one day, such as from Ikwa to Makurdi. If we started late, we'd go at least to Enugu and then drive the last two-thirds of the trip the next day. We'd stay at various hotels and eat meals there. Sometimes we'd arrange to lodge with American missionaries, like Andy and Patty Hunt, who served with the Navigators in Enugu, or with Nigerian Christian friends, like David and Rose Iordaah, in Makurdi. We'd make these trips six to eight times yearly. The rough roads took a big toll on our car.

Truck (lorry) accident toward Jos

On our journeys to and from Jos, we'd stop at stores where we could use the bathroom and get a cold soft drink or some snacks. Occasionally, on the way, we'd buy a roasted ear of corn, bean cakes, or suya (grilled beef seasoned with spices). We had to be aware of how these items were cooked, or we could have loose bowels later. For drinking water, we checked that the bottle caps were still sealed, as sometimes people refilled water bottles and resold them with water that wasn't processed.

After Dwight went to Hillcrest, we bought our first Nigerian cell phone. They were beginning to be used by Nigerians but were expensive. A SIM card alone was over $50 (N9,500). In our area, the few phone towers were adversely affected by rainy weather. As a result, we often had to go outside or upstairs to Brother Joshua's veranda to try to call Dwight. Despite these obstacles, we did our best to call him at least weekly.

Sometimes we were successful, sometimes we weren't. If we were persistent, we could usually chat with him, even if it was one or two days later than planned.

In 2004, we wanted Stephanie to join Dwight at Hillcrest to begin her seventh-grade studies. Most of her closest girlfriends her age in Ikwa were going to local high school (secondary) boarding schools. That would have made Stephanie the only girl her age in our village if Coletta homeschooled her. We didn't want that but wanted the children to learn how to intermingle with other mates their age, whether they were Nigerians or expatriates. This would help to develop their social skills. So, Stephanie went to Hillcrest for seventh grade.

Along with homeschooling the children, Coletta continued to serve part-time as a nurse at the FMH. In an email of October 31, 2004, she wrote to Mike and Dee Lindsey:

> We had a very busy week at the hospital. I ended up putting in a lot of overtime, eating just a few bites on the run, and having a tension headache. We had really bad pediatric cases. We lost an 18-year-old girl and a ten-year-old boy. The boy was a younger brother to one of our farm staff. Both cases came to the hospital way too late and were complicated. The boy had typhoid fever, and I think other things besides. He looked like he had been sick for a long time. The girl had resistive cerebral malaria/meningitis and had been sick for a week before she was brought in. These people are so poor. Most are subsistence farmers. When someone gets sick, they don't have any money for treatment. Hardly anyone comes in a timely fashion.
>
> We had another ten-month-old who was admitted, but the father came in the evening and said that there was no money for treatment, so he took her and the mother home. I wonder if she survived. Another six-month-old came in with sepsis.

At Hillcrest School

For each break from Hillcrest during Stephanie's seventh grade, just before we'd travel to take her back, she'd get all worried and worked up emotionally. She didn't eat or sleep well, became sick to her stomach, and dreaded going back to school.

However, in May 2005, while bringing Stephanie and Dwight back home to Ikwa with their belongings for summer break, Coletta asked if Stephanie would like to return to Hillcrest the next year. Surprisingly, Coletta looked back through our car's rearview mirror. Stephanie gave a thumbs up with a big smile, confirming that she was ready to return to Hillcrest for eighth grade. Her response thrilled all of us!

That August, after we had just taken the children back for the fall semester, I developed some issues with an irregular heartbeat. I traveled several times to see a heart specialist in Port Harcourt, 60 miles from Ikwa. After several tests, he checked me as far as he could go with the equipment he had on hand and advised that I go to the U.S. for further tests.

Coletta and I quickly arranged the flights. The children were already in good hands at Hillcrest. Soon after we arrived in Lancaster, we saw a cardiac electrophysiologist. She believed that she could help me with a heart ablation. Her first attempt wasn't successful, but the second one on the same day worked, and my heart became more regular. We kept in touch with the children through letters and phone calls. After two months in Lancaster, the doctor gave us the okay to return to Ikwa to continue our ministries.

During their Hillcrest years, Dwight and Stephanie lived at Pine View and later Niger Creek compounds. They had various dorm parents: Howard and Pip Michael and Ray and Jeanette Wilkinson from Australia; Robyn Bailey from New Zealand; and Chuck and Tracy Eddy, Aunt Beaj Beacham, and Toby and Alicia Abts from the U.S.

The children learned much from these different families and their parenting styles. These international interactions helped them for their futures to learn to be flexible and live amicably with people from various cultures and worldviews. This was a big plus because it enabled them to become more confident in themselves and intermingle well with their age mates, as well as their teachers, other missionaries, and adults. Their dorm parents and guides helped them when we couldn't be there in person.

Dwight continued to improve in his studies and extracurricular activities, especially sports. His favorite was soccer! The Hillcrest campus had standard athletic facilities: a big soccer field; a track; and courts for tennis, basketball, and volleyball. His ability to do well in soccer helped him make friends easily. Soccer was the most popular game being played in Nigeria. Hillcrest had a good soccer team and gave students opportunities to play basketball, volleyball, and track.

Dwight had already received good counsel to improve his skills from his LCS and LMS soccer coaches. Then he joined Hillcrest's soccer team and did well. Being on the team helped him learn how to work together under various coaches and learn many valuable life lessons.

Dwight's sports award night

One special blessing for Dwight at Hillcrest was to become close to his coach, Jay Tolar. Coach stood out as a godly leader interested in seeing his students grow in the Lord. He was particularly interested in discipling Dwight and several of his Hillcrest buddies. He gave the boys various Christian books to read and invited them to his house on various occasions.

Coach's impact through Bible studies and hanging out together significantly impacted Dwight to live faithfully for the Lord. Dwight followed Coach's example by spending quality time with various boys when he later returned to Hillcrest after his LBC studies to become the youth pastor for four years. This is what II Timothy 2:2 is all about: "And the things you have heard me say in the presence of many witnesses entrust to reliable people who will also be qualified to teach others."

Hillcrest is a small high school. This helped almost every student interested in various extracurricular sports to become involved, even if they didn't excel. This probably wouldn't have happened in a big U.S. high school, where only the most talented students would have made the teams or been involved in school activities. Thus, both Dwight and Stephanie joined various groups while they were there.

Dwight became the setter for the boys' volleyball team. He wasn't the tallest but did well in that position. In soccer, Dwight became the team captain in his senior year. In track, he ran in long-distance races.

When Stephanie enrolled at Hillcrest, she joined the girls' volleyball, soccer, and basketball teams and threw the shot put in their track meets. Their teams did well when competing with other Jos high school teams during various games and tournaments.

Stephanie didn't have someone like Coach Tolar to be there for discipleship interaction.

Stephanie throwing shot put

Still, she had some close girlfriends in her classes. In addition, some of her dorm parents reached out to her.

One mother, Julie Petersen, had three daughters who attended Hillcrest. Two of them were twins and became Stephanie's good friends. The Petersen's often invited her to their home for a weekend or on special occasions. These connections meant much to Stephanie since Coletta and I were far away in Ikwa and later in Kagoro.

During each trip back and forth from Ikwa, we passed through some police or army checkpoints. We became used to them and weren't usually intimidated by the police, whether traveling with our Nigerian staff or by ourselves. On one trip to Jos, we recorded 98 police checks one way. Several times on that trip, we could see the next checkpoint ahead of the one where we had just stopped, so that trip was longer and more stressful.

Depending on the time of year, on specific stretches of the roads, we'd drive through mud or deep water to continue our journey. More than once on the expressway at Aba, we needed local youth to tell us which way to go through water that was more than a foot deep. Otherwise, we'd hit a big, submerged stone or deeper water and then need to be pushed out or get out of the car and be helpless in the situation. After the youth would help us, they'd expect us—especially since we were whites—to thank them by giving them some money for their efforts. In such cases, we gladly gave some cash to them and continued driving.

Often on the way, policemen or army soldiers would greet us by saying, "Happy Christmas," "Happy New Year," or "Happy weekend." This didn't always mean that they were just very friendly. On the contrary, it implied that I—as a white person (bature)—was to give them money or alcoholic drinks to help them celebrate or cool down under the hot sun. Their black police outfits didn't keep them cool.

We often would respond, "We don't have money to give you, but here's something from the Bible that you might like to read." We'd then give them a gospel tract or some Christian booklet to read. They were probably Muslims, Christians, or non-religious. Some took them; some refused. One soldier replied, "How are we going to eat this?" They had hoped for money, but still allowed us to drive on.

One thing that helped us when we met police or army officers at these checkpoints was that I knew enough basic words in several main Nigerian languages that I could at least greet them when I saw that they were from the Yoruba, Hausa, Ibo, Efik, Igala, or Tiv tribes. When I said, "Hello," or "Greetings," in their language, they were greatly surprised, and their serious faces usually turned to big smiles. Right after that, they usually were happy to let us pass.

Our faithful 1999 Toyota Camry served us well from 2004 through all our trips to Hillcrest for Dwight and Stephanie's schooling. Being low to the ground was its biggest problem on long trips when going through deep water. It would also scrape its bottom when going over rough roads or a high railroad track crossing. We sometimes wished we had a higher four-wheel drive vehicle for those long journeys, but the Camry did well on gas mileage.

We saw God guiding and protecting us through those long trips. Now and then, we'd have car problems, which would delay us in reaching our destination as planned. However, we especially saw God's hand on us several times when we had engine problems or a flat tire. When those times happened, we weren't happy, but in retrospect, we thanked God for the delay.

On two specific trips from Jos to Ikwa, our car was delayed in getting repaired. We learned that if we had driven ahead that afternoon or the following morning, we would have met armed robbers on the road. When we could finally drive through those areas, the robbers had already left, and we were free to continue our journey.

Farmers often used the slash-and-burn technique during the dry season to clear their farms and areas where uncut grass and weeds had grown tall over the past year. Some of this grass along the main roads grew to be ten feet or taller (three meters). Because most Nigerian areas didn't have government tractors or vehicles to clear the grass along the roads, the local people used fire to burn it and then allowed the fire to stop on its own. Unfortunately, if the winds blew strongly, sometimes those fires got out of hand and burnt homes and destroyed farms and property.

During one particular daytime trip, I was driving to Ikwa after leaving the children at Hillcrest. Suddenly, we realized that brush fires were burning out of control on both sides of the road. We could either stop and turn around or drive quickly through the fires and hope that nothing terrible would happen to us and our car. The fires were so high that they looked like we were entering a tunnel. We chose the latter. We immediately felt the fire's intense heat as we drove through that area, but at least we reached the other side safely. As we traveled throughout Nigeria, we often felt that God had extra guardian angels protecting us.

On various trips between Jos and Ikwa, we met government workers trying to collect yearly tax rates for vehicles. Some groups were legitimate. Others just wanted to get money from us. Once near Lafia, Plateau State, one group of tax workers wanted us to pay about $50 (over N4,000) for a pile of plastic stickers because we drove through their state. Since we lived in Akwa Ibom State and not their Nasarawa State, we told them, "No." However, they had a two-by-four long pole with long nails sticking out of it that they put right in front of our wheels, so we couldn't move forward. We eventually were forced to buy the stickers, and they allowed us to pass. The stickers did us no good after that.

The government's vehicle inspections were more often to present us with a current registration paper, which was paid yearly. Usually, the workers wouldn't physically inspect our car for actual safety violations. We tried to keep our car in good shape, so that such inspections wouldn't cause us problems with these workers or cause us to receive a fine. They'd often look for a problem with our car or tell us that we needed an additional paper that we didn't have.

The workers in places near Gimi, Plateau State, were known as the "nail boys." They also used the two-by-four poles with nails under our tires to stop us and try to charge us for not having the correct driving papers. We were always happy to drive through those areas and not be blocked or delayed by them. We didn't like to give them money.

Two other times government workers wanted to delay us. Once one worker fined us because one of our brake lights wasn't working. We had repaired it that morning in Enugu, but it failed us when he checked it. It was late on Friday afternoon, and we were taking the children home for a holiday break. He wanted to take us back to Jos, more than one hour away, to his headquarters to charge us. We said, "No." We did give him the fine he wanted, and he let us go. He probably never reported to his commander that he received that money.

In 2010, Dwight completed his first year of studies at LBC. He returned to Nigeria on his way to join an LBC soccer team that was going for ministry during the World Soccer Cup in South Africa, so he could attend Stephanie's graduation at Hillcrest.

After graduation, we began our return to Ikwa with our Camry fully loaded with Stephanie's belongings. A group of policemen was checking cars and taxis on the right side of the road. Since some cars were bypassing them on the left, we slowly followed them. One policeman saw that we were whites and yelled to one of his mates to quickly stop us and pull us to the side. He was a big man and began arguing with us. He didn't like the fact that we had gone ahead without their permission.

Suddenly, the officer jumped into the front passenger's seat on top of Dwight and told us we had committed an offense, and that he was going to take us back to his headquarters in Jos. This was also late afternoon. We knew if we went back with him there'd be a big delay and trouble at the police station. We told him we'd pay him some money for the offense. After several offers, with the amount rising each time, he finally agreed, took the money, and let us go. This is why we didn't like driving long distances in Nigeria and dealing with the police.

Dwight and Stephanie gained much from their years at Hillcrest School. Both became members of the school's honor society and received Hillcrest's coveted Citizenship Award. In addition, at his 2009 graduation, Dwight received sports awards in soccer and volleyball, as well as in service and leadership.

They both keep in touch with some of their Hillcrest buddies worldwide. We don't regret sending them to study there and thank God for the positive impact that it had on their lives.

2010 - Stephanie's graduation

Coletta's thoughts:

I knew sending the children to boarding school was the best for them. My first and only question to the Hillcrest School superintendent was about how often we could visit them. He replied, "Anytime you want." That was what I needed to hear. We tried to keep in close contact through our weekly emails and phone calls. That first semester it seemed like Dwight grew two inches taller.

The first year that Stephanie joined Dwight was hard for her and for me, as I knew it wasn't her first choice. Dennis traveled for a seminar in Kaduna City that year. I announced that I wanted to travel along and have him drop me off in Jos, so I could spend a week at their Pine View hostel. We received permission from their house parents, Ray and Jeanette Wilkinson. Dennis did a lot of extra driving to grant my request, but I felt it was a gift from the Lord to encourage Stephanie.

We tried to visit near Dwight and Stephanie's birthdays and take a birthday cake for them to enjoy. We tried to be present for some of their athletic events and their end-of-year awards assemblies. When they returned home for school breaks, I'd put up "Welcome Home" signs and cook some of their favorite meals.

I looked forward to those long trips. They gave me a chance to get out of the village, buy items in Jos that I couldn't find in the local markets, meet other missionaries, and best of all, spend time with Dwight and Stephanie.

Chapter 20

U-Turns in Ministry and Location

"Obey your leaders and submit to their authority. They keep watch over you as men who must give an account" (Hebrews 13:17a).

In May 2006, FIM General Director Dr. Steve Wilt, and FIM's Board Chairman Don Clark visited us at Ikwa for several days. Their observations and interactions were taken back to the U.S. for them to prayerfully seek God's direction for our family's future ministries. The FIM leaders shared their findings with our Calvary Church missions pastor, Steve Beirn. They saw that the CWT ministries weren't moving well, and that I was spending too much time doing administrative work for BMTC and CWT. They wanted me to focus more on using my main gift of teaching.

Our family had already planned to return to the U.S. that summer for a one-year home assignment. Stephanie needed to have braces on her teeth. We also wanted Dwight and Stephanie to attend an American high school for one year to become more acquainted with life in the U.S., where they planned to return for their college studies.

In late January 2006, I developed an inguinal hernia on my right side. The Nigerian doctors didn't want me to have the surgery in Nigeria. They said that because the hernia was very large, they didn't have mesh to keep it from coming out again.

In my March 25 email to our family members back home, I wrote:

> My hernia is very persistent. If I wear my truss, it keeps the hernia from coming out, but then the tightness of the truss over time causes me to be very hot and gives me a rash. If I don't have it on, then the hernia comes out, and I must lie down four or more times a day to have it go back in again. I can't win. Waiting until I get home in June to have the operation is a long way away, but we want to try it, as it will only be a day procedure, and the healing and results will be much better than if we have the operation done here.

In March, we brought Dwight and Stephanie home for their mid-semester break. On the way home, we had problems when a rubber cup got caught at the back of our wheel. It was 7 p.m. when local mechanics fixed the problem, so it was too late to drive more. We stayed at the best hotel in the town, but they didn't have a restaurant and their generator was only on until midnight. The screens in the room had holes in them, and we used buckets to take our baths. We had a soft drink and a peanut butter sandwich for supper and then tried to go to bed, even though it was very hot.

The next morning, Sunday, we drove for several hours and were about one hour from Ikwa. At one police checkpoint, the officer warned us that some youths up ahead were shooting guns, but police officers were going to solve the problem. Maybe if we hadn't had the car problem the night before, we would have run into those youths or robbers. God's guardian angels were working again!

In June, we wrote in one letter to our family:

> We had a safe trip to the U.S., traveling Tuesday evening and all-day Wednesday [June 13–14]. The Lufthansa flight was very nice. The flight from Frankfurt to Philadelphia was smooth overall, but the video system didn't work, so we couldn't get any news or watch our flight status on the video screen, etc. That made the flight more boring, but we did get a little more sleep that way.
>
> Our main problem on the trip was that the airlines made us repack our five suitcases at Port Harcourt Airport. Our travel agency had told us that we could have up to eight suitcases weighing 70 pounds (32 kg) each, but at the airport, the workers said that wasn't true. We needed to lighten our suitcases to 50 pounds (23 kg) each. However, we could have up to eight pieces of luggage.
>
> So, we had to buy three Ghana-Must-Go bags (strong plastic bags with handles). Repacking took us about one hour or more of shifting our suitcases and about two hours to get through Immigration and Customs. Dwight was very sweaty until we got everything in order, as he was lifting suitcases onto the scale to check them for their correct weights.
>
> Immigration wanted to make trouble with Dwight and Stephanie's passports, as we didn't have their old ones with us. They had their entry stamps on them from when they entered Nigeria back in January 2003. We told the officials that both children were born in Nigeria, and he was kind to let us go. Otherwise, that could have kept us from traveling. Praise the Lord!

> Also in Frankfurt, the computers said we only had six of our eight bags or suitcases. We said there were eight. They put a tracer on them. We kept praying. At Philadelphia, all eight pieces arrived safely. We got through passport checking and customs very quickly and easily. God worked out the details, and we're safe in the U.S. We know many were praying.

Although our bodies were just beginning to adapt to American time from jet lag, Coletta and I were able to attend my Uncle Harlan Shelly's funeral service on June 15.

I had my hernia operation in late June and recuperated well. In mid-July, we drove Dwight and Stephanie to New York near Buffalo for them to attend a one-week course for TCKs. Interaction International, a Christian ministry specializing in care for missionary kids (MKs), offered this program. The goal was to give Dwight and Stephanie the tools to adapt better when they returned to the U.S. for college. Some MKs found it very difficult to return to the U.S. and fit into the American culture after living many of their formative years in overseas cross-cultural contexts.

While the children were taking that course, Coletta and I stayed in the home of two good friends, Tom and Linda Cribbs, in Rochester, New York, as they traveled for the week. They visited us at Ikwa in February 2005 and served on the CWST for some years. It was a good time of rest for us.

Dwight and Stephanie both enjoyed their week and made new friends. It was amazing that wherever they'd travel and meet other MKs, they'd bond almost immediately and have great times together. Their accent and vocabulary even changed when they talked to some of their Nigerian friends. They'd begin to speak in pidgin (rough, simple, trade language) English or add a Hausa word or two to their conversation. They both learned to speak English with a Nigerian accent so that their friends—many of them Nigerian—could understand them better.

During that year, we lived at Calvary Church's missionary farmhouse. We lived in the main section of the house. At the same time, some couples or single missionaries stayed briefly in the back section, which was made into a one-bedroom apartment.

The children were permitted to enroll at Lancaster Mennonite School (LMS) as ninth and eighth-grade students. It was a stretch for them. Some of their schoolmates had very different world views.

During that semester Stephanie had braces put on her teeth, with some follow-up visits with her orthodontist. Dwight tried out for the LMS soccer team and quickly made the team. He received much good advice from his coach. He enjoyed his practices and games. We tried to attend as many games as possible. Stephanie tried out for the girls' softball team and was selected. We watched some of her games, even though her team lost most of them. Some of her mates were afraid of the ball when it came to them, but the team tried. She enjoyed the experience.

During the next few months, Dr. Wilt and Pastor Beirn dialogued on what was best for our family's future ministry. In December, they met with Coletta and me at our home church. Finally, they asked our family to leave the CWT and prayerfully find another ministry. They wanted me to be relieved of many administrative and financial duties, so I could use my teaching gifts more fully, and for Coletta to serve as a nurse. Both of us, especially me, were shocked and surprised at this decision. That decision brought many mixed emotions, including some tears.

Ikwa was the only place of ministry that I had ever known from my first summer of teaching at BMTC in 1973 until 2006. Coletta joined me in 1988 when we were married and faithfully served by my side. What was God trying to teach us? Where did He want us to go for our next phase of ministry? How were we to know?

Following our FIM and Calvary Church leaders' directives, we prayerfully sought the Lord to find a new ministry and location in Nigeria. We felt that the Lord could still use all our experiences in Nigeria in another Christian organization. God gave us peace that He would show us our next step. We explored several ministry opportunities that would fit my teaching gifts.

In the past, God had used Bible verses to guide us. The same verse He used to direct us was Psalm 32:8, "I will instruct you and teach you in the way you should go; I will counsel you and watch over you."

We received good counsel from Pastor Beirn. He had shared our situation with SIM's East Central Regional Director Ray Hutchison. During a visit to our church farmhouse, Ray told us of an opportunity to teach at the ECWA Theological Seminary in Kagoro (ETSK), in Kaduna State, Nigeria.

We kept praying. Ray encouraged us that it wouldn't be selfish or wrong for us to consider a ministry that would be closer to where Dwight and Stephanie were in school. He told us, "In the right place of service, God can make some of your challenges lighter, especially if they can help you have a stronger family. God knows your best interests and wants you to have joy and happiness where He leads you, not sadness and regret." Kagoro was only one and one-half hours (50 miles) from Hillcrest. Ikwa was 550 miles and one and a half days away. So, living in Kagoro would be a significant advantage.

ETSK in 2007 had over 300 students in all its programs, including its Master of Arts programs. Receiving my Ph.D. in Intercultural Studies (Missions) would enable me to teach some of their master's degree-level courses. Some of their B.A. classes had up to

50 or 60 students attending, compared to many at BMTC, which only had one or a few students.

Through various phone calls and emails in the U.S. and Nigeria, God gave us peace about saying yes to serving the Lord at ETSK. Ray's prayers and advice helped us immensely. Since ETSK was under ECWA and ECWA had a close relationship with her mother ministry, SIM, we proceeded to apply as SIM associate missionaries.

Following this process required that Coletta and I attend SIM's March 2007 SIM candidate orientation program in Charlotte, North Carolina. Since we had already been FIM missionaries for many years, SIM was lenient with us. They told us we could attend their candidate orientation program for only one week instead of their regular two- or three-week course. We enjoyed that training, met many SIM missionaries, and began to build some good relationships with them. SIM soon officially approved and welcomed us as SIM associate missionaries. We would still be formally under FIM but would be on loan to SIM. We proceeded to learn more about our ETSK duties.

FIM officially wrote to the CWT and BMTC leaders that we were leaving Ikwa for good. Their Nigerian leaders had mixed feelings about this but didn't have a choice. We had been one of their primary sources for raising support for their salaries, student scholarships, and projects. We had also been the only U.S. family at Ikwa who had served with them for so many years and seen BMTC grow.

Many close relationships were made. We were grateful we could keep in touch with some of the BMTC staff and alumni through improved phone and email services. No matter where they live, we're always happy to see how God has been using many of our alumni for God's glory as they live for Him.

Our church wanted each of us as their Global Partners (missionaries) to form a Prayer and Care Team (PACTeam). Our team included four Christian couples who had known us for many years: George and Mary Duff, Earl and Kathy Mogel, Walt and Lois Zigrang, and Larry and Connie Laughman. Larry and his son, Dale, had come to Ikwa for one month in 1999 to do maintenance and electrical work for the CWT. The Duff's had visited us at Ikwa in 2003.

Our PACTeam since 2007

They met bimonthly to pray for us. When we'd return to the U.S. for home assignments, they'd buy and set up some basic food and household items in our house to help us settle in when we'd arrive directly from the airport. Up until 2020, they faithfully met bi-monthly on our behalf. We'd join them when in the U.S.

We couldn't have an official send-off at Ikwa. If the Ikwa villagers had known that we were staying at Ikwa, they would have misunderstood why we were leaving. I had been the treasurer of Ikwa village's United Nations Development Program committee for the past years. I handled their finances and made many reasonable efforts to help their Ikwa cooperative become a model for others.

Our return to Ikwa in late July 2007 was bitter-sweet. We left Dwight and Stephanie in Jos with friends. SIM helped to arrange for a small truck owned by the Evangelical Missionary Society (EMS) of ECWA and an EMS driver to come with us to bring our belongings back to Jos. In addition, we hired another Nigerian driver from another mission and his van to take us to Ikwa since we had left our car there during our home assignment.

When we all arrived at the CWT compound in Ikwa on Monday morning, some of the BMTC faculty advised us to go quietly to our house to sort out what belongings we'd take to Kagoro and what would stay. We worked throughout that day, then traveled to Uyo, about 45 miles away.

Tuesday morning, we all returned to Ikwa to finalize packing up our belongings into our vehicles. We had our car quickly serviced at Ikwa to drive to Jos. It wasn't easy to say goodbye to our CWT and BMTC staff. We had known some of them for over 30 years. They were very sad to see us leave. At about noon, we finally left for our journey to Jos.

Our car was the lead vehicle for the journey north to Kagoro, with the EMS truck in the middle and the van following. It went well, although we did have one minor accident. Once, the EMS truck didn't see my brake lights when I had to stop abruptly. It was at a spot on the expressway with two lanes on our side and two on the opposite side—from Port Harcourt to Enugu—where the entire two lanes on our side of the expressway suddenly dropped about eight inches.

He ran into my car's rear bumper. The impact didn't hurt my car much, so we continued driving, leaving a wider gap between each vehicle for the remainder of the trip. We all stayed overnight at an Enugu hotel and continued the journey on Wednesday morning.

We arrived at Kagoro early Wednesday evening. Students helped us unload our vehicles in the rain. Then we drove to Jos to see Dwight and Stephanie. We thanked

God for caring for us and helping us close one significant chapter of our lives and begin another at Kagoro. We believed God was going to use us in new ways!

Coletta's thoughts:

We enjoyed the year in the U.S., although we passed through great transitions. Stephanie was a trooper with her braces. Dwight enjoyed being part of a good soccer team at LMS. I enjoyed having all of us under one roof for a year. Dennis spent many hours taking computer lessons to improve his skills in PowerPoint presentations. He also studied to complete the Perspectives on the World Christian Movement course while I bussed the children to their many activities.

I wasn't as shocked as Dennis was about having to leave Ikwa. I had slowly watched things go downhill over the years. Brother Joshua Ekpikhe's deteriorating health had added heavily to Dennis' responsibilities. Still, it was hard to say goodbye to long-standing friendships.

I was pleased to have a fresh start at Kagoro and was able to find some household decorations in the U.S. on clearance and discounted drapes to take along. I was thrilled to have a large screened-in porch. When morning arrived, I could see the mountain peaks behind the seminary. They reminded me of Ecuador.

Chapter 21

Settling in at Kagoro

"There is a time for everything, and a season for every activity under heaven: a time to be born and a time to die, a time to plant and a time to uproot" (Ecclesiastes 3:1–2).

Our years at Kagoro from 2007 until 2020 were overall peaceful and enjoyable. However, no matter where we lived, everyday life wasn't easy for us as expatriate missionaries or for the local people. In pidgin English, the local people would say, "Eh hardo," meaning "life is hard."

Daily life when we first arrived at Kagoro in late July 2007, was in some ways easier than at Ikwa. At Ikwa, we had been used to living each day without many hours of electricity from NEPA.

Our home at Kagoro

At Ikwa, when we needed power, we'd go and use our generator, lantern, flashlight (torch), or candle to give us light, especially after sundown. A high-tension NEPA line went right by the CWT compound on the main road. Still, the NEPA leaders demanded that our village pay for a transformer before we'd be connected.

When we moved north to Kagoro, we knew that we'd also not have a steady NEPA supply at our home. Our home church helped us buy a new gas-run generator, a refrigerator, and a stove to use at Kagoro. We left our old ones at Ikwa for the CWT or BMTC staff to use, so we wouldn't have to transport them to Kagoro.

During our years in Nigeria, we never had to worry about sleet, ice, or snow. Nigeria had only two annual seasons, rainy and hot. Ikwa, in the Southeast, was always extremely hot and humid, often in the 80s or 90s °F (27–32 °C) in the shade. The climate at Kagoro was drier and less sticky. Their lowest temperature was about 70 °F (20 °C). When it was that cool, many of the nationals wore winter coats, gloves, and caps to classes to keep warm.

The Ikwa rains continued most of the year. In Kagoro, the rains began in March or April and continued only until mid-October, when it seemed like God turned off the faucet, and the rains immediately stopped. At Ikwa, we'd often have to change our wet clothing at least once during the day because of perspiration. At Kagoro, Coletta's kitchen thermometer often showed the low 90s °F (32 °C) during the day.

At Kagoro, SIM assigned us to live on one of the largest missionary compounds at ETSK. It was about 75 yards square along a main two-lane highway going to Kaduna and the North. Big trucks (lorries), buses, taxis, cars, and motorcycles drove by at all hours of the day or night, many going as fast as they could with horns often blowing loudly, even in the middle of the night. Many of them drove with only one working headlight or no taillights working at all. Most vehicles and motorcycles were old and in poor condition.

More than once in our travels, we saw terrible accidents when a bus would drive head-on into a truck, taxi, or vehicle. Suppose a tractor-trailer had only one headlight working on the passenger's side, without any other lights shining on his truck or trailer. In that case, oncoming drivers could easily mistake it for a bicycle or motorcycle. If one wasn't careful, a terrible accident could occur. This was one reason we tried our best not to drive at night. We thank God for keeping us from such accidents.

Rock formations in Plateau State

When driving to Jos, we saw unique stone formations in hills and mountains. Some stones appeared ready to fall if someone blew lightly on them. Yet, they stood still. We knew that God had allowed these formations to show that He was the great Creator and could form land and stones any way He wanted.

Kagoro was only 50 miles from Jos but could take two or more hours to get there depending on whether it was the dry or rainy season and if a road construction company was making a new road or only repairing it.

We were happy when the road through a big mountain was finally opened. However, some sections before the mountain were impassable. Villagers had cut out part of a big hill, so we could drive around one section of the road, which was deep mud. We had to pay a little money to the villagers when we'd pass. However, the construction company hadn't kept up repairs well. Some parts of the macadamed road were better to avoid completely by driving along the side of the road.

Location of Kagoro in Nigeria[9]

From 2007 to 2010, living at Kagoro allowed us to visit Dwight and Stephanie more regularly at school. They could also come home more often than just on holidays to spend a weekend or free days with us. Several times when they were home, some of their friends from Jos came as well. They would spend part of the day climbing Kagoro mountain. Dwight went to the very peak several times. Stephanie also went close to the top.

We'd go to Jos every four to six weeks to shop at several supermarkets and vegetable markets. When the new road to Jos was paved, we could get there about 45 minutes faster. However, with many potholes (gallops) in the road, along with some police checkpoints along the way, driving was much slower.

The genuine vs. the fake

In Jos, we could buy items that we could buy in the U.S. However, Nigerian prices for imported goods were usually double. We bought things like frozen hot dogs, butter, American cereals, peanut butter, and cheese.

We needed to be careful to buy genuine and not fake items. One example was buying Skippy peanut butter. Once we bought a jar, thinking that it was a genuine item. When we arrived home, we realized that the spelling on the label was spelled "SKKIPY" instead of 'SKIPPY."

Another company had made similar peanut butter. We did eat both jars with no bad effects. In addition, the Jos supermarkets had fixed prices compared to most open-air market sellers, who'd bargain with us on the price before we'd finally buy the item.

We'd usually stay one or two nights in Jos over a weekend at SIM's Woyke Guest House. This occasionally allowed us to attend some of Hillcrest's annual weekend activities or fundraisers—such as their Nigerian craft show—musical concerts, graduations, or some of Dwight and Stephanie's sporting or extra-curricular activities. Sometimes we attended SIM's Friday potluck dinner, where many of the SIMers came to eat and have a time of fellowship. We'd also interact with some of the students' parents and attend Sunday morning worship services in Hillcrest's chapel.

We'd sit with Dwight and Stephanie for the service, then go out for Sunday lunch at a nice restaurant before we'd drive back to Kagoro to prepare for the new week ahead. Such short breaks refreshed us and helped us return to Kagoro more prepared to meet the many knocks at our door and the constant challenges of facing life in the village.

Security wasn't a big concern when we first arrived in July 2007. When we moved into our house, we inherited a big, black dog named Buma. He had been owned by several past missionaries and had bitten a few people over the years. He did well with us but tried to bite some of the nationals. The local people didn't like black dogs, as they were considered evil. That was to our advantage to keep local thieves or curious intruders away.

The only security around our compound was two rows of old, dark green, roofing sheets erected by former missionaries. These sheets were about 26 inches wide and 6 feet long (66 centimeters by 1.8 meters). They were turned sideways and nailed together to short, wooden posts that were not more than three feet tall (one meter). We could see everything that was happening outside along the main road. Everyone could also see us easily as they drove or walked by our compound. We lived directly across the main road from the seminary, which also had the same type of short fences to protect it.

In late August, one month after we arrived at Kagoro, we were sleeping when we heard several loud gunshots. They came from the seminary near the deputy provost's home. Any noises at night usually sounded louder than they did during the day. We were afraid and didn't know if we'd be attacked that night.

The following day, we learned that robbers had attacked our deputy provost's house to try to get money and personal belongings from him. We learned that the day before, he had gone to the bank. Maybe some people watched him at the bank and then decided to rob him at night. We decided to avoid going to any Kafanchan banks personally, so we'd not be targeted as expatriates.

The deputy provost and his son lost much blood from the attackers. He had tried to fight one of them and used a wooden pestle from a pounding mortar to retaliate. The robber, in turn, grabbed the pestle and hit the deputy provost and his son on their heads and bodies. Both had to get numerous stitches at the Kafanchan and Jos hospitals, but they recovered over time.

Over the following days, these robbers attacked several other local places. The police became involved. We learned that the robbers were later killed. After that, the area had peace again for a little while.

We shared these events in our news updates and with Calvary Church. They responded quickly by sending us some funds to build a concrete wall around our entire compound. SIM learned of our project and asked if they could add some funds to expand the borders to go around one vacant lot and a second compound, where our SIM mates, David and Debbie Colvin, lived. Our church agreed.

Our new security gate and wall

Cutting down some large trees, burning the brush, and constructing the wall along the main road began. Nine-inch concrete blocks were molded and erected about eight feet high on three sides of our compounds. Sharp pieces of broken glass bottles were embedded into the concrete at the top of the walls to discourage robbers from coming over them. In the middle of our compounds, the workers built a six-foot chain-link fence.

Having a dog—and later up to three dogs—helped us deter robbers from entering our compound during our 13 years of ministry at Kagoro. The Colvin's, who didn't have dogs, did experience two robberies, as the wall at the back of their compound was initially lower than our sides.

One night, robbers climbed over their wall, used their shotguns, and had other robbers positioned to shout in Hausa for people to stay away. Our students patrolling that night, along with our young dogs, were all scared and couldn't chase the robbers before they stole some personal items from the Colvin's compound and fled. No one was hurt, but there was trauma. We believed that some Kagoro youths coordinated the robbery. One of them was later captured and taken away by the police. We never heard about that boy again.

During the summer of 2008, Dwight returned to the U.S. to attend several soccer camps. He stayed with my sister and brother-in-law, Bonnie and Denny Sharp. Stephanie didn't want to come to Kagoro for the entire summer, since her friends were at Ikwa, and she didn't know any of the Kagoro youth. We discussed this with Pastor Beirn at Calvary Church. They graciously gave money for an airline ticket for Stephanie to also go to the U.S. for the summer since she did know some teenage friends from the church and LMS. Tim and Darlene Farrell, Calvary Church members, kindly allowed Stephanie to live with them for the summer. It was helpful for her. In the end, she was refreshed and ready to return to Nigeria.

Eating a grasshopper

During that summer, Coletta and I were encouraged to enroll in a six-week Hausa language school in Jos. It was quite demanding, because we stayed during the week at Woyke Guest House, then drove back to Kagoro each weekend. To learn Hausa well, we needed to spend much more time in classes and then use our Hausa in real life with Hausa speakers. At least we were able to learn many words and short sayings.

One day during our lessons, someone brought us fried grasshoppers with some hot pepper sauce as a dip to eat. Since I was usually willing to try new things, I took several. They were very crunchy. Coletta also ate a few. We were able to get some extra protein that day. We've enjoyed telling that story over the years!

In early August 2008, we took Dwight and Stephanie to Jos to begin their fall semester. Just after our return to Kagoro, on August 7, we received word that Daddy had passed away at Pleasant View Communities in Manheim. SIM advised us to return immediately to the U.S. and helped us quickly get re-entry visas. FIM approved our travels for the funeral, and we bought airline tickets. The children continued to live in SIM's Niger Creek dormitory near Hillcrest.

We arrived in the U.S. just in time to attend Daddy's August 15 funeral service at Pleasant View Communities. He had been moved there in late June after he had had a stroke. We joined the family for the public viewing, where we met many friends and relatives who appreciated Daddy's life of service to the Lord. Our two-week visit to the U.S. enabled us to encourage Momma and the family.

Later that year, the Shelly family helped Momma sell her home and belongings at 405 W. High Street, Manheim. That same November, she moved to live in Pleasant View. She continued living there until she went to be with the Lord on February 28, 2023, at 100 years of age.

Several ETSK faculty started our courses for us while we were away. Back in Jos, Dwight and Stephanie were in good hands while we traveled. Coletta and I returned to Nigeria about one week after the funeral to both continue ETSK teaching and other duties.

ETSK taught all its courses in English. Our goal was to help our students speak and write better English, so their future ministries could be more productive in teaching, preaching, leadership, or writing. Some of our ETSK students knew four or more languages, but most didn't know English well. During one chapel, the Wycliffe Bible Translators' speakers recorded at least 42 different Nigerian dialects among the faculty, staff, and students who attended. One could see the challenge we had teaching our students in English!

At our house, Coletta hired several ETSK students' wives to help her with household chores, washing clothes, and basic cooking, like making our dog food, which had to be made from scratch. We also hired several male ETSK students to mow our grass, help in our garden, and be our night security guards.

Their working at our house was a big asset to us. The U.S. dollar was usually stronger than the Nigerian naira. That helped us pay these workers without too much cost. Yet the students benefited greatly from this salary. It helped them buy some items to feed their families, pay for part of their ETSK tuition fees, and pay the expenses of their younger children living with them.

On most Saturdays, Coletta would drive seven miles to Kafanchan to buy her weekly vegetables and a hunk of several pounds of beef (cow meat). Sometimes Debbie Colvin or one of our house helpers would accompany her. Traffic continued to increase on the main market roads in Kafanchan. On one trip, when Coletta was driving, she accidentally bumped into a man. She stopped and gave him some money to go to the hospital to get minor abrasions cleaned up. After that, she usually asked me to drive and accompany her.

We could buy almost any part of a cow or goat at the local meat market. Pieces were laid on wooden tables under small tin roofs, exposed to flies and heat. We'd show the seller which part of the cow we wanted to buy—part from a big leg or a piece that wasn't as fatty as the others. He'd then cut it off and put it on his scale for us to see and agree on the weight. Often, he'd add a small piece of meat as "extra" (jara) to say thanks for our business, hoping that we'd return to buy from him again. He'd also be willing to cut up the hunk of meat into small pieces with his sharp knife.

Helping Coletta grind meat

After returning home, it often took several hours for Coletta to clean the vegetables and meat she bought (sometimes the students' wives would help her). For the pieces of meat, she'd wash them, cut off the fat, and then cut them into smaller pieces or use our electric grinder to make ground beef. I'd occasionally help her. She'd then put them into small bags to freeze in our small refrigerator's freezer. Life and survival in Kagoro took much longer than back in the U.S.

Since we were usually in survival mode at Kagoro, we didn't have much leisure time, especially on weekdays. So, between classes, Coletta would spend several mornings or afternoons a week serving at the ETSK medical clinic, seeing sick students and their family members. Their main sicknesses were malaria, dysentery, upper gastrointestinal burning, respiratory problems, and minor injuries. She sent more significant problems to the local ECWA Medical Dispensary about one block from our campus or the Kafanchan General Hospital, seven miles away.

A typical daily schedule during the week would be from 6:30 a.m. to 10:30 or 11 p.m. First, Coletta (more of a morning person than I am) would get up and make coffee for herself (I haven't learned to drink coffee yet). Then, we'd get dressed. Coletta would get the dogs back into their pen by feeding them, and we'd eat breakfast afterward. The ETSK faculty and staff had two prayer meetings from 7:30 to 8 a.m. on Tuesdays and Thursdays. We tried attending them as much as we could. We'd head off to the ETSK campus to teach a class from 8 to 9:50 or 10:50, depending on if it was a two- or three-credit-hour course. If it stopped at 9:50, Coletta would walk home to get a few items ready for lunch.

Chapel time was from 11 a.m. to noon, Mondays through Thursdays. Coletta would try to sit with me then and in church services. Afterward, we'd drive back to our house for a quick lunch, especially if we had a 1 p.m. class. Our afternoon classes were from 1 to 3 or 4 p.m., depending on whether the course was two or three credit hours. Afterward, I'd return home, see some staff in their offices, or check how things were going at the fishery or garden. I'd usually check our email, correct papers, or prepare for the next day's classes. We often struggled to get email because of our location and the lack of phone towers in the area.

Each day, late in the afternoon, Coletta would prepare supper. After washing the supper dishes, she'd feed the dogs. We'd then prepare for the next day's classes, correct homework, or send emails to our family and friends.

Coletta caring for our three dogs

At about 10:15 p.m., two students who were night security guards would arrive at our compound. We'd pray with them before they began patrolling between our compound and the Colvin's with the dogs loose. By 11 p.m., Coletta and I, usually exhausted, went to bed and prayed together before we slept on our waterbed.

On Friday nights, Coletta and I intentionally tried to have a date night. We'd stop working for at least one or two hours to play a game or watch a video or film on TV. If NEPA gave us electricity that night, we'd watch a movie on TV. More than once, the power stopped just before the movie ended. If we wanted to try to continue watching without missing the final minutes, I'd quickly run outside to our generator house and turn it on.

However, since it took about ten minutes to start up the generator and have it ready to give power, the film had usually already ended when I came in to watch. Even these short breaks were occasionally interrupted because of some health emergency that demanded Coletta's nursing skills, or the occurrence of another unavoidable issue. Therefore, going to Jos for an occasional weekend was the best way to take a short break.

Often at night, the sky at Kagoro was perfectly clear. We could see various constellations in the southern hemisphere, like Orion and Pleiades. The Milky Way was beautiful, looking like one bright cloud from one end of the horizon to the other. Crickets would be chirping; bats would be flying (often fighting with each other over a ripe mango); owls would be hooting; dogs would be barking; and vehicles and motorcycles would be zooming past our compound, using their horns to try to get a passenger, a person, or a stray dog out of their way.

Fulani herd outside our wall and gate

During the dry season, we'd often hear the Fulani herdsmen move their cows and sheep along the main road in search of grass and water. The cows would be mooing, and the dust stirred up as they'd walk on and along the road outside our gate. We'd also see these herds as we'd drive to Jos or Abuja. When driving, we'd need to be careful so we wouldn't kill any of their animals. Some people said the Fulanis often valued their cows more than their children.

When we moved to Kagoro, part of our 75-yard square compound was quickly cultivated to grow sweet corn, cucumbers, tomatoes, green beans, and leaf lettuce. I used some gardening ideas that I had learned from my parents. I also experimented with growing other vegetables to see which would produce the best in our soil. While on home assignments in the U.S., we'd buy various vegetable seed packets or would receive gifts of them, so we could try to grow more food or give others the seeds.

When we first arrived at our compound in July 2007, we found banana and plantain stands, along with mango, orange, guava, and grapefruit trees already growing. They were planted by previous SIM missionaries. We later added papayas, along with other varieties of oranges, plantain, and bananas. In addition, some Nigerian vegetable leaves like spinach (ogu) and moringa (zogale) were grown. It was great to pick fresh fruit from a tree or vegetables from the garden to eat or pass on to needy students or staff.

Our Kagoro compound garden

I registered as a voluntary development worker with the Educational Concerns for Hunger Organization (ECHO), based in North Fort Myers, Florida. Their website is echocommunity.org. This status allowed me to receive ten free packs of various seeds or small cuttings every year to bring to Nigeria to plant in our garden or at the ETSK fishery's garden to see if they'd grow in our climate. Some of these seeds, like Leucaena, grew into trees over 40 feet tall (12 meters) on our compound. They provided our students with firewood, smaller branches to make fences on our compound, or stakes to hold up spinach or vines.

While we lived at Ikwa and Kagoro, I was always burdened to help our students learn practical skills to support their families or church members. This could enable them to eat better foods or supplement their ministry salaries. God led us to begin the ETSK Skill Acquisition Center (SAC). Its purpose was to empower interested faculty, staff, students, youth, and adults from the community to come and learn basic skills. This could help them partially support themselves when they left ETSK or would help them discover if these skills could be turned into a small trade or business. Chapter 25 gives more details on this.

During all our years at Kagoro, from 2007 to 2020, we never had power from NEPA for 24 consecutive hours for even one full day. The day that the chief of Kagoro was buried in 2008 was the closest we ever came to achieving that feat. He was one of the oldest reigning chiefs in Nigeria, holding his position for over 60 years.

Former President Babangida and other key government leaders from Abuja and around the country came for that burial. The village enjoyed electricity during the entire celebration. Unfortunately, Nigeria's "shame" culture often forced people to do extra things or spend money that they didn't have to look good in public. So that day, the NEPA managers rationed and shifted electricity to Kagoro from other areas for the day to look good in the eyes of the leaders. However, when everyone returned home that Saturday night, the NEPA managers felt less pressure to direct the power to Kagoro. So, they turned off the power after dark, and we returned to our normal irregular supply.

There were often challenges with accidents or mishaps at ETSK as well as for Coletta and me. Once I bumped a vein above my left ankle. Blood began squirting out from it without my knowledge that it was from me. I quickly called Coletta for help. We even looked up at the ceiling in our bathroom to see where the blood was coming from. Finally, we saw that it was coming from my leg.

Coletta had me lie on our waterbed and tried to stop the bleeding. Our ETSK driver, Jolly, was called to take us to a Kafanchan private hospital to see if they could cauterize the vein. The Nigerian doctor told us he couldn't help us. So, Jolly drove us to Jos to the ECWA-operated Bingham University Teaching Hospital (BUTH). The medical staff saw me and said it wasn't necessary to cauterize it, and that it would heal on its own. I was told to be careful of my movements. The wound opened again one week later, but I haven't had problems since.

One other scary event happened late one day when I visited the ETSK fishery. I bent my head down to see something and caught my forehead on some barbed wire. It immediately started to bleed. I quickly went home for Coletta's help. She tried to clean me up and saw that I had a small gash on my forehead. She wanted us to go to BUTH in Jos. The doctor on duty put only one stitch on my forehead. Often cuts on foreheads bleed a lot, so it looked worse than it was. We stayed at Woyke Guest House that night and returned to Kagoro the next morning.

On May 24, 2009, we attended Dwight's Hillcrest School Baccalaureate service and a special SIM tea honoring eight SIM-related seniors, including Dwight. In the awards chapel, Dwight received five awards: most valuable soccer player, most valuable volleyball player, service and leadership, and citizenship. The Citizenship Award was the highest award any senior could receive. On May 28, Dwight graduated with 22 other seniors. As their class president, he presented his speech well.

As a junior, Stephanie was inducted into the National Honor Society. As a senior, she was elected senior class treasurer and also received the Citizenship Award. She graduated from Hillcrest in 2010. SIM also had a tea to honor her and several other SIM-related seniors. We were very proud of both Dwight and Stephanie.

When Stephanie came home to Kagoro, she'd often pick a bouquet of flowers from our compound and put them in a vase to set on our dining room table. Depending on the season, she could pick flowers from our trees and bushes: red flame, hibiscus, bird of paradise, or plumeria. She needed to walk around the compound carefully, as we had some bee hives near some of those bushes and trees.

Living in Kagoro had various challenges when it came to getting my three-month prescription drugs from the U.S. Since most of them were unavailable in Jos pharmacies, we had to order them from the U.S. We'd either have them sent to us through the U.S. Post Office, or friends coming from the U.S. would bring them to us. Surprisingly, the U.S. Post Office informed Denny Sharp that we were no longer allowed to mail prescriptions through them.

After that, Denny sent our prescriptions through UPS to be delivered directly to us at Kagoro. Once their van dropped a note by the seminary gate informing us that our package was at their Lagos office, but we had to pay a 100 percent customs duty before they'd deliver the small package of prescriptions to us. They gave us three days to pay for it, or they'd destroy the parcel.

I had to promptly scramble to find the money to pay the worker. We received the parcel safely several days later. We never sent them through UPS again. We either brought them with us from the U.S. or found SIM missionaries or visitors coming to Nigeria to personally bring the prescriptions to us.

The Kagoro Post Office received many boxes of donated library books for ETSK while we were at Kagoro. Some men like Neil Holliker and Bob Hopper helped us greatly by shipping various bags of books from their personal libraries to the ETSK library. Zada Shearer, from Word of Life Chapel, sent us regular boxes of old "Our Daily Bread" devotionals and left-over Sunday school papers for children and youth and "Power" papers for adults. We gave them to the children in our Sunday schools, youth in high schools, prisoners in the local prison, and policemen and army officers at police checkpoints when we went on long trips. The recipients didn't worry about the dates on these items but were very happy to read them. The results of church members sending Christian literature to countries like Nigeria will only be known when we get to heaven!

In our final years at ETSK, as Coletta and I grew a little older, and our energy wasn't as much as when we first arrived in 2007, we learned to say no more than in the past when asked to speak or travel for a ministry. We were always happy to see God blessing the ministries at ETSK and watch how God was using the faculty, staff, and students to continue to be witnesses for the Lord!

Coletta's thoughts:

Kagoro was a farming community. We decided to have big gardens to improve the diets of the staff and students by adding more fruits and vegetables. We introduced new crops from Dennis' involvement with ECHO.

Dwight and Stephanie were at Kagoro only several weeks before leaving for Hillcrest School. While they were away, I worked hard to get their rooms in better order, so they could enjoy them on their mid-semester break. Dwight chose red curtains; I added a border with African animals.

Steph chose pink curtains; I added a border with kittens and yarn balls. To the bathrooms, I added a border of frogs and lily pads. To the kitchen and dining area, I added a border with coffee, teapots, and berries. All of that was an effort to help us adapt to a new home.

We moved many times over the years as we transitioned overseas and to the U.S.. We always stressed that home was wherever we were all together.

In preparation for ETSK graduations and seminary-wide special dinners, I enjoyed cooking with the national staff and faculty ladies. We drove seven miles to the Kafanchan market to buy the ingredients. The next day we spent hours chatting over the huge cooking pots set on wooden fires.

Chapter 22

Using Our Spiritual Gifts at Kagoro

"It was he who gave some to be apostles, some to be prophets, some to be evangelists, and some to be pastors and teachers, to prepare God's people for works of service, so that the body of Christ may be built up until we all reach unity in the faith and in the knowledge of the Son of God and become mature, attaining to the whole measure of the fullness of Christ"
(Ephesians 4:11–13).

Starting Ministry at Kagoro

Although we had a rough start living in Kagoro, Coletta and I firmly believed God would use our spiritual gifts to be a blessing to many. According to Bill Hanks, "Discipleship" is defined as "beginning to pour your life into another, and training others to a reproducing and growing ministry that will glorify Christ."[10] We wanted to pour our lives into the lives of hundreds of ETSK students and others from Nigeria and Africa for more effective Christian ministries. They could then return to their people and church ministries to pass on what they had learned. We also looked forward to good Christian fellowship and partnership in ministries.

Whether at Ikwa or Kagoro, we had many challenges as expatriate missionaries serving cross-culturally. Problems with electricity, weather, medical issues, limitations in communication, obtaining visas and resident permits, and learning to prepare and eat different types of food were all issues that needed God's grace.

At Kagoro, we learned how to adapt to various leaders' styles at ETSK. From 2007 to 2020, we served under three provosts, with different accountants (bursars) assigned from the ECWA headquarters in Jos. Sometimes ECWA transferred various faculty and staff, often our best ones, to serve in another ECWA ministry or seminary. Other faculty chose to move on to become leaders in the ECWA leadership in their local areas.

Teaching and Ministries

Teaching Evangelism and Discipleship

Coletta and I enjoyed our years at Kagoro very much. In August 2007, being our first semester to teach, I was assigned courses on The History of Missions, Pastoral Theology, and Personal Evangelism and Discipleship. Our classes were much larger at Kagoro compared to Ikwa. At Ikwa, there were rarely over 20 students. At ETSK, several of my classes had up to 50 or 60 students.

Coletta taught Community Health, HIV-AIDS, and Basic English. In addition, she began serving several mornings or afternoons weekly as a volunteer nurse at ETSK's medical clinic to provide essential medicines and care to staff and students who had malaria, colds, or diarrhea.

She referred more serious medical issues to the ECWA College of Health Technology Comprehensive Health Center, Kagoro, or the Kafanchan General Hospital, seven miles away. We'd drive the 50-mile trip to BUTH when Coletta or I faced a medical problem that she couldn't solve. Coletta was always ready to help those who were sick or needed medical advice. Sometimes this was at inconvenient hours, early in the morning or late at night.

Coletta at the medical clinic

Occasionally, she spoke in the chapel to enlighten the ETSK leaders and students on a critical medical topic: malaria, hypertension, hepatitis, monkeypox, AIDS, handling stress, typhoid fever, domestic violence, diabetes, sickle cell anemia, and meningitis. She ended with time to answer questions. Those who attended greatly appreciated what she shared.

In 2016, my largest class was How to Study (Research Methods I), with 105 students in our new classroom that could hold up to 150 students. Many of my other classes had from 15 to 60 students. My M.A. and M.Div. courses had between one and five students. These smaller classes gave me more personal involvement and discussion opportunities than my larger classes. We'd sit in a circle in the classroom or on the porch of our house.

At ETSK, Coletta and I enjoyed attending student chapels, Sunday evening services, and various weekly meetings: Monday evening dorm devotionals, Tuesday night missions department meetings, and Thursday student prayer chapels. I presented various PowerPoint presentations in chapels to help students improve their English writing, especially for their theses. I also preached in chapels on missions or in the ETSK Church Sunday morning services.

ETSK morning chapel

During my first years, I had more energy to coordinate Sunday evening competitions for students and some of their teenagers and children. These included Bible quizzes—who could read the best five-minute Bible passage, answer questions on various Bible verses or topics, or spell Bible books and names of Bible characters—and leading the best hymns.

These were fun ways to sharpen students' Bible skills and give them more confidence in leading in their present and future ministries. Several judges helped us choose the winners. Several times I teamed up with Rev. Yusuf Gajere in a chapel to teach a new song or to show how to lead singing confidently using various time signatures.

If I preached for the ETSK Church Sunday morning or evening worship service, I'd squeeze time between everything else that week to prepare. I often used PowerPoint presentations. They took more time to prepare than just preaching, but they helped those listening and watching to be more attentive and to improve their English.

Over the years, some of my favorite messages I have preached various times were (and still are) the following: *How Are You Passing the Test* (I Corinthians 3:10–15; II Corinthians 5:9–10); *God's Faithfulness Should Cause Us to Be Faithful* (I Kings 8:54–61); *To Be Great Is to Serve* (Mark 10:43–45); *Qualities of a Growing Christian* (Romans 1:9–16); and *You're Strongest When You're Weakest* (II Corinthians 12:1–10). Most of these messages have been made into PowerPoint presentations; I'd be glad to share them with anyone interested.

Some preachers have said that one shouldn't preach the same passage a second time. I disagree. If I were to preach a sermon a second time, I would do some fresh study to sharpen my points and update my illustrations and applications instead of depending mainly on my past studies. If the passage spoke to me in new ways, I'd depend on the Lord to first speak to me, so that I'd be fresh in what I'd share with the congregation.

I've enjoyed teaching various book studies in church settings: Colossians, I Timothy, and I John. I've also enjoyed conducting several seminars: *Developing Christian values among our youth*, based on Josh McDowell's book, *Right from Wrong: What You Need to Know to Help Youth Make Right Choices; Six ways to reach God's world*, with the main points from materials from Overseas Missionary Fellowship; and *I am N*, from Voice of the Martyrs on how we can pray for the persecuted church.

I've also enjoyed sharing in various chapels and chats on *How to Be Happy Though Single*, *How to Use Your Time Wisely*, and *Personal Hygiene and Appearance*.

In my M.A. Mass Communication class, one of my assignments was for each student to prepare a PowerPoint presentation and present it to his church or a Christian group and then to our class before the end of the semester. Some of the men strongly resisted this because they had never prepared one before; I still required it. One of the men who had resisted this idea later shared in class that when he used the presentation in his church, his church members were so excited that they took an offering and raised enough money to buy a video projector so he and others could use it in future messages and teaching.

We learned that it was best to use the chapel's generator when giving these PowerPoint presentations. Otherwise, the lights would often go off if we depended on NEPA to give us power. We'd then have to start the chapel generator and restart the computer and the video projector equipment. Such delays took at least ten minutes. The service leader would often fill such time gaps by leading the congregation in singing several choruses.

Missions Emphasis

In 2008, I accepted the position as the head of the Missions department. The academic dean gave me three or four courses to teach each semester in the diploma and B.A. programs. In the beginning, I taught Evangelism and Discipleship, Pastoral Theology, Introduction to Missions (History and Science of Missions), Cultural Anthropology, How to Study (Research Methods I), and Research Methods II. I taught the last two to help students learn how to write their theses. As I taught and served at ETSK, my prayer for every student, no matter their major, was for each one to become "missions-minded" missionaries, teachers, pastors, or Christian workers and be bright lights for Christ daily.

We enjoyed partnering with the ETSK faculty and staff as we tried to strengthen the seminary in any way we could. Some of the best lessons we taught them were while working together on a committee or project, at our house, in the garden, at the fishery, or just interacting with them casually on campus. We also learned much from our national brethren.

Most departments planned for one weekend each semester to travel to an unreached village in their region that needed the gospel. As head of the Missions department, I was always happy to see our Missions department students and the other ETSK Pastoral and Christian Religious Studies departments go out for weekend outreaches to areas in our region for personal evangelism and discipleship.

However, I wanted them to focus first on doing their best in their studies, not wanting them to go out for ministries too many times in a semester and then do poorly in their studies. This would help them form good habits and be more productive once they graduated and went into actual ministries.

Some weekends, 20 or more male and female students would volunteer to go. Each student took only a small backpack with needed personal belongings for the trip. They were willing to sleep on the floor in a church, school, or home. They'd walk for a mile or more over rugged paths off a main road to go into the targeted village or would be willing to fight the mosquitoes as they tried to sleep. They weren't looking for luxuries but went because they felt God wanted them to go and tell others about Christ.

Most students donated some money to buy gas for a taxi or van to take them to the targeted village on a Friday afternoon. When the ETSK van was in good condition, they'd fuel it to transport them. Often a church near their target area supplied housing and food for them. They'd take a small generator and equipment to show *The Jesus Film* or other gospel films on Friday and Saturday evenings. During the meeting, they'd either prepare a drama to present, or a student would testify about becoming a born-again Christian, while another student would preach.

They'd spend their Saturday visiting villagers or doing a practical project to reach out to them. They invited those whom they had counseled or who had come to know Christ to attend their Sunday morning worship service. They'd return to Kagoro on Sunday afternoon to prepare for Monday morning classes.

When they returned, they shared encouraging testimonies with us about how some adults, youth, and children came to Christ or how some Christians rededicated their lives to the Lord. Their love for witnessing and discipleship, along with their simple trust in the Lord to meet their needs, challenged us to do the same. However, sometimes these groups received resistance from village heads and church leaders who thought they might want to steal their members.

Another way we tried to motivate our ETSK Missions department students and faculty was to begin a yearly Missions Day involving both our ETSK and Jos ECWA Theological Seminary's (JETS) missions departments' students and faculty. The Missions departments in both institutions were much smaller numerically than the Pastoral and Christian Education departments. One year, ETSK would be the host. The next year JETS would host the day.

We'd have a special theme for the day, have several speakers or students speak, and have reports from each school on what they had done in missions during the past year. Lunch and refreshments would be provided by the host, with a small charge to help toward the expenses. In 2018 and 2019, Missions departments' students and faculty from several other seminaries in the Jos area were also invited to attend.

Sending out ETSK students for holiday outreach

My prayer for many of these new Christians was that they'd not just be "Sunday Christians"—come to church on Sunday, not be involved in any other church or Christian services during the week, show up again the next Sunday, thinking that was all that Christianity was to be—but that they would make Christ a part of their everyday lives.

Students interested in cross-cultural missions proceeded to work with the EMS of ECWA. We worked with the area EMS coordinators several times to have interested ETSK students serve during the Christmas or summer break in missions ministries or for their required ten-week practical field service assignment with an EMS missionary. This gave them practical experience and helped others to hear the gospel or become more serious about serving the Lord. Some ETSK graduates have also chosen to apply to EMS of ECWA for full-time ministries. Other EMS of ECWA missionaries have come to ETSK to study in the Missions department to receive a certificate, diploma, B.A., or master's degree.

Probably the largest audience I have ever spoken to in Nigeria was at the 2019 EMS of ECWA Missions Conference in April in Jos. I shared what we were doing at Kagoro in the areas of skill development and how the delegates could benefit from learning a skill when ministering in an area that was dominated by Muslims or animists. Although I spoke in the dark that night, I received one of their daytime pictures of the delegates. Most of them came from all over Nigeria, with some coming from other countries where EMS served. This was a great privilege!

2019 EMS of ECWA Missions Conference

Theses and Writing

At ETSK, we enjoyed our teaching. Many of the students were very zealous about their studies. Unfortunately, many didn't have suitable elementary (primary) or high (secondary) school backgrounds, especially in their English studies, which adversely affected them when they were required to write assignments or type a paper.

Many of the students had to hire a typist to type their papers, especially during our first years at ETSK. Most didn't have the luxuries of knowing how to type or of owning a personal typewriter, computer, or printer. Some students who knew how to type worked part-time to type other students' theses, or some owned a printer and a small generator to print papers for them. In our later years at ETSK, more students saw the importance of buying their own laptops, which empowered them to become more independent. However, finances kept many students from buying one.

Right from my first courses taught, it didn't take much time for the ETSK students to learn that I was one of the most rigorous faculty members on campus. I had always been demanding at BMTC by expecting my students to complete their assignments on time and do their best in writing. Plagiarism wasn't allowed. I wasn't going to change now.

I used a red pen (biro) to correct writing or grammatical mistakes on their papers. I wasn't afraid to ask them to rewrite what they had written, especially if they had more than 10 or 20 mistakes on any given assignment. Even if there were many mistakes on the paper, which was often the case, I usually marked them one by one and rarely overlooked any.

Since English wasn't their first language, most of them had to rewrite many of my homework assignments and small papers in my courses. Some liked my style; others hated it. I was told that sometimes when students would look at the semester's schedule and see that I was to be their instructor, they'd be told by their friends to switch to an easier course.

However, some students were brave enough to register for my courses. If they stayed with me until the end of the semester, many later returned to say, "Thank you for taking the extra time to help me improve my written and spoken English." They saw some improvements and were proud of themselves. They wished that more of the faculty would follow my example.

Once one older student asked me about his paper on which I had marked many mistakes with red, "What will happen if I show my papers to my children? There are too many red corrections on them." Of course, he didn't want to be embarrassed. However, I didn't let that stop me from continuing my style and requirements. I wanted him to learn to write better. I believe that my commitment to excellence benefited all my students in ministry and life.

Correcting student homework or major papers took me many hours, but I believe that my efforts over the years helped many of the students to do better in all their ETSK courses and later studies. We were happy to see many complete their master's programs at ETSK, with some going on to begin or complete their doctoral programs in Nigeria, South Africa, or the U.S.

Several times I had more than a one-foot pile of papers and exams from my courses to correct during the Christmas break. It took me until early March to complete those corrections between teaching new courses and carrying on regular duties.

One of the most challenging assignments for Coletta and me as ETSK faculty members was to be student thesis advisors for the B.A. and master's degree students. The thesis was to be about 65 pages double-spaced on a topic relating to the student's major. Doing a thesis was one essential requirement of every B.A. or master's degree student. After serving for several semesters, Coletta asked the ETSK leaders not to give her more theses to supervise since this wasn't one of her strengths. It took time away from other ministries in which she was uniquely gifted. They agreed.

I started with theses from some B.A. students and later added on master's level students. To do an excellent job as an advisor demanded many hours over many months or longer to edit each of their five chapters until the student could present a credible thesis. Most of those I supervised were Missions majors.

Any student under my supervision had to write with good English grammar, with proper footnoting and form. Typically, students did much better in speaking orally than in writing. However, I usually didn't overlook many of their mistakes. After much hard work and following my suggestions, which usually were many, the students joyfully handed me their final copy. Finally, with my approval, they happily handed in their theses to get bound to present to the academic dean. I was happy, too!

One day, a female B.A. thesis student began crying as she sat at my table on our screened-in porch. Previously, she had presented me with several past drafts. I still had many red marks on her latest draft for more corrections and page retyping. She told me that she didn't have any more money to print her pages and didn't know what to do. I asked Coletta to join me to comfort her. Somehow, she returned later with a revised draft. I accepted it, and she graduated. Overseeing students' theses also wasn't my favorite ministry responsibility!

ETSK graduates

Graduations

One of our greatest yearly joys was attending ETSK's annual November graduation. While in their studies, some excelled, and others struggled. Some faced complex family issues and financial hardships. However, finally, most graduated. That thrilled each student, the faculty, the staff, and the graduates' families. Several times family members were so happy for the student to graduate that they danced and shouted so loudly when the student's name was called that it disturbed the ceremony and the master of ceremonies had to ask them to stop.

ETSK has seen over 3,500 men and women graduate from its programs since it began in 1930. Over the past few years, we've seen over 150 students graduate yearly, including various M.A. and M.Div. students. The new Ph.D. program began in 2019. Its first graduating class hopes to graduate in 2024 or 2025.

While serving at ETSK, one rewarding benefit was seeing our students and alumni use what they had learned from their classes. Some used the principles gained from their Personal Evangelism and Discipleship course to continue connecting with their disciples over the years. Some ETSK graduates who were in our B.A. and master's level courses have gone on to do their Ph.D. studies in various Nigerian universities or South Africa. Others are close to completing their Ph.D. studies or are now ETSK faculty or faculty in other ECWA Bible colleges throughout northern Nigeria.

One example is Rev. Yusuf Gajere, our current ETSK deputy provost. He attended my History of Christian Missions course in 2007. We've served together on various committees, such as the Work-Study Scholarship Committee, and in developing our SAC. He has just completed his Ph.D. studies in New Testament at one of Nigeria's universities and has been a full-time ETSK teacher for many years.

Many others have graduated with certificates, diplomas, or their B.A. or master's degree in theology, Christian education, or missions. Many are pastors of ECWA or other denominations. Some are missionaries with EMS of ECWA or are teaching Christian Religious Studies in Christian or public elementary (primary) or high (secondary) schools. Others teach God's Word in their local churches whenever needed. No matter how far they've gone academically. God is using them to touch lives for Christ!

Campus Development and Public Relations

During my years at BMTC as a teacher and provost, I enjoyed working in the areas of public relations and printing. These interests continued when I was at ETSK, where I served for several years either as a graduation program committee member or their chairman.

As I adapted more to life at ETSK, I served on several committees to raise funds to construct and renovate old buildings and to expand the capacity of ETSK. In addition, with God's leading and grace, we teamed up with some of our faithful supporting churches, especially MABC in Mount Airy, Maryland. They played a major part in supporting various projects all over the campus, such as providing funds to begin the concrete tank fishery project to raise and smoke catfish. They were major supporters of funding dorm and building projects, buying a new electric transformer to help us get more steady electricity for the campus, strengthening our computer center, buying more library books, funding the student scholarship fund, and resourcing a classroom reroofing project. Many individual and church sponsors also rallied with us over the years.

We began the ETSK Student Work-Study Scholarship fund to help students work part-time and have that money paid toward their semester tuition fees. About 50 students continue to benefit each semester from these scholarships.

Although I never took professional training in writing project grant proposals, God opened doors for us. One Christian ministry matched a partial grant to build the two Grace Dormitories, each housing eight families. Because of limited buildings on the campus for student housing, there were more single men than families who wanted to live on campus. Sometimes up to ten students shared one of these family apartments.

Grace Dorm dedication

Other donors gave funds to renovate seven old student dormitories, reroof the old classroom block and chapel, and buy library books and resources. Supporters also helped ETSK paint various buildings and buy classroom chairs.

We continue to connect with many of these Nigerian brethren. We're encouraged by how God uses them, sustains them, and protects them under difficult economic and political tensions. Some have been persecuted and martyred for their faith! Others are widows and widowers. They are great examples of keeping on, being strong in the Lord, and doing what is right, no matter what! Coletta and I thank God for leading us to serve at ETSK and using our spiritual gifts and training to equip more men and women for His service.

Coletta's thoughts:

I did a lot more teaching at ETSK than at Ikwa. My first set of nine students in Basic English was either French-speaking from surrounding countries or Hausa-speaking from the far North of Nigeria. Many had poor educational backgrounds, and a few had learning disabilities. I enjoyed teaching English to them, as they had positive attitudes and were very grateful for the opportunity to improve their English. The class was small enough that I could work individually with them.

Later, I taught students in ETKS's one-year program of Preliminary Studies that had 40 or 50 students. Their attitudes weren't as good, and I couldn't do any individual work with them. Just keeping up with marking assignments, tests, and papers was overwhelming. Dennis and I developed this program for students who didn't pass ETSK's entrance exams the first time. They needed skill building. A second opportunity was given after their one year of studies to retake the exams and be considered for official admission. Many who went through the year of studies passed the exam and were admitted into various programs according to their results.

It was our great joy to see our students progress from one level to the next and finally graduate into ministry at their ability level. Many served in small village churches. Others served in large city churches. Some became country-wide leaders.

Most of them faithfully served God under very challenging conditions and in survival mode with limited salaries, threats from terrorist groups, and poor infrastructures for water and electricity. We thank God that we had a small part in training them and encouraging them along the journey.

Chapter 23

Serving with SIM and Other Missionaries at Kagoro

"I always thank my God as I remember you in my prayers, because I hear about your faith in the Lord Jesus and your love for all the saints. I pray that you may be active in sharing your faith, so that you will have a full understanding of every good thing we have in Christ. Your love has given me great joy and encouragement, because you, brother, have refreshed the hearts of the saints"
(Philemon 4–7).

During our years at Kagoro, Coletta and I used our spiritual gifts to help coordinate trips to Nigeria for various American visitors and groups. We had our FIM General Director Dr. Paul Barreca visit us. Other FIM leaders, Dr. Francisco DeSouza and Dean Ressler, came on one trip.

One of our Calvary Church missionaries, Phil Morrison, who served with Africa Inland Mission in Kenya, came to teach a seminar based on his book, *The Multi-Church Pastor*. Our Calvary Church missions pastor, Steve Beirn, and his wife, Lorraine, visited us for one week in 2016. Several other SIM missionaries, such as Ralph Sauers and Jon Banke, stayed overnight with us on trips to Jos to or from Abuja.

We worked with Bible Centered Ministries International (BCMI) and the ECWA Christian Education Department in Jos to have various BCMI trainers come to Nigeria to equip many of ECWA's children's workers throughout the country. Some trainers who came were Stephen and Jane King, Olga Zaitseva, Pat Black, and Marion Brandt. They traveled to various parts of Nigeria before it became riskier for them as expatriates to travel southward in the country. Later they remained in Jos and led seminars for invited ECWA children's workers from various regions of the country. These national workers are now using the BCMI curriculum: In Step with the Master Teacher.

We greatly appreciated the fellowship and bonding with various SIM-Nigeria missionaries and ECWA national leaders during our years at Kagoro. As SIM associate missionaries, SIM gave us full privileges to visit their Jos offices during regular weekday work hours to use their facilities and services, obtain assistance in applying for our resident permits or visas, or take us to or from the Abuja airport. They reached out to us when we'd face a problem, like sending two SIM missionaries to debrief us when robbers attacked the Colvin's compound next to us.

David & Debbie, Dee, and Cheryl & Donna

In addition, when we visited Jos, we joined other SIM missionaries for their first Friday of the month potluck supper and time of praise, prayer, and fellowship. This was usually at Peter and Miriam Fretheim's home. This helped us build close relationships over the years with various SIM missionaries and their families.

We also enjoyed close bonds with our SIM missionary colleagues at Kagoro and Samaru. David and Debbie Colvin lived next to our house. During our years at Kagoro, the families of other SIMers—Dr. Rick and Alanna Creighton and Kevin and Alexis Stokes, along with Dee Grimes— lived on the campus.

Periodically, we'd drive 12 miles to the compound of Cheryl and Donna Pridham, SIM Canadian missionaries, who taught at ECWA's Widow's School in Samaru for many years. Judy Strand occasionally visited us from Gure. We'd celebrate one of our team's birthdays or have a special holiday potluck meal. They were great cooks and bakers. As a result, we always left their home with extra-full stomachs.

2019 - With the Creightons at Christmas

We who lived in Kagoro tried to meet weekly for a Thursday night prayer meeting and fellowship. We occasionally entertained various U.S. visitors who were passing through.

As SIM associate missionaries, Coletta and I were each asked to serve on a board of governors in one of ECWA's educational institutions. I represented SIM for most of my years under SIM as a member of the JETS Board of Governors. Coletta served on the ECWA Widows' School Board of Governors in Samaru.

SIM allowed us to stay at their Woyke Guest House in Jos for a small charge for overnight accommodations. In addition, under SIM's umbrella, we paid lower tuition for Dwight and Stephanie during their high school years at Hillcrest. SIM gave us discounts at their Miango Rest Home (MRH) when we'd attend their annual January Spiritual Life Conference or other yearly events, such as their Easter "Fun in the Sun" weekend getaways, to provide us with spiritual and physical refreshment. Miango was 45 miles from Kagoro and 15 miles from Jos.

SIM required that we attend SIM's Spiritual Life Conferences. Excellent SIM guest speakers, often those who had served around the world, ministered to us. We had great meals and fellowship with other SIM missionaries from all over Nigeria. A special treat was being able to choose various types of doughnuts to eat from several hundred freshly made by the Pridhams. In the afternoons, participants could rest, attend a seminar, hike in the rocky hills around Miango, or go swimming at a resort hotel near Jos.

One of the U.S. SIM missionary families at MRH, Dr. Steve and Ruth Porter, ran a dental clinic for SIM missionaries, other non-SIM expatriate missionaries, and some Nigerians with dental problems. Steve was a professional dentist who was trained in the U.S. Ruth and several Nigerian-trained workers assisted him. They spent over 30 years ministering at Miango. Under SIM, their dental charges were about half of what we'd pay for similar dental care in the U.S.

The Porters used their spiritual gifts well in serving, giving, hospitality, and member care. They had a particular burden to provide rest to us SIM missionaries, so we wouldn't burn out. With the help of various supporters, they renovated the MRH Grace Cottage.

Steve and Ruth allowed SIM couples or singles to stay in Grace Cottage free of charge for up to three days per year. They had upgraded this cottage with enough solar power to run its refrigerator and provide hot water for our showers when NEPA wasn't on. It had well-kept screens to keep out bugs and mosquitoes. Upon arrival, we'd find some notes and snacks on the counter with more snacks and cold soft drinks in the refrigerator. A microwave was in the kitchen to help us warm up food quickly or pop some microwave popcorn. Christian DVDs, music tapes, and messages from prominent groups and speakers were there to listen to or to watch on the TV.

Before our arrival, the Porters would send us a detailed, well-laid-out menu of a full-course supper they would provide during our stay as their special guests in their screened-in outside pavilion next to their home. We could choose our appetizer, beverage, main course, type of salad, and a fancy dessert with something to drink. Steve and Ruth were the servers. All this was for them to say thank you for our service to the Lord in Nigeria and provide us with some much-needed downtime and rest from our busy ministry schedules.

Many people were blessed through their ministries. They had a fruitful discipleship ministry over the years and were examples of how to care for their daughter, Julie, who was an adult in her 30s with special needs. They'd take Julie to some of the church services and activities at Miango. Julie was loved by both the missionaries and the nationals.

Memories like these continue to bond us with many of these missionaries and Christian friends. God is using them wherever they are, whether overseas or in their home countries, to equip nationals for ministry and challenge others to go and reach others for Christ. There's still much to do for the Lord!

Coletta's thoughts:

We had a few missionary colleagues at Ikwa, but for most of my years there, our family members were the only expatriates. That certainly helped to create deep bonds with our national brethren. At Kagoro, we had several expatriate colleagues from different countries. I was used to working with international teams in Ecuador, so it was a pleasure to develop new friendships. Some of them have developed into life-long friends.

Grace Cottage was our number one destination to celebrate our wedding anniversary. If our anniversary fell during the work week, we went there either the weekend before or after. It was so much fun to be thoroughly spoiled. We spent our last few days in Nigeria in February 2020 at Grace Cottage.

Ruth also had a food ministry for missionaries living off the plateau. She froze large quantities of vegetables that didn't grow in other areas. We took an ice chest and filled it with frozen veggies and berries bought at a moderate cost from

Ruth to take back to Kagoro to provide quick meals in an environment where food preparation and cooking were all from scratch.

On my way to the corner shop at Kagoro to buy groceries, I would stop by Debbie Colvin's compound to have a cup of coffee on her back porch, while Debbie drank tea and offered chocolate cake.

Chapter 24

Dwight and Stephanie Off to College and Beyond

"Cast all your anxiety on him because he cares for you" (I Peter 5:7).

Over the years, Coletta and I saw God continually lead us one step at a time. Sometimes it was scary. Other times we moved ahead, confident that God was moving us in the right direction. We saw the same for Dwight and Stephanie relating to their education. During their senior high school years at Hillcrest, we prayed for God's guidance for them as they considered taking their next step to attend college in the U.S.

Hillcrest School's high academic standards helped Dwight and Stephanie learn to handle much homework and other requirements proficiently. As a result, they both received Hillcrest's Honor Society and Student of the Year awards. In addition, they were learning how to independently handle each challenge that came their way.

Seeing them off to college was a big step for us. Coletta and I didn't have much money saved to send them to a big college or university. Dwight wanted to play college soccer and searched for some small U.S. colleges that offered sports scholarships to help him pay his tuition fees.

2011 - Our family

In the back of our minds, we would have liked both Dwight and Stephanie to study at a Bible college for at least one year before going on to another university or college. To our surprise, one day Dwight asked us, "Dad and Mom, what would you think if I went to LBC for my studies?" We happily replied, "That would be great,

Dwight." He informed us that LBC had offered him more scholarships than any other college he desired to attend.

A year before, while we were in the U.S. on home assignment, we had arranged to have an LBC staff member take Dwight and us for a tour around their campus. We met one of their athletic coaches, who encouraged Dwight to consider studying there.

LBC Soccer Team after they won

Since Coletta and I were still full-time missionaries serving at ETSK, we were excited to see the children move on to college. When Coletta's parents went to be with the Lord in 1996 and 1997, they had left some funds from their estate, which we invested in mutual funds.

We used these funds for each of them to buy a good, used car, with the balance to be used for personal needs or college tuition. This was a big boost for them to become more independent while we were in Nigeria. They both developed good friendships with Christian friends at college. They also kept in touch with some of their Nigerian and expatriate friends from Hillcrest through Facebook and email.

Dwight accepted LBC's offer and chose a double major: Bible and health education. It would take him four and a half years to complete instead of the regular four-year program. It all worked out well for him. He enjoyed his studies, did some part-time work on the LBC campus, and traveled for two summers with LBC's Team Chargers ministry team. They visited various camps along the northeastern U.S. to recruit potential LBC students. He joined LBC's men's soccer team, which had a winning record.

As for Stephanie, she had much interest in becoming a nurse, like Coletta. She gathered information from various nursing colleges. During one of our summer visits to the U.S., we took her to Messiah College to see their nursing department. Later, she decided to attend Eastern Mennonite University (EMU) in Harrisonburg, Virginia, for their four-year nursing program.

Whether Coletta and I were in Nigeria or the U.S., we worked hard to prioritize calling or emailing Dwight and Stephanie at least weekly. As a result, God helped us have very close relationships with them. It took a lot of effort, but it was all worth it. Other groups from our supporting churches, such as the Word of Life Chapel, sent care packages to Dwight and Stephanie while they were in college. They included snacks, school supplies, and toiletries. That was one way to let them know that the church members were thinking about and praying for them during their studies.

During the fall of 2011, Dwight and a team of LBC students had an interest in coming to Nigeria for a 2012 two-week summer ministry trip with SIM's City Ministries in Jos. To research this possibility, LBC sent Bob McMichael, one of the LBC recruiting staff, and Dwight to Nigeria. They came to attend our ETSK graduation and see where the team would serve at Kagoro and Jos. They were happy at what they saw and enjoyed meeting many people at the graduation and in Jos.

That following summer, Dwight and Stephanie came to Nigeria with the LBC team of 17 students. Bob was their leader. Mrs. Naomi Rhoads, the wife of one of the LBC faculty, and Scott Harrison, the husband of one of the LBC staff, were two chaperones.

The day after the team arrived at Kagoro, the LBC men played ETSK in a friendly soccer match. The LBC men beat them 5 to 0. The Nigerians had never played a team with so many white people on the opposing team, which also beat them!

Their schedule was packed with variety and exposure to various ministries at ETSK and City Ministries in Jos, Plateau State. Scott, who was the father of eight children, preached the first Sunday at the ETSK Church. Many who had large families at ETSK hit it off well with Scott since most Americans had much smaller families.

At Jos, the team reached out to various arms of City Ministries. They visited outreaches to widows and orphans and stayed in Jos nightly at the Baptist Guesthouse. One of their most memorable events was visiting a village near Jos, where hundreds of people had been massacred by Boko Haram militants. The Voice of the Martyrs had erected a unique memorial to remember those killed. Some living family members shared testimonies with the team about horrific events that had happened then. Many tears were shed that day.

While in Jos, Naomi Rhodes played soccer and badly injured her ankle. At the Jos Hospital, it was confirmed that she had broken it and needed a cast. We were happy that this event didn't cause Naomi to leave Nigeria before the team ended its ministries. Instead, God used it to bond the team members together.

Coletta and I visited the LBC team for one night in Jos. At 8:50, the flying ants began coming toward the guesthouse's outside fluorescent lights by the thousands. Dwight and Stephanie, who had learned how to catch them at Ikwa when they were younger, showed the team how to catch them, take off their two sets of wings, and then fry them the following day, so they could eat fried flying ants. Dwight said some of the team liked them, some were indifferent, and others thought they were gross.

LBC team after ETSK Church service

The day the team left Kagoro to return to the U.S., they joined us for the ETSK Church service, which ETSK Provost Rev. Prof. Sunday Agang concluded by serving communion. Dwight was asked to preach. This was one of the first messages that he had ever preached in a church service. He did a fine job. Like me, preaching became one of Dwight's greatest joys in ministry.

When the team said their goodbyes from our house that afternoon, they wondered why Coletta and I hugged Dwight and Stephanie tightly and cried as we saw them go. It was because we weren't expecting to see them for another 18 months. However, little did we know that I'd have back issues that would make us return to the U.S. one month later.

During Dwight's senior year at LBC, he was captain of their men's soccer team. He was also chosen as the LBC Male Student of the Year. The LBC leaders informed us just before the event. They invited us to attend personally or to recommend some people to represent us if we couldn't come. Since we were involved in teaching in Nigeria and couldn't quickly adjust our schedules to travel home, we chose the latter option.

Dwight with Coach Tolar

Dwight asked Coach Jay and Heidi Tolar to come from Charlotte, North Carolina. Others who represented us were Denny and Bonnie Sharp (my brother-in-law and sister) and Mike and Dee Lindsey (Coletta's brother-in-law and her sister). They all willingly accepted.

What made that occasion so special was that Coach Tolar played a big part in discipling

Dwight at Hillcrest during Dwight's high school days. Coach was then battling advanced Lou Gehrig's disease. His acceptance to come with his family to attend that banquet was a great honor for Dwight.

Coach's godly example encouraged Dwight to continue passing on to others what Coach had taken much time and effort to pass on to Dwight in discipleship. Many others learned much from Coach at Hillcrest over the years that he and Heidi served with SIM in Nigeria. Coach went to be with the Lord in September 2014.

2014 – Stephanie's EMU Graduation

Stephanie joined a group of EMU students to travel for one semester throughout the Middle East and Italy to be exposed to living in other countries. She later took a short-term trip to Thailand with a team from Calvary Church. They ministered to missionary kids who attended a missionary conference with their parents. She enjoyed going with another team from Calvary Church to serve at Camp Nathaniel in Kentucky.

Coletta and I attended both Dwight and Stephanie's college graduations. We tried to support and encourage them as much as we could. Life for us as cross-cultural missionaries and for the children as TCKs was definitely different. Their worldviews as MKs were broader and more balanced than most of their contemporaries, many of whom had never lived or traveled outside their state or the U.S.

After Dwight graduated from LBC, he returned to Nigeria to teach at Hillcrest School for four and a half years, four of them as Hillcrest's youth pastor. Along with these duties, he also coached several school sports teams. During those years, he met Amy Kringle, Hillcrest's fifth grade teacher. They began dating. He proposed to her on Valentine's Day, 2017. They returned to the U.S. in May and were married in the Minneapolis, Minnesota area on July 30, 2017.

Stephanie graduated from EMS in April 2014, then worked at Lancaster General Hospital in their behavioral health department for several years, before moving on to several other health-related jobs. She lives in an apartment in Lititz, Pennsylvania.

While on home assignment in the summer of 2016, Coletta was diagnosed with breast cancer. She had surgery, followed by radiation from October through December. Then she began five years of hormone therapy. This required us to return yearly for follow-up. She has been cancer-free for the last seven years.

We thank the Lord for how Dwight and Stephanie have desired to follow God's leading and to use their talents and spiritual gifts to be a blessing to many. We know many Christians were not only praying for Coletta and me but also for God to bless and direct Dwight and Stephanie.

June 30, 2017 - Dwight & Amy's wedding

Coletta's thoughts:

I loved being closer to Dwight and Stephanie during their last few years at Hillcrest. Before we knew it, they were off to attend college and university in the U.S. Once again, we were separated by long distances. Our weekly phone calls and emails continued.

We are grateful to friends and family members who took them in during those summers and holidays. SIM advised us to physically see our adult children once a year while they were in college. We either went to the U.S. for a short holiday or home assignment, or they came to visit us in Nigeria. My need to get yearly checkups for five years after having breast cancer helped us come home to see the children.

I found separations more difficult as the children grew older and had bigger issues to deal with. For me, in-country separations were easier than being continents and days of travel apart, especially if some kind of crisis was in progress. Thankfully, cell phone and email services did improve over the years.

I found this prayer, which was a hymn written by Isabella S. Stevenson, when we sent Dwight and Stephanie to boarding school and college. I still use it today:

Holy Father, in Thy mercy,
Hear our anxious prayer.
Keep our loved ones, now far distant,
'Neath Thy care.

Jesus, Savior, let Thy presence
Be their light and guide;
Keep, oh, keep them, in their weakness,
At Thy side.

When in sorrow, when in danger,
When in loneliness,
In Thy love look down and comfort
Their distress.

May the joy of Thy salvation
Be their strength and stay;
May they love and may they praise Thee
Day by day.

Holy Spirit, let Thy teaching
Sanctify their life;
Send Thy grace, that they may conquer
In the strife.

Father, Son, and Holy Spirit,
God the One in Three,
Bless them, guide them, save them, keep them
Near to Thee.[11]

Chapter 25

Skill Acquisition Training at Kagoro

"Make it your ambition to lead a quiet life, to mind your own business and to work with your hands, just as we told you, so that your daily life may win the respect of outsiders and so that you will not be dependent on anybody"
(I Thessalonians 4:11).

My interest in gardening and using the soil around my house to grow things continued from working in my parent's garden. When I went to Nigeria, I tried to grow cucumbers, sweet corn, and tomatoes in the tropical soil of Ikwa. Over the years, we involved our BMTC students in growing crops such as yams, cassava, and rice. Later we raised broiler chickens, pigs, and catfish. At one time, we raised about 100 pigs of various sizes right behind my house. Sometimes the smells weren't the best. We wanted our students to try to grow similar crops and raise animals back in their home areas to help support themselves after they graduated. Some did just that.

Computers at BMTC and ETSK

At BMTC, we wanted our students to learn to use computers. One Christian foundation from the U.S. helped us obtain funds to begin a small Computer Studies Center in 2003. It was run by one of our graduates who became a faithful faculty member, Mr. Moses Oluwole.

At ETSK, we were later able to receive a grant from a U.S. Christian foundation to buy some computers and a satellite dish to connect to the internet from our village. As a result, we expanded the small computer café. We faced challenges of poor connections, bad weather, and unreliable computer repairs to keep everything working well. However, we never gave up. With the help of MABC, we bought some computers and further expanded the café.

Strategic Cross-Training and Its Benefits

My attitude toward a more holistic ministry changed over the years while I was in Nigeria. In my first years of teaching, I thought that unless someone came to Bible college and then went on to study mainly Bible-related majors, they were out of God's will. This bubbled up when 19 of our BMTC graduates had the opportunity to go to WBC in Lanham, Maryland, to complete their B.A. studies. I was unhappy that some wanted to further their M.A. or Ph.D. studies in other disciplines, like education and business administration.

However, over the years, I've changed my perspective and seen that God leads each believer differently since we're created differently by Him for a unique purpose. We need faithful, committed Christians with their B.A., M.A., or Ph.D. in various disciplines to live faithfully for the Lord in the secular workplace. Nigeria would be a much better place if we could encourage and support more influential Nigerian Christians to serve the Lord in politics, business, and the workplace without yielding or compromising their values and following the corrupt practices around them. We've seen some of our BMTC graduates return to Nigeria from their U.S. studies with their master's or Ph.D. degrees, while others have remained in the U.S. to be used by the Lord in education and other areas of work.

ETSK's Strategy and Expansion

In July 2007, our interest in training our students in practical ways continued from Ikwa to Kagoro when Coletta and I began ministry at ETSK in Kaduna State. Our belief was even stronger that God could use our students and Christians trained in these areas to help tackle some of today's challenges in Nigeria. We saw the need to train our students in skills, like computer studies, to complement their theological studies.

In 2010, MABC gave funds for us to begin a fishery to raise and dry catfish. We wanted to see this project help more of our faculty, staff, and students get more protein and better food in their families' diets. Some of them could also learn how to raise catfish and begin such projects where they'd live after graduating.

During the long holiday break of 2017, I saw that we needed to expand training our ETSK students in other practical skills. We began to share this opportunity with our Christian friends and supporters in my monthly email updates. Our vision for this SAC was to empower more students to learn at least one essential skill to complement their theological studies before graduating. In addition, our faculty and staff could also benefit from learning these skills.

Right after this, I shared this vision with a Christian couple from New York, Peter and Chris Mason. They wanted to play a part in supporting this new endeavor. They had previously supported a SAC in another country, but the center's teacher left that ministry. Thus, they stopped supporting it. However, they still had much interest in supporting our vision at ETSK and gave $5,000 (about N1.7 million) to help us start.

With these funds and several other gifts, we renovated a storage room and bought various new and used equipment. Examples were hand saws and a new, small diesel generator on four wheels to move around to places where welding was needed. In addition, we repaired some of the ETSK Women's Institute sewing machines.

ETSK diesel generator for welding

Our training of 30 ETSK students and staff began in the January to May 2018 semester. Students in seven skill acquisition sections spent at least three hours weekly learning one skill in carpentry/furniture making, masonry/building construction, welding, raising catfish, computer studies, men's tailoring, and women's sewing.

Each week these students met with their SAC trainer. This training didn't take many hours daily or continue for months or years, so it wouldn't conflict with their theological studies. Our main goal was to expose the students to basic principles to get them started in that skill. It could challenge them to continue with part two of the SAC training or go on to future skill acquisition training after ETSK.

Initially, the section with the most interest was men's tailoring, with ten men benefiting from it. They learned to make shirts and trousers. They were very proud of their work and wore these items to chapel as they learned from Bukar Adamu, one of our ETSK B.A. seniors.

In early 2018, another gift of $7,000 (about N2.5 million) from the estate of Harold Brandt, a U.S. Christian businessman who named ETSK as a beneficiary, helped us begin a new SAC building.

Other Christians have since given toward this to complete the two-floor building in 2019 and purchase more tools and electrical equipment to empower our current

The ETSK SAC building

sections. It has six rooms for individual training sections.

In my October 2018 ETSK chapel talk on *Skill Acquisition*, I asked the students, "What would happen if your ECWA District Church Council or another ministry interviewed you and another candidate for a job? The other candidate had learned some skills like computer studies, carpentry, and welding. Being compared to him, you didn't know how to use the computer or have any other skills. Who would that ministry be more likely to hire? Could having at least one skill, along with your theological studies, help you better support yourself and your family now and in the future?"

Their answer was obviously, "Yes." The ministry would hire a candidate with more skills and training. Such skills could supplement their needs at ETSK and afterward in their ministries. I encouraged students and adults not to wait until they had enough money or could take out a large agricultural loan before becoming involved in a small farm or business project. They should start with what they had and see God bless it as they faithfully used what God had already given them.

In that same chapel, I challenged staff and students not to hide from us the training they had in specific skills. They could use this to help us teach others while at ETSK. I had chats with several of them later. One had skills in photography and video production. Another knew how to make insecticides, disinfectants, hand soap, and detergent. Several other students wanted to enroll immediately in one of our SAC sections. We told them they had to wait and register when we began our next semester. This was very encouraging.

SAC Working Hand-in-Hand with Work Scholarships

During one chapel, several student testimonies were given by students who had learned skills before coming to ETSK. They shared how their training had helped them to work in the ETSK Student Work-Study Scholarship Program so they could work part-time to raise money to pay for part of their school fees. We used some of these same students as trainers in these sections.

The SAC Program is closely connected to our ETSK Student Work-Study Scholarship Program. Over the past few years, we've seen at least 50 students each semester benefit from doing some part-time work on campus to supplement their school tuition fees. Some students were already trained carpenters, masons, builders, plumbers, tailors, or seamstresses. As a result, they had a better chance of working in needed areas on campus and receiving scholarship funds from donors than those who never had such training. Rev. Joseph Jeraba is the SAC coordinator now.

Success Stories

The response by the students and some of the faculty and staff who've taken these SAC courses so far has been very encouraging, especially in the men's tailoring and women's sewing sections. The men made a man's shirt and a pair of trousers. The ladies sewed a new dress that gave them the enthusiasm to learn more.

We have other examples of present and past alumni whose skills helped them pay their tuition fees.

Rev. Jeraba with ladies and their sewn dresses

Engine Repair

One example is Rev. Daniel Gufwat. He learned how to repair engines when he was young. While at ETSK for his B.A. and M.A. studies, he worked hard and successfully repaired generators and lawnmowers. He helped our family repair our lawnmower, car, and generator.

Now as an ECWA minister in Barkin Ladi, Plateau State, he is a friend and witness to Christians and Muslims in his

Rev. Daniel Gufwat repairing our mower

area. They go to him to repair their engines and generators.

Welding

Beds made in the welding section

Samuel Sheyin was a professional welder for more than five years with Power Works Construction Company in Jos. God led him to do his B.A. in Missions at ETSK. He used his welding skills to support himself through the ETSK Scholarship Program.

While a student, Samuel was the welding trainer under the SAC. He taught basic welding skills to different students and our Deputy Provost Rev. Dr. Yusuf Gajere. With ETSK's portable diesel welding machine, Samuel repaired doors and chairs and constructed metal beds and doors for ETSK. The students under him wanted to learn more, so they continued with part two in welding during their next semester.

Sewing and Tailoring

Pastor Bulus Maitalata, an ETSK alumnus, has used his past carpentry, construction, sewing, and tailoring skills to support himself. While at ETSK, he taught sewing at the ETSK Women's Institute. Such skills continue to help him in his current ministry as an ECWA pastor.

Construction

Pastor Andrew Bature, another ETSK alumnus, has personally been hired by ETSK with contracts to build various projects on the campus over the years. He returned to do his B.A. studies at ETSK. As a builder, his name is indirectly engraved in many of our current buildings, such as the 16-family unit Grace Dorm, seven renovated dorms for married students, and the new SAC.

He would often be seen working in the hot sun after his afternoon classes or during a school holiday to see progress on these buildings. In addition, his skills have helped him teach some students in construction and masonry work. The program has benefited him by gaining partial scholarship funds to help pay some of his B.A. tuition fees and support his family.

Raising Catfish

Dried catfish from the fishery

MABC's gift to build our catfish tanks has helped many of our students, staff, and local villagers get good protein (and vegetables from the fishery's garden) for themselves and their families. Since it began in 2010, we've raised many lots of 500 to 1,000 or more catfish at a time of different sizes to later sell. Sometimes we've bought lots of catfish up to one or two pounds (0.5 to 1 kg.) each and kept them in our fish tanks to sell fresh or to smoke.

Smoking fish helps many people to preserve what they buy since many don't have a refrigerator, freezer, or steady electricity. ETSK has never made any significant profit from the fishery. This is because of poverty and many people not being able to pay the cost of raising them. However, some have bought fresh, dried, and smoked catfish. ETSK has learned much and still is learning. They've bought a small machine to make pelleted fish feed. The fishery staff taught the students how to dry and smoke fish and hatch catfish fry (babies).

Another Christian ministry from Jos has assisted us financially to expand the fishery. They gave us a used generator to pump water when the fishery needed more water. The power could also give light to the SAC building. Several students learned the basics of the fishery over two semesters. One lady from the Gidan Waya College of Education also did her internship at the fishery with us in early 2018. Kagoro indigenes and local restaurant owners have patronized us regularly.

Run-off water from the fishponds is an excellent fertilizer, which we used in our Kagoro gardens. One papaya variety from Israel that we bought from Kaduna Vom near Jos and planted in our ETSK garden next to the fishery produced fruit from their short trunks about two feet off the ground instead of eight to ten feet off the ground. We tried to grow some seedlings from these papaya seeds to sell to interested buyers. Papaya is an excellent fruit to eat. From this garden adjacent to the fishery, we've sold spinach (ogu), Kafi ogu (chaya), papaya (popos), and other seedlings for people to grow in their gardens.

Beekeeping

Several years before we left Kagoro, we had an interest in beginning a beekeeping section. One of the Kagoro indigenes helped us get started with a hive on our compound. We bought a beekeeper's outfit and some basic beekeeping tools from the U.S. We also worked with several ETSK students who had learned beekeeping from their parents or others in their home villages.

Enjoying a harvest of honey

One of our students, Pastor Tanko Baba, led one SAC beekeeping section while studying for his B.A. and M.A. Several men had to stop their involvement because they were allergic to bee stings, becoming very swollen or sick. Tanko has been overseeing eleven beehives on our compound and another adjacent compound. Some hives were made by local carpenters, while several were large clay pots made by village women. Those hives were turned upside down with a small hole in the front and back for bees to enter and depart. Some who've taken this training have made hives back in their home villages.

Having one or more beehives in one's garden or farm can help produce 30–40 percent more crops, as the bees help pollinate the crops that have blossoms. The types of crops that the bees get nectar from will determine the color of the honey. That's why honey from the forest is often darker in color. Nectar coming from fruit trees is lighter.

Being a Model in Caring for the Environment and the Local People

Coletta and I used our compound to be an example to our faculty, staff, and students in what they could grow back at their homes or places where they would be posted to teach, preach, or do church planting. We raised various varieties of papayas (popos), oranges, mangoes, tangelos, avocados, guava, plantains, bananas, tomatoes, cucumbers, leaf lettuce, mulberries, sweet corn, and sweet potatoes. Other greens raised were moringa (zogale) and spinach (ogu). One other local vegetable we grew was Kafi ogu (chaya). It was known as "more than ogu" or "hospital is far." If a person ate it, it would give good iron and vitamins, so that they wouldn't need to go to the hospital so often.

We also bought palm kernel seedlings from contacts with the Nigerian Institute for Palm Oil Research in Warri, Delta States, to help some of our local people grow palm trees to produce their palm oil. Most of it came from the South and was very expensive to buy around Kagoro. We raised some ginger and turmeric on our compound. We made a small snailery and sold some to Ibo and Yoruba staff and students whose tribes liked to eat them.

Growing these items on our compound helped us save money at the local markets during certain seasons of the year. When we had more fruit or vegetables than we could eat, we often gave them to the students who worked on our compound or to the faculty or staff. We often took several large feed sacks of oranges to ETSK chapels or Sunday morning services to give several oranges to each member who attended. Sometimes 200–300 people at one service benefited from these efforts.

Sometimes when a student or a child was sick, we'd give them some food from our garden. Other times some students' money had all been spent, and we'd help them dig some sweet potatoes or cut some ogu or Kafi ogu leaves to put in their soup. We didn't sell these items. However, if students learned to grow them on their compound or for their church back home, it would be easy for them to eat some and sell others in the market for a small profit to get some cash in hand.

We also tried to be good examples of keeping the environment clean and putting back some of our harvest into the soil. For example, we didn't burn our leaves and grass on our compound but put them in compost piles for them to decay. Then, after some months, we'd have a good compost as fertilizer to put back into our garden. This contrasted with the typical slash-and-burn method, in which many Nigerian farmers would burn off leaves and chaff from harvested grains and rice.

ECHO Connections

Since I had connected with ECHO while at Kagoro, I brought some seed packets from the U.S., planted them, and had some good results to show on our Kagoro compound. Examples were African moringa (zogale), Leucaena, tomatoes, Malabar spinach, and lettuce. In addition, ECHO helped me get cuttings like Elephant (Napier) grass and one variety of Kafi ogu (chaya) which does not scratch when harvested. Some are good for humans, some are good for goats and cattle, and some are good for compost.

In 2016, I attended one of ECHO's four-day seminars at their international headquarters in Florida on *Raising small-scale livestock in the tropics*. I not only learned much from the hands-on sessions but also the importance of networking with other Christian development workers around the world. I attended ECHO's 2017 forum on *Sustainable agriculture* in Jos, hosted by Calvary Ministries CAPRO. We had about 70 participants from all over Nigeria and some from Burkina Faso, where ECHO has its West African office. They had another profitable forum in May 2018, in which Rev. Joseph Jeraba represented ETSK. Their presentation on raising rabbits was of great help to us.

Chickens and Rabbits

Noiler vs. local chicken eggs

Bantam vs. Noiler cock

Through financial assistance from one Christian ministry in Jos, we began two new SAC sections on raising chickens and rabbits. We experimented with a new poultry variety called Noilers. They are a new breed in Nigeria in which a cockerel is crossbred with a broiler. They grow two and a half times larger than a local Bantam variety. Their eggs are also much larger than the Bantam eggs. A Noiler hen can lay over 200 eggs yearly compared to about 75 from a Bantam hen.

We were told that the Noiler hens were not good setters. We placed some fertilized Noiler eggs under a local Bantam hen with some success. They crossbred the Noilers with their Bantams. Better varieties proved to give better results. ETSK leaders gave over 50 Noilers to help some Christians in the Manchok area, ten miles from Kagoro, who had lost everything from Fulani herdsmen attacks.

The Noilers also have fewer problems with disease and feeding than agricultural chickens. We wanted to show our students the importance of raising such small-scale livestock. Caring for them could help our students and staff, internally displaced persons, widows, and orphans with an opportunity to eat eggs and meat right from their own small farms or projects. This could also provide them with some extra income. It could help to pay for some of their school fees and family needs and help them to give more to their church and other Christian organizations. Having eggs and meat to eat could help them raise healthier children and help with hospitality when meat was needed for a meal.

Coletta tried to teach the ETSK student wives that one egg given daily to each of their children could help them be healthier. However, because of their limited finances, many of the students could only give their children an egg several times a month.

Home Skills – Baking, Hairdressing, and Sewing

One of our faculty, Mrs. Deborah Bonat, was the principal of the ECWA Widows' School in Samaru, Kaduna State, for many years. God used her to train many other widows to make home products, such as cocoa mix (Bournvita), Vicks (Rub), disinfectant (Izal), and bath soap. She has also been the ETSK B.A. Entrepreneurship teacher and the ETSK dean of students for several years. Several other wives of faculty members and female students have taught SAC sections in baking, hairdressing, and sewing.

As a widow, she said:

> My skill acquisition training has helped me in my home to pay for my children's school fees and support new converts. I've been able to train some widows in many churches. An ETSK student produced Rub and used the proceeds to pay his school fees. Such training will help families with upkeep while waiting for employment in the ministry. It can be a medium for preaching the gospel.

Reaching Out to the Community

As ETSK was benefiting from this training, we felt God leading us to expand this outreach to help develop and empower some of the youth, widows, orphans, and adults in the Kagoro community and the surrounding villages. The ECWA District Church Council challenged its youth in late January 2018 at their youth conference to consider taking SAC training.

They asked for sponsors to pay their fees, so they could get some basic training with us at ETSK. Three donors—leaders in ECWA and the Kagoro community—made pledges to sponsor up to 33 ECWA youth to get weekly training in a practical skill for one semester. In addition, several local Christian entrepreneurs were willing to give their time to educate these youth about thè importance of entrepreneurship and business plans.

Progress over the Past Few Years and the Future of the SAC

During the January to May 2020 semester, more than 100 students from ETSK, along with youth and adults from the Kagoro community and other local villages enrolled to learn these basic skills.

Since Coletta and I left Kagoro in late February 2020 to continue serving ETSK as FIM missions advocates based here in the U.S., ETSK continues to keep the SAC moving. We want the program to assist more of our students, staff, and community members to support themselves financially and be more empowered to live in their homes, churches, and communities. If this happens, our efforts will have been worth it.

ETSK layer chicken project

Learning these skills can provide income to benefit a student's lifestyle, family, or church, especially in an area dominated by African Traditional religion or Islam. Despite most of our students being good subsistence farmers, they can always learn something new as life-long learners to do a better job now and in the future.

Since 2020, another Christian foundation's grant helped ETSK develop one large plot of land behind some of the faculty homes. Several buildings have been built there. One contains about 500 layer chickens and the second one contains rabbits. These efforts can give training to some of our students and the Kagoro community. Eggs, chicken dung, and meat from the chickens and rabbits can be sold to those at ETSK and in the community. They have the potential to provide some income for ETSK.

It is exciting to see God lead in these efforts. We pray that God will direct the ETSK faculty, staff, and students not to be afraid to think outside the box. If it's legitimate, is God-honoring, and can help others to meet their physical needs, we trust God to move them forward one step at a time and to help them conquer their fear of doing things that have not been done before. God promises to direct us as we stay close to Him (Psalms 32:8; James 1:5–6). We will continue to pray for the right supporters and workers to come alongside our ETSK leaders to strengthen this program.

These ideas will greatly benefit our ETSK population and the many young people and adults in the Kagoro area and beyond. For example, one ETSK M.Div. alumnus, Rev. Femi Olowu, is an EMS of ECWA cross-cultural missionary serving the Lord with his family in Ghana. Before coming to ETSK, he helped young Christians whom he was discipling to raise rabbits, pigs, and goats to support themselves. He's now aiming to reproduce these ideas and implement some of the SAC training in Ghana that he saw at Kagoro. In addition, he's using some of his limited support to buy land, animals, seeds, and trees to be an example to Ghanaians living close to him. He wouldn't raise pigs in an area where Muslims live, as that would be offensive to them.

Our facilitators are mostly ETSK students or faculty who can give only about three hours weekly to train these students. We're praying that God will raise more local entrepreneurs or skilled technicians—welders, carpenters, tailors, or seamstresses—to work with these youth one or two days a week. Additional financial support could expand weak areas.

I learned that in the provost's report at the November 25, 2023, graduation, he shared, "With the kind approval of the board of governors, we have named some key buildings at the seminary after some individuals whose legacies we are enjoying today." One of the four buildings, the ETSK Skill Acquisition Center, was named after me.

This is a real honor. We were able to start this vision at ETSK in 2017, but it would

Dennis Shelly Skill Acquisition Block

never have happened without the support of many of you. Though we're not present, our prayer is that more students will benefit from this training and use it for God's glory wherever He leads them to serve!

We'd love to see someone—from Nigeria or overseas—who is skilled in areas of construction, industrial arts, or has a flair for entrepreneurship come to be a trainer for longer than a week or two, which is the time it takes to complete a small building project or need. Training usually takes more time than this. There will be longer-lasting results if someone can come for a longer time.

We hope that more of our pastors and church planters from ECWA and other denominations will see the importance of learning and using at least one essential skill besides their theological education. This could give them at least one tangible means besides their salary to provide funds for themselves, their families, and their churches. It could open other ways for outreach in the town or city where they're ministering. We believe He will do more great things through this training for His glory and honor.

Coletta's thoughts:

I never worked directly with the SAC projects, but I used and bought various products from their sections for our kitchen to improve our own diet. We routinely used honey, various green leaves, and dried fish in our African soups or served them with rice. We used eggs from the chickens, Rub to treat colds, and hot cocoa to warm and nourish our security guards at night.

Chapter 26

Connecting with Family and Supporters

"I thank my God every time I remember you. In all my prayers for all of you, I always pray with joy because of your partnership in the gospel from the first day until now, being confident of this, that he who began a good work in you will carry it on to completion until the day of Christ Jesus"
(Philippians 1:3-6).

From my first trip to Nigeria, one of my priorities was to work hard to keep in touch with my family and friends who were praying for and supporting me. In the 1970s, it took two to three weeks for my family or others to receive a letter from me or send one to me. Often when I'd receive a letter, I'd have to remember what questions I had asked them in my last letter. Fortunately, things have changed for the better in that area today!

When we first lived in Kagoro in 2007, we had to travel about ten miles to get a signal from a phone tower to make phone calls or send out emails. Back at Ikwa, Brother Joshua Ekpikhe made some international calls when he went to Lagos, about 400 miles from Ikwa, or from Kaduna, about 600 miles away. Once I had to fly to Lagos just to make a phone call to the U.S. Before we left Kagoro in 2020, we were able to use our cell phones to call and send out emails right from our bedroom.

Daddy and Momma won the prize for the two people who wrote me the most letters over the years. They often used Sunday afternoons to write me a weekly letter while watching the Philadelphia Phillies or Philadelphia Eagles games. Daddy especially had a very commendable habit of writing to me weekly beginning in 1977 when I began full-time teaching at BMTC. He continued this after Coletta and I were married in 1988.

His handwriting was usually more challenging to read than Momma's neater style. Still, I always looked forward to receiving their letters. Later when his handwriting wasn't so clear, he'd tell Momma what to write, and she'd type the letter before sending it.

When Momma wrote a letter, she'd often put a Bible verse reference on the back of the envelope. Some examples were: I Peter 5:7, "Cast all your anxiety on him because he cares for you;" I Thessalonians 5:18, "Give thanks in all circumstances, for this is God's will for you in Christ Jesus;" and I Thessalonians 5:17, "Pray continually."

I don't know whether anyone read these verses in transit. However, when I saw them, God used them to encourage me. I was reminded of His promises. I've tried to follow Momma's example when writing letters to friends by including similar verses beside my signature or on envelopes. Now that technology has improved, I include them at the end of my emails and text messages. God's Word will never return to Him without some results (Isaiah 55:11).

When I was single, I was always happy to receive aerograms, letters, or cards from friends or supporters. Receiving them was a highlight of my day. After various trips to Nigeria, I gained more insight into the saying, "Out of sight, out of mind!" I didn't want that to happen to me.

On several of my first trips from Lancaster to New York, I had some heart-pounding experiences. On one of my first trips to Nigeria, Daddy and Momma took me to the Lancaster airport. While checking in, I realized that one of my big suitcases wasn't with me. "Did we leave it back at our house?" I asked. We concluded that the answer was yes. Daddy quickly hopped in his car to return to our house in Manheim (about seven miles away) to find it. He drove on all the back roads as fast as he could. Yes, it was left behind at our house. He sped back to the airport with it. We had just enough time for me to check in and load it on the small airplane! We made it!

While in the air on another flight from Lancaster to New York, I realized that I had a set of Daddy's car keys with me. "What should I do now?" I wondered. Daddy did have a spare set of keys with him, so he could drive Momma back home. I worked out details with the pilot to kindly take the keys back to Lancaster on his return flight that day. The airport staff called Daddy to collect them. I flew on to Nigeria.

When I was approved as a missionary under FIM in 1977, FIM's leaders advised me to find a Christian newsletter ministry that could print my regular newsletters and manage my mailing list at a minimal cost. Missions, Inc., in Bellefonte, Pennsylvania, was just what I needed. The owners were Richard and Dorothy Shope. We connected by telephone calls and regular mail.

The Shopes were most helpful over the years in printing my newsletters. Most of them were monthly; some were bi-monthly. Occasionally, I'd include a picture or two to be part of the newsletter. Black and white photos with captions underneath helped to keep my costs down. My main objective was to regularly share praise and prayer items with those who wanted to hear from me.

My mailing list slowly grew. First, it included my immediate family, extended family members, and other Bible college and seminary friends. It later expanded to include members from my supporting churches and others I met over the years, such as friends from CEF.

I wrote to help my readers get a feel of what it was like to live in a rural village in southeastern Nigeria and to help them see how God cared for me and those working with me at Ikwa. I'd usually divide the newsletter into "Praise" and "Prayer" items. For the next newsletter, I'd review the past month's items and often move some of the "Prayer" items to the "Praise" section because God answered our prayers.

26 Christmas letters at one time!

The post office was my primary means of communication back in the 1970s and 1980s. I often would buy 10 or 20 blue aerograms from the post office and Nigerian stamps to write letters to send home to our family and supporters. The Shopes also continued faithfully printing and sending out our newsletters. I tried my best to always keep a copy of these newsletters. Daddy and Momma kept many of them too. This data helped me greatly in writing this book.

Over the years, I learned much about the local culture, often from firsthand experience rather than being warned or taught. For example, once at the Ikot Abasi Post Office, I wanted to add a note to one of my letters. I was going to use my red pen (biro), but the post office worker shouted, "Don't do that! Writing in red will alert the reader that someone has died or there was a crisis in the family." So, I didn't write in red that day.

We often needed prayer in working with the Nigerian Embassy. Usually, it took several visits for me or one of our CWT or SIM staff to work with the Nigerian Immigration department to complete our visa process. Most of the time, a key Embassy worker would be out of the office and couldn't sign or approve what we needed. When the delay became too long or near our travel deadline, we shared the situation with our friends and supporters for prayer.

The U.S. Embassy was also based in Lagos then. Dealing with them was a completely different experience. I needed to fly there several times to renew my passport or those of our family. What I especially liked about going to the U.S. Embassy was that all the staff—from the lowest worker to the ambassador or his assistant—were always there to handle or sign what I needed. One visit took me only 30 minutes from start to finish. That was great! Yea, America! People did not usually need to pray for us much for these visits.

The Federal Capital Territory of Abuja was created in 1976 in the middle of the country. It became Nigeria's capital in 1991. Brother Joshua visited Abuja early on in its development. Since he had a great heart to see people coming to Christ, once he asked someone along a road, "Do you know about Jesus?" The person said, "Maybe he lives in another area nearby." That showed that there were great needs and good opportunities to share the gospel there.

Our schedules were often very demanding, from teaching, correcting papers, and preparing class notes or messages for classes, a chapel, or a Sunday morning. We'd watch for any chance to send letters overseas or with friends. Because it usually took two or three weeks to get a letter from Nigeria to the U.S., when a CWT leader, friend, or missionary was flying to the U.S. or driving to a large Nigerian city, we went into crisis mode called "Operation No Mercy." We'd often stay up late the night before the person traveled to write as many letters as possible for them to carry by hand. When they'd arrive at their destination, they'd mail our letters at the post office for speedier deliveries.

Back then, we didn't have a Xerox copier. We used a mimeograph machine to make copies for class notes, church ministries, graduations, conferences, or newsletters to be mailed in and beyond Nigeria. We had to first type a master copy on a long, legal-sized (foolscap) duplicating sheet, then make copies on the machine by keeping enough black ink on it. Finally, we'd turn the machine's handle round and round to make individual copies.

We'd use correction fluid if we made a mistake typing on the sheet. It had an orangish color and a strong, alcoholic smell when the applicator was opened. We'd use the tiny brush at the end of the applicator to cover the mistake. When done correctly and after the fluid was dry, we could retype over the error. It took much time and patience, but we didn't have other options.

If we took CWT letters to the U.S., once we arrived and settled at our home, we'd take the pile of letters to the post office. We'd buy stamps, dampen each stamp since there weren't self-adhesive stamps then, stamp each letter, and put the letters into the mailbox. It's incredible how much information we shared during those years.

On my first trips to Nigeria, Daddy and Momma saw me off at Lancaster airport. While waiting in the small waiting room for the small plane to arrive, I'd use those minutes to write a few final letters to friends or supporters. When finished, I'd give them to Daddy to mail. I did the same while waiting at Kennedy Airport in New York. Once written and stamped, I'd find a mailbox to drop off a few letters before boarding my flight. Otherwise, once in Nigeria, it would take me some time to settle. Any letters from Nigeria would take another two or three weeks to get to the U.S.

During those years, keeping in touch with our family and supporters wasn't easy. Daddy worked hard behind the scenes as our durable power of attorney, with Momma assisting him. They wrote weekly letters, paid our U.S. bills on our behalf, helped us get our income tax returns completed, mailed and shipped packages and drug prescriptions to us, and contacted our doctors when needed.

Daddy and Momma carried out these duties until 2007. Because of his health limitations, Daddy felt that another family member should take over this vital role. As a result, Denny and Bonnie Sharp (my sister and brother-in-law) agreed to begin carrying out these duties. They faithfully served us in that role until early 2020, when we returned to live in Lancaster.

One challenge that faces all cross-cultural missionaries is figuring out how to visit those who support them financially, whether individuals or a church. I took this responsibility very seriously. While I was single, my parents were accommodating in allowing me to use their car to drive to my supporting churches. Most of them were based in Pennsylvania or Maryland. One was in New York; another was in Virginia; and one was in West Virginia. After we married, one church in California joined our support team. Several times during my home assignments, I rented a car from a local church or flew to New York.

During our home assignments, my schedule included visiting supporting churches. Over the years, many church members and friends, such as my CBS mate, Dr. Todd Beall and his wife, Sharon, used their gifts of hospitality to allow us to stay in their homes for one or more nights when we came to speak in their churches or for their missionary conferences.

Except for my original deputation in 1977 to raise support, only once did we have to ask our supporters to prayerfully increase our financial support. Our home church and several individual supporters responded positively to help us meet what FIM required for us each month. Since then, God has continued to use our supporting churches and individuals to meet our monthly needs. After that, if we mentioned finances in our

Our display table at a supporting church

newsletters and correspondence, it was on behalf of the CWT and BMTC, and then ETSK after we moved to Kagoro in 2007.

My base during many of my home assignments while I was single was my parent's home on 405 W. High Street in Manheim. I also used their home phone to call various friends and supporters.

Daddy and Momma were happy to have me serve overseas as a cross-cultural missionary. Like most other families, I know that sometimes they would have liked to have me closer to them and our family.

Various Christians and several pastors, like Pastor Abram Gish, from Word of Life Chapel, in Bainbridge, Pennsylvania, either gave me or allowed me to choose books from their libraries to send to Nigeria for BMTC's library. The librarians from WBC and LBC also donated many books to be shipped to BMTC and ETSK's libraries. I also bought books at library sales.

Daddy and Momma helped me package many of these boxes to take to the post office to send. Kathy Mogel, a long-time friend of Coletta, also helped us. Over the last few years, when mailbag rates were stopped and books could only be shipped at about $4.00 per pound, this greatly decreased the number of good library books that could be sent to ETSK's library.

I also tried to think ahead about what items I'd need to buy for the next year or two. That included clothing, items to improve the house, medical needs, and items that were requested for the ministries or Nigerian friends. This became more complicated when we became married and when the children joined us. Homeschool items later added much weight to our suitcases.

For our trip back to Nigeria in 2003, we took 19 suitcases with us, which included a guitar. God helped us get the money to buy all our tickets and pay for extra suitcases. We also didn't lose any children or suitcases on the way. The Lord helped us get these items safely to Ikwa. We wonder how God gave us the energy to buy what we needed, pack it all in suitcases, and then get it all safely to Nigeria!

As Daddy and Momma aged, it became more challenging for our family to live with them for more than several weeks, especially when our children were young. In 1990, after we came to the U.S. with Dwight, who was about one year old, we lived in one of

Calvary Church's missionary homes on Princess Avenue in Lancaster from August to December. At that time our home church had six different homes or apartments for us as their missionaries (Global Partners) to live in when we returned from overseas. This was such a blessing to us. We also rented a church missionary car for our use during several home assignments.

During our stay in the Princess Avenue home, we saw Dwight learn to walk, experience his first snowstorm, and enjoy colder weather than he was used to in Ikwa. Also, Coletta became pregnant with Stephanie. We returned to Nigeria right after Christmas to resume teaching at BMTC.

It was always with mixed emotions that we returned to Nigeria. Saying goodbye to our close-knit families, especially to our parents, was one of the hardest things we faced as missionaries. It never became easier. In some ways, it became even more problematic. We didn't know if we'd see relatives or friends again when we'd return a year or more later.

When leaving, our emotions were always stretched. Over three days, we'd sadly say goodbye to our families and friends in the U.S. Then over 6,000 miles from home, we'd soon happily say hello to our Nigerian family and friends and the CWT, BMTC, and ETSK faculty, staff, and students. We had known some of them for over 40 years. Saying goodbye and hello many times over the years was part of being cross-cultural missionaries.

My records show that I had personally traveled 29 total times back and forth from the U.S. to Nigeria from 1973 to 2020. While single, I took 9.5 trips; while married I took 17.5 trips with Coletta, and later with the children. On one of those trips in 1995, I went to Nigeria alone for seven weeks. On several trips, we returned with other missionaries or visitors.

2019 - Leaving the farmhouse apartment for Kagoro

During these various home assignments, our family stayed briefly with Daddy and Momma. However, we lived mostly in different Calvary Church missionary homes: on Sunset Avenue, the church's farmhouse and apartment, their new townhouse in Kissel Hill Commons near the Lancaster airport, several times in their Princess Avenue home, as well as in their duplex on Pleasure

Road. Wycliffe Bible Translators allowed us to live twice in their Willow Street apartment, four miles from Lancaster.

The Calvary Church staff gave us helpful assistance when we came to the U.S. for home assignments. It also gave some stability to Dwight and Stephanie when we came to the U.S. Several times Calvary Church arranged for us to live in one of the missionary homes where we had lived before. This especially helped Dwight and Stephanie become more comfortable because they remembered the house.

Our U.S. mission, FIM, allowed us to be associate missionaries under SIM from 2007 until 2020. Both missions provided our family with member care and counsel. Calvary Church, as our home church, has been our key accountability partner.

Many missionaries don't have a supporting church, like Calvary Church, that has missionary homes and vehicles available to rent while on home assignment. From the time Coletta and I went full-time to Ecuador and Nigeria, we had faithful financial supporters, including about ten churches. This contrasted with many other missionaries who had to travel to visit 20 or more supporting churches and individuals throughout the country during their home assignments. All of this was good but often exhausted them before their return overseas.

Our home church was a great example of caring for us as their missionaries. This was part of what Pastor Steve Beirn and Dr. George Murray wrote about in their book, *Well Sent: Reimagining the Church's Missionary-Sending Process*. We were the goers, while others on our team were the senders.

Coletta's thoughts:

Dennis did our official writing, while I did the personal writing. He did the letter writing to our supporting churches and individuals. I wrote weekly personal letters to our families, filling them in on our daily living activities, Dwight and Stephanie's growth and development, home school activities, and later about their activities at Hillcrest School and college.

When the children were young, Dennis made frequent videos of our family life to send to both our parents. This helped them to see me pregnant and see the children as they grew.

Every night we prayed with them, naming each grandparent, aunt, uncle, and cousin. That way each grew up knowing the names of their blood relatives. We also called adults in Nigeria "aunties" and "uncles" to show respect. Our children never became confused about who were their blood relatives and their other aunties and uncles.

Most missionaries know how important the whole team is to their success. We thank God for the many people who've faithfully served and partnered with us over the years.

Chapter 27

God Is Always in the Details!

"Consider it pure joy, my brothers, whenever you face trials of many kinds, because you know that the testing of your faith develops perseverance. Perseverance must finish its work so that you may be mature and complete, not lacking anything" (James 1:2–4).

Over my years at Ikwa, I had chronic back problems. By God's grace, I tried not to allow those pains to keep me from doing ministry. I heard someone say that a successful missionary needs three qualities: a good sense of humor, a good sense of humor, and a good sense of humor. With my health issues, and the many challenges that required us to be in daily survival mode at Ikwa and Kagoro, we needed to trust the Lord for the strength to keep moving and the ability to see how He would guide and protect us and the ministries. With a good sense of humor, I often said and still say, "Except for all of my problems, I'm doing great."

At Kagoro, my back problems increased. In June 2013, I attended a Nigerian Theological Educators' Conference in Jos and stayed at Woyke Guest House. One evening upon returning with several of the guest speakers, I removed my heavy briefcase from my car. Immediately, I felt a sharp pain in my back. The speakers assisted me to my room. I could hardly walk or get comfortable on my back that night and had great difficulty sleeping. The next morning, after the SIM leaders learned of my situation, they had one of the SIM drivers take me to Kagoro.

Arrangements were made for Coletta and me to return to the U.S. several weeks later. Before our departure, I managed to complete teaching one summer Research Methods II course, using crutches to move around.

Once in the U.S., I was seen by a back surgeon in Lancaster. He prescribed some physical therapy, which didn't solve my problem. He therefore concluded that I should have surgery on one broken and one herniated disc in my lower back—L-3, and L-4—that same August. After much rehabilitation, we returned to Kagoro in late July of 2014.

The operation wasn't entirely successful. My back since then has caused me much chronic pain. Walking continues to be one of my biggest struggles and least favorite activities.

Calvary Church rotated us as their Global Partners (missionaries) to be assigned to different Adult Bible Fellowships (ABFs)—like Sunday School classes—every three or four years. While in the U.S. that spring of 2014, Coletta and I were assigned to Crossroads ABF. We tried to attend their Sunday morning sessions as much as possible. Their ABF leaders asked me to teach on various Sunday mornings. I used some PowerPoint presentations and enjoyed the opportunities.

Before we returned to Kagoro, the Crossroads ABF gave us $3,400 to buy a gas-run generator with a battery and self-starting switch. This system would save me and my back from having to start it by pulling a rope. Coletta could also start it on her own.

August 2014 – Our new self-starting generator

Once in Nigeria and settled, we bought the generator in Jos. It cost much less than we had estimated. The ABF members agreed that we could use the unspent balance to buy an electric washer and a small electric, upright freezer. Coletta had never had any of these before in Nigeria. We kept the remaining funds to purchase gas and engine oil. It lasted for more than one year. Wow! That was quite a gift! We thanked God for those class members whenever we turned on the generator (which was almost daily) or when Coletta used the washer or opened the freezer.

Managing our generator indeed brightened our days and nights in more ways than one. Coletta used the electric washer at least weekly. When NEPA didn't supply us with more than six hours of light a day, which happened much of the time, we'd turn on our generator to run our small freezer in the kitchen to keep our meat and vegetables frozen. This was a great help to Coletta in managing our kitchen and home with little frustration.

I'd make my special homemade ice cream when we had electricity for more than 12 hours a day. I'd mix two cans of evaporated milk, some sugar, a little vanilla extract, and some full cream powdered milk in water. If we had mulberries or bananas that we grew on our compound, we added them. We'd have ice cream for dessert for about ten days until it was time to make another batch. I didn't follow a set recipe but made it to taste. Coletta would taste one spoonful before we froze it to see if it was sweet and thick enough.

Since my back operation, I haven't slept or walked well. I usually sleep on my back for most of the night. Before I go to bed, I take two pain capsules to ease my pain level, so I can sleep as well as possible for at least six hours. My left leg often wants to drag along when I walk. I must lift it intentionally and keep it as straight as possible to avoid tripping or catching it behind my right leg. During the daytime, if I take two pain capsules at breakfast, stay active, and take a pain pill when needed, I usually don't think much about these challenges.

After 2014, back in Nigeria, I fell several times on the ETSK campus. One time after morning chapel, I was walking toward our car. I looked ahead to see several faculty members chatting about 50 feet ahead of me. Before I knew it, I was on the ground. There was a big, long tree root that was sticking up several inches high right in front of me. I tripped right over it, giving me brush burns on my knee.

Another day the seminary driver took our car to Kafanchan for repairs. Coletta and I had to walk from our house after chapel across the main road to the campus. While walking home, I wasn't watching where I was going and tripped over some stones sticking several inches high out of the unpaved driveway on the rustic campus. The fall caused some scuffs on my arm. Most of the campus didn't have concrete walks or paved streets.

Another time we visited Cheryl and Donna Pridham at Samaru, 12 miles from Kagoro. We were touring their campus. While walking together, I looked up at some of the trees, since I loved to see nature, birds, and the sky. Before I knew it, I tripped and was on the ground.

Then on Tuesday, May 21, 2019, Rev. Joseph Jeraba and I attended a conference in Jos for an agricultural forum run by ECHO. The conference was held on the campus of the international headquarters of Calvary Ministries, also known as CAPRO. Brother Joseph, as an ETSK faculty member, also had much interest in farming and agricultural ministries. He has been overseeing the SAC at ETSK. I was to give a late morning PowerPoint presentation to over 50 Christians from Nigeria and several other African countries, like Burkina Faso. I wanted to share developments in our ETSK SAC sections relating to farming and animal husbandry.

After we all had breakfast, I walked back to our main hall to prepare. On the way, I chose to walk on their brick path instead of an uneven, grassy section. Upon entering their beautiful building, I walked through a hallway leading to our venue. The area was dark. Somehow, I missed seeing a step and fell very hard on their shiny, granite-type floor.

As soon as I fell, I looked at my foot and saw that I couldn't move it. I knew something serious had happened. Some conference participants quickly came and tried to get me up and on a chair. I was in so much pain that I was unable to give my presentation. The conference staff quickly called for medical help to come from the ECWA BUTH hospital about four miles away in Jos.

When they arrived, they tried to move me. When this happened, I was ready to scream because of the sharp pains around my hip. They transported me in a van to the hospital, where I was admitted. The hospital staff took X-rays and found a room for me. One of the SIM missionaries, Dr. Adam Lee, who is a surgeon from South Korea, visited me.

While this happened, Rev. Jeraba tried calling Coletta, who was back at Kagoro. After various attempts, he connected, telling Coletta that I had fallen. She worked with our ETSK provost to have the seminary driver, Jolly, bring her to Jos. She knew that I was in trouble. She arrived that afternoon to meet me in the hospital.

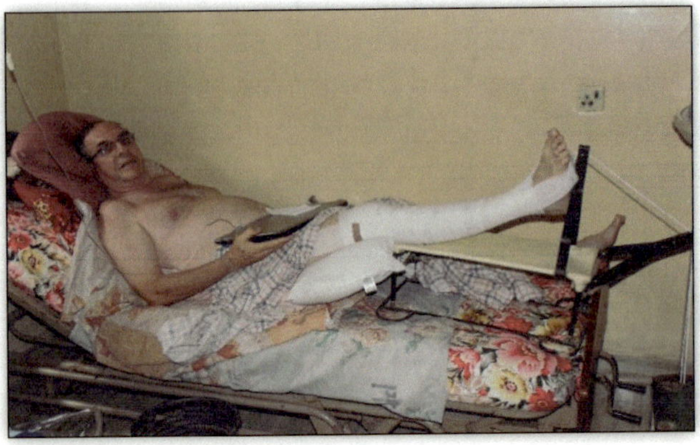

In traction in Jos Hospital

The X-rays showed that I had broken my right hip. Dr. Lee wrapped up my leg and hip and put me in traction. I had to lay on my back with my leg in the air. It was very hot in Jos, so I kept my shirt off. Dr. Lee knew that I'd need surgery. However, he didn't want it done in that hospital.

SIM-Nigeria's staff leaders quickly contacted our FIM leaders and our U.S. health insurance company on what to do. They all decided that Coletta and I should be evacuated to Nairobi, Kenya, on a medical flight. After many calls and planning, SIM-Nigeria's leaders arranged with a Kenyan company to have a medical team fly from Nairobi to collect us on Thursday morning.

On Wednesday, Rick and Brenda Naatz's driver drove Coletta back to Kagoro for her to hurriedly pack some of our clothes and personal items, including our passports and traveling papers. I had her turnover some of my duties to others to carry on for me. Then, she returned to Jos so we could fly to Kenya. After that, we didn't know if we would be able to return to our home in Kagoro or ever see our ETSK staff and student helpers again.

The medical team from Nairobi arrived in Abuja on Wednesday night, then flew to the Jos airport to collect us on Thursday morning. Two pilots, one doctor, and one nurse were on board the small eight-passenger jet. The U.S. medical insurance staff assured us that the Kenyan medical team would come from Jos airport and collect us at BUTH. That sounded too good to be true since they had never come to Jos before, nor did they have a good ambulance to use to collect me.

Our SIM-Nigeria missionary staff wisely made a plan B in case this didn't work. You guessed it! Early Thursday morning, Dr. Lee received a call from the team from Abuja saying that plan A couldn't work. So, SIM quickly shifted to plan B, which was to prepare a van to take Coletta and me to Jos airport, about 40 miles from the city.

Being lifted into the jet for the Nairobi flight

I was wheeled out of the hospital, put in SIM's van, and laid on a giant mattress. Coletta was with me. Once at the airport, they strapped me on a stretcher that came from Nairobi. With various workers slowly lifting me toward the jet's narrow entry door, they squeezed me through with only a few inches to spare.

They straddled me over several passenger seats, causing me to lie parallel less than two feet from the top of the jet's ceiling. Coletta, the doctor, and the nurse couldn't stand fully upright, so no one had much extra space. I have some claustrophobic tendencies, but I made it. Getting some painkiller shots helped me manage the 12-hour trip.

It took about an hour to clear immigration in Jos and later in Abuja. Then, finally, we were on our way to Nairobi, landing briefly in Bangui in the Central African Republic to refuel. We arrived in Nairobi after 9 p.m. Coletta took about one hour to check in with the Kenyan immigration workers to obtain visitors' visas.

All this time, I was still strapped to my stretcher in the jet until I was lifted into a Kenyan ambulance. By this time, Coletta was exhausted from all she had been through over the past few days. From the airport, the ambulance, with its siren blaring, delivered us to the Aga Khan University Hospital. I was taken on another stretcher to a booth while Coletta had to check us in. This took another hour or more.

Coletta and I kept wondering why our health insurance company had abruptly decided to have us go to Nairobi for my care. Only later would we find out.

Kenya's time was only two hours ahead of Nigeria's. The staff eventually shuttled us to my hospital room. It had a space next to a big window with cushioned seats and room for more than two people. The hospital staff members were very kind to allow Coletta to sleep in my room on those seats instead of requiring her to go into the city to find a local hotel. The staff went out of their way to help us get something to drink and eat, even though it was the middle of the night. We tried to sleep a little before morning. This room was to be our home for the next three weeks.

Several international doctors were assigned to oversee my case. The orthopedic hip surgeon and cardiologist had Indian backgrounds, even though I think they had lived in Nairobi much or all their lives. They knew that I needed a hip operation promptly. First, I had some X-rays taken. Then, they arranged for me to be operated on at noon that same Friday. Coletta was highly impressed with the high quality of care the doctors, nurses, and staff gave us while we were in the hospital. She thought I received better care in Nairobi than I would have received had we been in the U.S. Our doubts about coming to Nairobi were turning to joy because of this excellent treatment.

My operation was successful. Afterward, I had more X-rays taken. It wasn't easy to turn different angles to get the X-rays done, but I somehow made it. Now began a long journey for me to start to walk and become somewhat independent again.

The hospital's good care spilled over into their food service. They had a menu that outdid many fancy U.S. restaurants. I could choose from various breakfast, lunch, and supper courses. A staff member would come ahead of time to take my meal orders for the next day. I could choose to take small, medium, or large food portions. I usually decided on the small one. Even with their small portions, I couldn't eat all the food. They served me an appetizer, the main course, and a dessert. It felt like I was being treated like royalty.

Coletta took most of her meals down in several small cafés connected to the hospital facilities. This helped to meet her needs. She learned to know her way around the hospital very well over the next few weeks.

Right after my operation, my right leg swelled up so much that it looked like an overstuffed sausage. It was also very black and blue. I didn't like anyone touching the area, especially from my knee to my feet. As a result, I was in much pain most of the time. This required me to take constant pain pills and get some shots to sleep at night, including morphine. I kept their staff busy at night since my first nights were rough. My energy level was also low during those first days. One staff member came to take my blood early every morning.

We made many good friends during those weeks. Various men came to give me a daily bath. I needed help to go to the bathroom because I couldn't hold myself up or move enough to sit on the toilet. Things had indeed changed for us since we were at Kagoro.

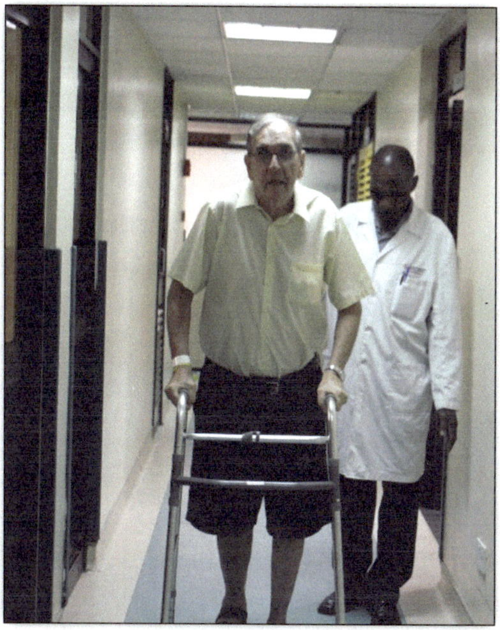

Doing physical therapy in Nairobi

We met some Kenyan hospital staff who were Christians. We still keep in contact with several of them. The team, from the surgeons and doctors down to the physical therapy workers and cleaners, were most helpful and willing to go out of their way to help us. The nurses checked on me every few hours around the clock, giving me a shot or painkillers when needed.

Right after my operation, I went for physical therapy twice daily. During my first few sessions downstairs in their physical therapy room, I could hardly hold myself up. My first assignment was to stand up and use my arms to move across two wooden parallel bars about 15 feet long. I barely made it. Then I was given a walker to begin to walk a few steps. Over the three weeks that I was in the hospital, I saw much improvement.

The physical therapy staff gave me various exercises in each session. I was to pull on some bars up to 20 times. Then they'd have me increase my numbers. One day they had me use one machine in which I put my arms inside some cushions. I was to pull them up to 50 times. I told myself I could do more than that. As an over-achiever, I thought, "If I can double the number, I can get double the results."

Little did I know that this pulled some of my shoulder muscles, which made me sore for about one month. However, each day my walking improved step by step. I appreciated the physical therapy staff who helped me through those weeks.

During my hospital stay, the SIM-Kenya director, Ben Colby, and his wife, Natalie, visited us. They helped us buy Kenyan phone cards, get some Kenyan money, and learn a few tips on living in Nairobi. Also, Andrew and Stephanie Onguka, SIM missionaries in Kenya from our home church, Calvary Church, found out about my hospitalization and came to see us. We appreciated their visit.

The hospital doctors tracked my progress and discharged me after three weeks. The Colbys helped us arrange to live at SIM's Southern Sudan Guest House. This allowed us to go to the hospital for periodic checkups, as I needed more physical therapy before boarding a jet to travel.

We said our goodbyes to the hospital staff, with whom we had made good friends. The next step of our journey was to stay three weeks at the guest house, about five miles from the hospital. After that, we used Uber taxis to move around the city quickly. They were usually very prompt and were not expensive.

We enjoyed our trips around the city during those weeks. We were incredibly impressed by how orderly the Kenyan drivers and motorcyclists drove compared to Nigerians. Kenyans followed the British system, where vehicles drove on the opposite side of the road compared to the U.S. or Nigeria.

Coletta was our cook in the guest house kitchen. She found several local stores and supermarkets that offered far more choices than in Nigeria. The hospital helped us connect with one nursing service where a male nurse would come to stay with us for 24 hours straight before another male nurse would relieve him. This helped us, especially during our first week there, because I needed help going to the bathroom and taking my daily baths. A physical therapist also visited us almost daily during those three weeks. He was happy with my progress.

I needed to use a walker to move around in the guest house. On our return from our first visit to my cardiologist at the hospital, I couldn't climb up the three steps to the entrance. It took Coletta and our male nurse all their strength to help me climb them. My next visit wasn't so eventful.

During our stay, we did a lot of correspondence by email on my laptop. We called some of our Nigerian ETSK staff as well as our family in the U.S. For some reason, my laptop's hard drive crashed. SIM-Kenya had a Christian technician come to install a new one.

After three weeks, with more steady progress in my walking and pain levels, the cardiologist and surgeon said it was time for Coletta and me to return to the U.S. However, my surgeon strongly advised me to travel business class for our two flights to have more room to move around. Our insurance company only paid for me to travel business class.

Before we left Nairobi, we hired an Uber driver to take us to one of Nairobi's game reserves. How could we come the whole way to Kenya and not try to see some of their wild animals? Unfortunately, we couldn't go on any trips that required much walking. One guide at a game reserve advised us to visit one section of the reserve to see wild animals recuperating from accidents or sickness. Because of my hip, Coletta pushed me around in a wheelchair. At least we were able to see some lions, hyenas, cheetahs, and monkeys inside their cages.

Lioness in a Nairobi game reserve

On the day we were to travel, June 24, the surgeon wanted me to use a catheter for the trip. At about noon, our male nurse helped to put it in. This was very painful. We realized later when I had to urinate that something wasn't right.

We had a Kenyan travel agent drive us to the Nairobi International Airport and drop us off. We had pre-arranged airport staff to help me with a wheelchair at each airport for quicker movement. After easy check-ins, we stayed in the Business Class lounge before boarding our flight. That way, we had more space to sit and could have some snacks and something to drink before boarding the jet.

Because Coletta's ticket was economy class, we had to pay $30.00 for her to stay with me in the lounge. I was still in tremendous pain when I urinated, enough to make me want to shout out loud. The pain continued during our first Lufthansa flight to Frankfurt, Germany.

While at Frankfurt airport, Coletta insisted that I see the airport clinic doctor. We had a seven-hour layover, so we were sure that we'd have adequate time to do this. Once at the clinic and after waiting about 30 minutes to see the doctor, she insisted that we go to the city to see a urologist. We asked ourselves, "How can we do this during our layover?" I was put in a bright, orange-painted ambulance and sped off to a local hospital about ten miles away.

Once at this hospital, the staff quickly helped me see the urologist. He easily pulled out my catheter at about 9:30 a.m. and inserted a new one. It still gave me much pain. Our layover hours before we were to board our flight to Philadelphia were ticking down.

Where was Coletta? The hospital staff didn't allow her to accompany me. Instead, she was asked to sit in a nearby waiting room, where other patients' family members were waiting. They were busy texting on their phones, minding their own business. They also spoke German, so no one talked with her.

After the urologist left me, I was lying alone on a table in a big room. One nurse did come to see me later. The problem was that she spoke Spanish and didn't know English well. She was using her cell phone to translate what she wanted to say in our conversation. Then she left me, and no one came to see me. I was the only person in the room for about two hours.

I asked myself, "Will we make it for our 1:15 p.m. flight?" Still, no one came. I began to shout, "Hello. Is anyone there? Help!" I shouted various times without any good results, getting louder each time. Now it was after 11 a.m. I had to remember to apply some of my theological knowledge about the sovereignty of God. If God knew I was here and wanted us to board the Philadelphia flight, He was the One who had to work it out.

Finally, another medical staff member came into my room and rescued me. He gained permission for me to be released and took me to the waiting room where Coletta was sitting. We were delighted to see each other, but we couldn't leave the hospital yet. She had to sign papers and arrange to pay for their services before we could leave for the airport. She couldn't find someone to help her at the desk for about 20 minutes. Time was ticking down!

While she was arranging to pay my hospital bills, I went ahead to find a taxi driver who understood English to take us to the airport. Coletta's delay made him restless, but he waited for us. As soon as Coletta paid my bill, he rushed us to the airport.

After the driver dropped us off at the airport departure area at about 12:30 p.m., Coletta had me wait outside, standing and propped up against one of the round, concrete barriers that keep vehicles from driving too close to the buildings. She hurried to find an airport staff member who could find a wheelchair for me to sit in. I waited for about 20 minutes, praying we could still embark on our 1:15 p.m. flight. There was still no sign of Coletta. I was getting tired of standing. Finally, Coletta came with an airport staff and a wheelchair. She was from Peru and was most helpful.

We didn't have any red flashing lights to move us through the airport, but the staff member aptly helped us check in and go through customs. Our suitcases were already checked through from Nairobi to Philadelphia, so we only had our carry-ons. Then, she wheeled us into an elevator. Before we knew it, we were at the entrance door to board our flight.

Wow! We made it just in the nick of time. All we could say was, "Thank you, Lord!" God was taking care of us! The flight to Philadelphia went well, although I still was in much pain whenever I urinated. Coletta visited me several times from her seat in economy class.

Once we collected our suitcases in Philadelphia, we were warmly welcomed by Dee and Mike Lindsey. They had arranged for us to stay overnight at a local hotel before they'd take us to Lancaster the next morning. That night Coletta removed my catheter, for which I was very much relieved.

Calvary Church farmhouse

Our home church housed us in their farmhouse apartment for the next few months until October. Once we stepped up the porch steps, the apartment didn't have any more steps for me to climb. This was one of four times we would live in this colonial house on home assignments. (It was built in 1732.) Another part of our journey was finished. We were confident that God would continue to lead us. He was again working out the details, even though we often didn't know how.

Coletta's thoughts:

May 21, 2019, was one of the most stressful days of my life. It was the day Dennis fell in Jos, a rainy day in Kagoro. Our simple cell phone didn't work well in rainy weather. When I received Rev. Jeraba's call, he told me that Dennis had fallen and injured his ankle. I thought, "Oh, I'm glad it was his ankle and not his hip." At the same time, I knew Rev. Jeraba wouldn't call me unless it was serious.

Immediately, I started to call Dennis' number, but I had great trouble connecting. For the next few hours, I continuously redialed his number, but couldn't connect. Finally, at about noon, Dennis called me and told me he was in terrible pain and couldn't move his hip or leg, and that he was stuck at the ECHO seminar venue. I assured him I would come to Jos as soon as possible.

My phone number for Dr. Lee was an old one. I had no numbers for SIM headquarters on my phone. I managed to find the number of another doctor we had seen, so I called her and asked her to please send the hospital ambulance to pick up Dennis.

Next, I called the ETSK provost and requested permission for the seminary driver, Jolly, to take me to Jos immediately. After I quickly packed an overnight bag,

Jolly and I headed to Jos. About 40 minutes into the trip, Dr. Lee called me to confirm that Dennis had broken the head of his femur and that he was arranging for a medical evacuation. He told me to bring our passports to Jos.

By then, the weather had cleared, and communication was easier. Jolly wasn't happy about us turning around because he wanted to be back in Kagoro before dark. However, I insisted on needing the passports. We turned back to Kagoro, losing precious time.

It was about 4:30 p.m. when we climbed to the plateau on the outskirts of Jos. The next call was from Dean Ressler from our FIM home office. He was surprised that I hadn't yet made it to Jos or seen Dennis. He relayed the message that FIM had sent all the evacuation information to SIM and that we were in their prayers. That was comforting.

Little did I know this was the beginning of a marathon that would last for weeks, even months. This would be another event that would forever change our lives. I spent the next two nights in an easy chair in Dennis' hospital room, helping him with hygiene and toiletry needs, keeping a watch on his IV infusion, and walking around to buy food. The mission told me to pack enough clothing for several weeks.

Wednesday morning, I returned to Kagoro to collect our green cards, more clothing, and a very long list of items Dennis wanted me to do or bring along. Everything but his CPAP machine and his computer had to fit into two overnight bags, as the air ambulance was small.

Thursday was an early morning start. Mrs. Lee kindly brought us breakfast and some coffee for me. Dr. Lee said that was good because I would need to be "strong." That word rang in my ears. Suddenly, our breakfast was interrupted by the news that the air ambulance had landed. The door-to-door service didn't end up happening, so Dennis and his mattress were loaded into the back of the van. We made our way over bumpy roads to the airport about 40 minutes away.

The trip was long but comfortable. I was seated at Dennis' head, directly behind the pilot and co-pilot. I heard them discussing the course they would take, where we would refuel, and how many times we'd stop according to the fuel gauge.

As soon as we landed in Kenya, I faced many decisions. I had to get temporary visas. We were in a country that was new to us, with a new language. The visa line was very long, but the man in charge marched me up to the front. I explained to the people around me that my husband was waiting for me in an air ambulance outside.

As soon as we arrived at the hospital, there were more decisions to be made. What kind of room should we stay in? The hospital didn't have the kind of room available that our insurance covered. It was after midnight. How would I find a hotel? How would I go there at this hour of the night? There were many permission papers to sign. I had eaten little food and hardly slept over the past 72 hours. I kept praying, "Lord, give me a clear mind and wisdom."

The hospital was incredibly clean. The staff were friendly, helpful, and skilled. I was put at ease and decided to just sleep on cushions in Dennis' room, instead of trying to find the hotel arranged by the insurance company. Everyone went out of their way to help us.

By morning we met the surgeon and the cardiac doctor. X-rays and tests were quickly done. Dennis was in the operating room by 1:00 p.m.

The first few days were particularly rough. There were times when I thought we might lose Dennis. His leg was so swollen and developed blisters. A scan ruled out blood clots and showed his circulation to be adequate. A dermatologist was consulted. Special daily dressings were applied.

Stephanie reminded me of my favorite Psalm, Psalm 20. I began reading it every day, and on every occasion, when feeling anxious, "May the LORD answer you when you are in distress; may the name of the God of Jacob protect you. May he send you help from the sanctuary and grant you support from Zion…Some trust in chariots and some in horses, but we trust in the name of the LORD our God" (20:1,2,7).

Rehab was brutal. An old back injury, a dragging left leg, and a poor gait left Dennis with no good leg to compensate for the right hip fracture. After the first week, I decided not to be present at rehab.

I kept in close contact with our nurse daughter, Stephanie, in the U.S. We could send texts easily. I relayed information to her and then depended on her to inform everyone else. Otherwise, it was too overwhelming to keep in touch with everyone. FIM called weekly to check on our progress. Very slowly, things improved.

Our next crisis was the catheter before boarding the flight home. I knew it was definitely not functioning as it should. Dennis was having bladder spasms and bloody urine. Should I cancel the flight at the last moment, after weeks of getting travel plans all arranged and with all the required medical clearances in place? I decided to move forward and hopefully deal with it in Germany.

I knew that international airports had medical clinics. Even though a urologist changed the catheter, the rest of our flights home were plagued by his bladder spasms and bleeding. I could only see the concern in the stewardess' eyes as I helped Dennis settle in his business class seat. She promptly arranged for me to be moved to the front of the economy class section so she could reach me easily if needed.

Once we reached the U.S., the rehab continued for several months. It never became easy. Progress was slow, but the Lord continued to help us day by day.

Chapter 28

Rounding Up Our Presence at Kagoro

"Keep watch over yourselves and all the flock of which the Holy Spirit has made you overseers. Be shepherds of the church of God, which he bought with his own blood (Acts 20:28).

Once we settled at our church's missionary apartment in Lancaster in late June 2019, one of our top priorities was to arrange for physical therapy to improve my walking. We received this at the Lancaster Health Campus. Several staff members helped me three times weekly for three months. Unfortunately, my health insurance policy only paid for part of our bills. We transferred to the Lancaster YMCA for one more month using their exercise equipment. By this time, my walking had improved some. I was promoted from using my walker to using a cane.

During those months, we communicated with our family, home church, PACTeam, individual supporting churches and individuals, other friends, and relatives. We were grateful for our prayer and financial supporters who had been behind us since we both first started summer cross-cultural ministries in 1973.

We made phone calls and had visits with Pastor Steve Beirn, our home church missions pastor, and Dr. Paul Barreca, our FIM general director. They strongly advised Coletta and me to prayerfully consider stopping our teaching at ETSK and returning to Kagoro to briefly round up our physical presence there. We were to pack up our house, say our goodbyes, and prepare to return to the U.S. to continue our ministries from here on behalf of ETSK and FIM.

Meeting with Dr. Barreca & Pastor Beirn

That was a shocker to me! However, we later saw that God was again using our leaders to wisely guide us to benefit not just us but eventually everyone at Kagoro. Because of my poor walking and past falls at Kagoro and in Nigeria, our U.S. leaders didn't want us to have another crisis resulting in another medical emergency. We agreed with their insights. The ETSK provost and management leaders also understood our leaders' advice and our situation. They fully agreed with their plan, although they were sad to learn that we'd soon be leaving them.

During those five months in Lancaster, we challenged MABC to have their associate pastor, Pastor Keith Surland, and one elder, Jim Rice, visit us while we were still at Kagoro. They gladly agreed to go speak at our December ETSK graduation and see what projects they had supported since 2007 when Coletta and I began our ministries there. They had previously supported us and BMTC in various projects at Ikwa over the years.

We returned to Nigeria on November 3, 2020. This was four weeks before the MABC men arrived for the graduation weekend. Upon arriving at our Kagoro home, we were greatly disappointed. Even though our ETSK student workers had tried to keep our house clean over those past four months, rats had invaded our house. Droppings were everywhere, causing a terrible smell. They had also eaten some of our papers and destroyed some of our household items and linens. It took Coletta and our household workers several weeks to clean up each room of our house, especially the kitchen, to be ready for the MABC visitors. Only after their visit could we begin to focus on packing our personal belongings.

Coletta and I hosted Pastor Keith and Jim in our two spare bedrooms. They immensely enjoyed their one-week visit. Part of the reason was that they toured around the campus and saw various projects that MABC had sponsored or assisted with since 2007. This included the computer studies department, the fishery, the library, and funds to put on a new roof for the classrooms. In addition, MABC supported the student scholarship fund and missions outreaches. We called their church "Our Project Church" since they were willing to partner with ETSK in so many ways for many years.

Pastor Keith and Jim Rice at graduation

We kept the men busy during their entire visit. Friday night, Jim spoke in the baccalaureate service. Saturday morning, Pastor Keith gave the graduation message to over 150 graduates and over 2,000 friends and family members who attended the occasion. Sunday morning, he preached in our ETSK church. In between meetings, the men listened to many stories of various students and staff. Many had faced trauma or were adversely affected by Boko Haram militants and Fulani herdsmen attacking their home villages.

2019 ETSK graduates

The men were visibly touched by these stories and had brought some funds to help selected people. We were sad to see both men leave, but their coming was very timely. They left Kagoro with a greater understanding of how God had been using MABC to assist many of our ETSK alumni and students in ministry.

Back in the U.S., the men shared their burdens. As a result, MABC began "Operation Mercy" to support ETSK students who had financial needs for their tuition, along with others who had trauma-induced, physical, or medical needs. MABC is a model church sharing the gospel worldwide and meeting our national brethren's spiritual and physical needs!

Once the men returned to the US, Coletta and I worked hard to reduce our personal effects in our house and turn over administrative duties and records to Nigerian staff. This turned out to be an almost daily activity. Coletta and I worked hard to sort through our course notes and files. We passed on many of our library books to a small Bible college, the ETSK library, and some of our faculty, staff, and students. Many at ETSK understood why we were returning to the US and expressed their sadness at our departure.

ETSK management members sending us off

We enjoyed Christmas and New Year's Day with some of our student workers and those at ETSK who stayed on campus during the holidays. We attended SIM's January Spiritual Life Conference at MRH in early January. We also spent every spare moment trying to sell or give away some of our personal belongings. SIM, at their Friday night pot-luck supper, gave us a beautiful Nigerian painting as a send-off gift.

In February 2020, we sold our 2006 Rav4 to a Nigerian Christian. We turned it over to him just before our departure. ESTK's provost and the management committee had an appreciation chapel for us. They came to see us off and prayed with us on the day we left. After that, we went to Miango for three days to sort many final files and get some physical rest before leaving Nigeria.

Dr. Steve and Ruth Porter allowed us to stay free of charge at Grace Cottage on the MRH campus during those days. They served us a special first-class supper with many selections of appetizers, main courses, desserts, and beverages for us to choose from during one of those evenings.

On the morning of February 24, we left Miango. It was chaotic right up until the moment we entered the SIM van. We completed packing our travel suitcases and left final items and notes for the ETSK staff. Kevin and Alexis Stokes, our SIM mates at Kagoro, helped us by bringing one suitcase of personal items to the U.S. for us when they later returned for their home assignment. SIM's driver drove us to Abuja airport, where we finally left Nigeria for the U.S.

We had many mixed feelings about leaving our many Nigerian friends at ETSK, throughout the country, and in several other African countries. However, one benefit of being cross-cultural missionaries was that we made countless Christian friends wherever we traveled and lived. With email, Facebook, Yahoo Messenger, and Zoom, we can still keep in connect with them and share what God has been doing in our lives and theirs. Now in God's timing, we would travel to the U.S. and step into our next assignment from the Lord!

Coletta's thoughts:

As we packed to return to Nigeria, I was happy. Happy that God had given us the chance to say a proper goodbye. Happy to physically see our friends and colleagues and drink in the sights and sounds of African villages another time. Humbled to see how God had returned us there, as He had so many previous trips. Humbled to remember how He had sustained us over many years. Humbled by the fact that God still uses ordinary people!

Chapter 29

New Assignments in the U.S.: Trusting God to Finish Well

"But I trust in you, LORD; I say,
'You are my God.' My times are in your hands"
(Psalm 31:14–15a).

As we returned from Nigeria on February 25, 2020, we didn't realize until later how God was working out more details for us. We had already booked our flights in January. We had a short layover in Frankfurt, Germany, from Abuja, Nigeria. A few Asians were walking around wearing masks on their faces. No other travelers had them on. We learned that some people were beginning to contract the new COVID-19 virus.

After arriving in the U.S., we settled into Calvary Church's missionary apartment in Lancaster. God was very kind in bringing us to the U.S. at that time. If we had booked our flights several weeks later, they may have been delayed or canceled because of COVID-19 international restrictions.

While we were on home assignment in 2013, we visited Calvary Homes in Lancaster, PA, to see if we could apply to live in one of their cottages. We visited with Carl and Sandy Hodges during the Calvary Homes annual open house day for visitors to consider living on their campus. We submitted our names to be placed on Calvary Homes' waiting list for admission. The Hodges advised us to put aside some money monthly so that when we finally returned to live in the U.S., we'd immediately have enough money in our hands to buy a good used car and furnish our home. This plan worked. Two weeks after we arrived in the U.S. in 2020, we bought a 2016 Toyota Rav4 with only 37,000 miles on it.

In May 2020, God opened the door for us to live in a two-bedroom cottage at Calvary Homes. There are about 360 residents in this continuing care facility. Lord willing, we can stay here until God calls us to heaven. I use one bedroom as my office to make contacts for FIM and ETSK. Coletta loves our kitchen, laundry room, and our prox-

Our RAV4 at our Calvary Homes cottage

imity to family, church, stores, doctors' offices, and hospitals. A one-car garage is convenient when it's rainy, snowy, or cold.

Our U.S. mission, FIM, emphasizes "God's Passion, Your Call: Declaring God's Glory Among the Nations." Their literature says, "FIM offers flexibility and freedom to obey God's call in your life."[12] As we returned to the U.S., FIM allowed Coletta and me to design our new job descriptions, as they saw God leading us into a new phase of ministry. FIM didn't tell us what to do or where to serve. We were happy about this freedom.

Coletta and I worked out the following job descriptions since we were not ready to retire yet. We are now missions advocates for FIM and ETSK.

Dennis' Full-Time Job Description

1. Serve ETSK from the U.S. in public relations.
2. Raise awareness and finances for them.
3. Keep in regular touch with the ETSK provost and management members to obtain current information and a list of needs to share with our friends and supporters.
4. Write regular newsletters and communicate with ETSK alumni and donors.
5. Represent FIM in local churches or Bible colleges/seminaries during missions conferences or public gatherings.
6. Make phone calls to encourage FIM missionaries preparing to go on the field.
7. Help support churches to strengthen their missions programs.
8. Write my autobiography to challenge more youth and adults in the U.S., Nigeria, and West Africa to become more mission minded.
9. Work to sort out many of my past preaching and chapel messages and compile them in a book or pamphlets to help ETSK and ministries like the EMS of ECWA in Nigeria.
10. Do several weekly sessions of physical exercise, like water aerobics, to improve walking.

Coletta's Part-Time Job Description

1. Accompany Dennis on any representation trips.
2. Join a team in the Cup of Water Ministry at Calvary Church. This could involve visiting church shut-ins, making a meal for them, helping Calvary Homes residents go to a doctor's visit, or doing shopping for others.
3. Join Calvary Church's team to welcome refugees and help them get settled.
4. Do several weekly sessions of physical exercise, like water aerobics and walking.

2022 - Dennis & Coletta

We're trusting God to continue to use us to be a blessing to others as God gives us strength and grace. I'm in regular contact with the ETSK leaders and students in Nigeria. God is working in many ways through the ECWA denomination in Nigeria. Presently ECWA has about ten million members throughout Nigeria. They have about 10,000 churches and 8,000 pastors.

Their missions society, the EMS of ECWA, has over 4,000 workers, mainly couples. Most serve in Nigeria, some in 18 other countries, including the U.S. in Maryland, Chicago, and Atlanta. Some of our ETSK graduates serve under ECWA and the EMS in Nigeria. One of our alumni, Rev. Femi Olowu, serves in Ghana with the EMS of ECWA.

I include praise and prayer items in our monthly email updates. In addition, some of our friends and supporters have sacrificially given toward ETSK's Student Work-Scholarship Fund, their SAC Fund, E-Learning Equipment Fund, and Relief Fund for Persecuted Christians in Nigeria.

Some of our supporters have thought outside the box to partner with ETSK. One supporter, Dr. Abimbola Adebowale, has set up a fund in memory of her late father, Robert Olutunji Adebowale, that assists worthy ETSK students with scholarships. MABC has set up an Operation Mercy Fund to team up with the ETSK Relief Fund for Persecuted Christians to provide relief for some Nigerian Christians who've lost loved ones, homes, and other property from Fulani militia attacks over the past few years, especially in the Middle Belt of Nigeria around Kagoro.

On December 17, 2020, there was an attack on one village about 20 miles from Kagoro. They lost seven people, with over 30 homes and buildings burnt. One of our ETSK B.A. Missions department students lost his father and mother, his brother and sister, and his six-year-old son.

Some Christian friends want to bless others through their giving and have given from retirement funds, family estates, and successful businesses. We thank God for each of you who've been praying for and giving to assist our Nigerian brethren.

I've asked some ETSK leaders and SIM missionaries serving in these areas how we can best pray for these Nigerian brethren. They've said, "Pray that the Christians will be strong," or "Pray for them to do the right thing." In the flesh, it would be so easy to retaliate against Fulanis or Boko Haram militants who've killed their loved ones, burnt their homes and churches, stolen their cattle or crops, or destroyed their property. Instead, they're praying for these people to be saved.

One Nigerian brother who saw us leaving Nigeria begged us, "Don't forget us here in Nigeria." I promised him, "With God's help, we won't forget you." We continue to pray for them, share praise and prayer requests with our friends and supporters, and do all we can to see them succeed at ETSK and in their ministries. We want to work together to reach more Nigerians and West Africans for the Lord and see the national church move on for the Lord for His glory. Thank you for your faithful part in these ministries over the years.

As we usually go to L.A. Fitness to do water aerobics two or three times weekly, we've made friends there with some Christians and non-Christians from various countries of the world. We're trusting that God will use these relationships to show Christ to them, so they'll be more open to hearing about the Gospel or connecting with some local Christian ministries.

As we continue to connect with many of our Nigerian brethren, we're encouraged by how God uses them, keeps them, and encourages them under complex economic and political tensions. They're great examples of pressing on and being resilient, being strong in the Lord, and doing what is right, no matter what!

Here at Calvary Homes, Coletta and I serve in various ways. I'm the secretary-treasurer for the men's fellowship and play the piano when needed. I preach or play my accordion when asked in their Sunday vespers services. Coletta reaches out to help some of the residents who need basic medical care or a ride to the doctor or store to buy some basic needs. She also has made efforts to help one immigrant family of seven.

At Calvary Church, as one of five teachers in our ABF, I am one of the regular teachers. I occasionally play the piano for the adults during their Wednesday night prayer meetings.

We are also within five miles of our children's homes. This allows us to visit Dwight's family and Stephanie easily. We get together for birthdays, holidays, and vacations. Coletta and I often babysit Isaac Deane and Annika Jean on Saturday mornings to allow Dwight to spend a few hours on his woodworking hobby and Amy to go shopping or connect with friends. Sophia Grace has just been added to the family, so we will enjoy time with her as well.

We can also join my four sisters and their husbands when they go on weekend cabin or seashore getaways. Mike and Dee Lindsey have just joined us to live in one of the Calvary Homes cottages. Living close together was a dream that Coletta and Dee had for many years.

We thank God for each of you who've faithfully prayed for and supported us financially. Some of you, like my mother, have prayed for me for many years. Others have watched God lead us since Coletta and I, as singles, began our overseas ministries for one summer in 1973, and as we've continued in full-time ministries since 1977.

You've been part of our team. Your prayers, financial support, counsel, and encouragement, as we served the Lord first in the U.S. and then in Ecuador and Nigeria, will all be rewarded by our Lord (I Corinthians 15:57–58). May God use each of us for His glory (I Corinthians 10:31) as we continue to serve Him, whether it's easy or difficult. We look forward to meeting all who know the Lord as Savior in heaven someday.

Coletta's thoughts:

Looking back, we remember how many times God kept us from all sorts of dangers. When we set our travel dates back in January 2020, COVID-19 wasn't even on the horizon. Two and a half weeks after we arrived back on U.S. soil, both Nigerian and American flights, schools, and public meetings were all shut down. God had once again intervened on our behalf to get us here before the shutdowns. After the intense work of closing our house and moving, we used those quiet months to recuperate from the emotional goodbyes and to get needed rest.

There are a few things I don't miss about Nigeria—rats, snakes, mosquitoes, and the lack of water and electricity. However, there are many more things I miss—

yams, rice and stew, African porridge and soups, the smoke rising from cooking fires, and most of all, the people.

Looking forward, we're happy to be near extended family, children, and grandchildren, and to be able to build into their lives. We remember our Nigerian brothers and sisters all the time and the grand privilege it is to have our sins forgiven and to serve the Lord with gladness, no matter what!

Contact Addresses for Your Convenience

Our U.S. Address:
653 Elizabeth Drive
Lancaster, PA 17601-4470
dshelly@fim.org

Our U.S. Mission Address:
Fellowship International Mission
555 S. 24th St.
Allentown, PA 18104-6666
www.fim.org

ETSK'S Nigerian Address:
ECWA Theological Seminary
PMB 35, Kagoro
Kaduna State, Nigeria 801005
https://etskagoro.edu.ng/

The Christian Witness Team, Inc.'s Nigerian Address:
P.O. Box 26
Ikot Abasi, Akwa Ibom State
Nigeria 534103

Contact us or FIM's website at www.fim.org on how to give a tax-deductible donation toward the ETSK's Student Work-Study Scholarship Fund, the Skill Acquisition Fund (SAC), Fund, the General Fund, or the Relief Fund for Persecuted Christians in Nigeria.

Chapter 30

The Romans Road: God's Simple Plan of Salvation

DO YOU KNOW THE WAY TO HEAVEN?

If you wanted to travel to New York or Lagos but didn't know the right way to go, what would you do? Most likely you would ask someone who has already traveled that way before. You might call someone who lives there presently and ask for directions. You could Google it or use your GPS to give you the correct directions. Otherwise, if you ask someone who sincerely would like to help you get there, but doesn't personally know the way, the directions given might lead you wrongly to Chicago or Abuja.

Many people in the world today sincerely want to go to heaven. They are searching for the right way. Some might tell you that the way to heaven is to join their church. Others might encourage you to give your money in the church offering, get baptized, keep the Ten Commandments, give to the poor, or just try to do the best you can each day, hoping that what you've done will be good enough for God to allow you to enter Heaven.

Figure 1

Everyone Has a Spiritual Need

When we look in a mirror, it helps us see ourselves, so we can make ourselves look good and respectable before others. However, when we look in the Bible, God shows us who we really are. To start with, the news isn't good. It shows us that every one of us is a sinner. Romans 3:23 says, *"For all have sinned and fall short of the glory of God."*

Whether we're five or 80 years old, each of us has done or thought something that is against God or that makes Him sad. None of us is good enough to get to heaven as we are, because God is holy, and no sin is allowed in heaven.

Each of us is on our way to hell because of our sins. That's what we deserve: "*For the wages of sin is death...*" (Romans 6:23a). "*Therefore, just as sin entered the world through one man [Adam] and death through sin, and in this way, death came to all men, because all sinned*" (Romans 5:12). That's the bad news. To fill this separation, man tries so many things—church attendance, religion, living a good, moral life, etc.— but man cannot save himself, no matter what he does.

God's Provision for Everyone

I'm so happy that God has given us good news to cancel the bad news. God has provided the only way to meet our spiritual needs. This is through the gift of His Son, the Lord Jesus Christ. "*But God demonstrates his own love for us in this: While we were still sinners, Christ died for us*" (Romans 5:8). Romans 6:23b states, "*...but the gift of God is eternal life in Christ Jesus our Lord.*"

The Lord Jesus Christ was God Himself. He came to earth in the flesh and never sinned. He willingly died for your sins and wants to give you abundant life now and forever (Romans 6:4). You will never be condemned because of your sins (Romans 8:1). God's Holy Spirit will come into your life and give you the power to live for Him (Romans 8:9). He will be with you whether things are easy or hard (Romans 8:35–39).

Your Response

How will you respond to this wonderful offer of salvation? God promises "*That if you confess with your mouth, 'Jesus is Lord,' and believe in your heart that God raised him from the dead, you will be saved. For it is with your heart that you believe and are justified, and it is with your mouth that you confess and are saved*" (Romans 10:9–10).

You can't buy or earn salvation. It's a free gift. God also says, "*Everyone who calls on the name of the Lord will be saved*" (Romans 10:13).

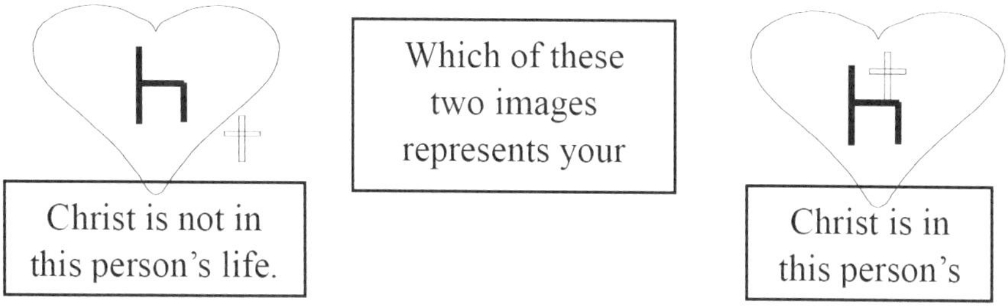

When someone offers you a gift, you can either receive it or reject it. I hope that as you hear this message from the Bible today, you will honestly see yourself as the Bible sees you—a lost sinner who is on your way to hell. Do you want Jesus Christ to come into your life today? If this is your desire, why not pray this prayer right now? "Dear God, I know that I'm a sinner and have done wrong things against you. I believe that Jesus Christ died for my sins, was buried, and that He rose again from the dead to give me eternal life. Help me to begin to live for you. Thank you for Jesus coming into my heart today. I pray this in Jesus' name, Amen."

If you have just sincerely prayed this prayer, God's promises from Romans 10:9–13 are for you. You can be assured of your salvation. You are saved. You can put your name in the blank spaces in Romans 10:13 like this: "*If_______calls on the name of the Lord, _______will be saved.*"

Today your sins have been forgiven and taken away. You are a child of God. You will not be condemned again. Christ by His Holy Spirit promises to be with you and empower you to live for Him each day (Romans 8:11,14,16).

If you have prayed this prayer, tell another Christian you know about it. Surrendering yourself to

Christ is the most important decision you will ever make in your life. That Christian can help you to find a Bible-believing church near you to attend. Write down today's date on a paper or in your Bible to help you remember when you invited Christ into your life. Begin to read the book of Romans and begin to claim the many promises God has for you. Another special Bible book for you to read after that is the Gospel of John. Begin to talk to God in prayer. Present your life to Him. He will help you resist temptation and give you victory in your life (Romans 12:1–2). As you see God working in your life, share this same message with your friends.

Finally, write to us so we can know of your decision. We will be praying for you and will try to send you some literature to help you live more for Christ. Our contact information is at the end of Chapter 29.

*The Christian Witness Team, Inc., in Nigeria has permitted us to use this adapted pamphlet in this book.

*Bible passages used above are from the New International Version.

A Short Romans Road Outline to Share with Others

The Romans Road: God's Simple Plan of Salvation

I. THE NEED: We are all lost sinners and are spiritually dead without Christ.
Romans 3:23; 5:12; 6:23a

II. GOD'S PROVISION: Christ Jesus came to give us eternal life.
Romans 6:23b and 5:6-8, especially verse 8

III. YOUR RESPONSE: What will you do with the Lord Jesus?
Romans 10:9-10, 13

IV. ASSURANCE OF SALVATION
Apply Romans 10:9-10 and 13
Romans 8:16

V. ENCOURAGE THE PERSON TO GROW IN CHRIST & YIELD TO HIM.
Romans 10:17: Read God's Word and share it with others. Attend church and pray.
Romans 12:1-2: Yield to the Lord and don't follow the world's ways.

Notes

[1] I heard this quote at a missions conference at Calvary Church, Lancaster, Pennsylvania.

[2] Sidney E. Cox, "One Step at a Time," in *Growing Songs for Children: 60 Excellent Songs of Faith*, (Warrenton: CEF Press, 1978), #41.

[3] Oswald J. Smith, *Be Sure of Your Salvation* (Oradell: American Tract Society, 1970), 1–4.

[4] *Nigeria Map: Regions, Geography, Facts & Figures*, "Infoplease," Updated October 4, 2023, accessed August 15, 2022, https://www.infoplease.com/atlas/africa/nigeria-map.

[5] Admin, "Meaning of Akwa Ibom." Aziza, Aziza Group, January 12, 2019. https://www.aziza.com.ng/meaning-of-akwa-ibom/.

[6] Harry Fletcher, "The Pastor as Counselor." (doctoral thesis, Luther Rice Seminary, 1976), 48.

[7]"Every Child, Every Nation, Every Day," CEF online, Child Evangelism Fellowship, 2001–2024, https://www.cefonline.com/about/history/.

[8] Josh McDowell and Bob Hostetler, *Right from Wrong: What You Need to Know to Help Youth Make Right Choices* (Dallas: Word Publishing, 1994), 94-99.

[9] *Nigeria Map*, accessed August 15, 2022.

[10] Bill Hanks and William Shell, *Discipleship: The Best Writings from the Most Experienced Disciple Makers* (Grand Rapids: Zondervan Publishing House, 1981), 18.

[11] Isabella Stephenson, "Holy Father, in Thy Mercy," in *The Lutheran Hymnal*, ed. W.G. Polack (St Louis: Concordia Publishing House, 1941), #643.

[12]"God's Passion Your Call," FIM Fellowship International Mission, fim, accessed February 10, 2023, www.fim.org.

Bibliography

Admin. "Meaning of Akwa Ibom." Aziza. Aziza Group, January 12, 2019. https://www.aziza.com.ng/meaning-of-akwa-ibom/.

Cox, Sidney. E. "One Step at a Time." in *Growing Songs for Children: 60 Excellent Songs of Faith*, #41. Warrenton: CEF Press, 1978.

"Every Child, Every Nation, Every Day." CEF online. 2001–2024. http://www.cefonline.com/about/history/.

Fletcher, Harry. "The Pastor as Counselor." Doctoral thesis, Luther Rice Seminary, 1976.

"God's Passsion Your Call." FIM Fellowship International Mission. Fim. Accessed February 10, 2023. www.fim.org.

Hanks, Bill, and William Shell. Discipleship: *The Best Writings from the Most Experienced Disciple Makers*. Grand Rapids: Zondervan Publishing House, 1981.

McDowell, Josh, and Bob Hostetler. *Right from Wrong: What You Need to Know to Help Youth Make Right Choices*. Dallas: Word Publishing, 1994.

Nigeria Map: Regions, Geography, Facts & Figures. "Infoplease." Updated October 4, 2023. Accessed August 15, 2022. https://www.infoplease.com/atlas/africa/nigeria-map.

Smith, Oswald. J. *Be Sure of Your Salvation*. Oradell: American Tract Society, 1970.

Stephenson, Isabella. "Holy Father, in Thy Mercy." In *The Lutheran Hymnal*, edited by W.G. Polack, #643. St Louis: Concordia Publishing House, 1941.

Made in the USA
Columbia, SC
14 July 2024

38184689R00157